PAUL ABELS
MICHAEL J. MURPHY
*Case Western Reserve University*

# ADMINISTRATION IN THE HUMAN SERVICES

## a normative systems approach

Prentice-Hall, Inc., Englewood Cliffs, New Jersey 07632

**Library of Congress Cataloging in Publication Data**

Abels, Paul, (date)
  Administration in the human services.

  Includes bibliographical references and index.
  1. Social work administration—United States.
I. Murphy, Michael, joint author.  II. Title.
HV41.A24      361.3'068      80-27056
ISBN 0-13-005850-5

*TO OUR WONDERFUL FAMILIES*

Sonia, Abigail, Beth, and Barbara Abels
Peggy, Michael II, Madeline and Maura Murphy

*FOR THEIR PATIENCE, UNDERSTANDING,
FORTITUDE, AND HUMOR*

Editorial production/supervision and interior design by Cyrus Veeser
Cover design by Wanda Lubelska
Manufacturing buyer: John Hall


© 1981 by Prentice-Hall, Inc., Englewood Cliffs, N.J. 07632

Printed in the United States of America

10  9  8  7  6  5  4  3  2

Prentice-Hall International, Inc., *London*
Prentice-Hall of Australia Pty. Limited, *Sydney*
Prentice-Hall of Canada, Ltd., *Toronto*
Prentice-Hall of India Private Limited, *New Delhi*
Prentice-Hall of Japan, Inc., *Tokyo*
Prentice-Hall of Southeast Asia Pte. Ltd., *Singapore*
Whitehall Books Limited, *Wellington, New Zealand*

# contents

## 3

## holistic administration: the systems view     45

## 4

## the agency in its contextual environment     70

## part 2

## THE MANAGEMENT CYCLE     89

## part 3

## CREATIVE ADMINISTRATION    167

# preface

While this book's emphasis is administration in the human services, its underlying concern is the improvement of all administrative practice. We maintain that administration, and especially administration in the human services, must always work toward the enhancement of human endeavor and the betterment of human society. As part of a larger society, an administrator must take action to nurture humane goals. This commitment must start with his or her own agency.

The welfare industry seems to be evolving into one of the largest "businesses" in the United States. While a business analogy may be helpful, it does not necessarily hold that the administrative techniques of business are the best approaches for an administrator in the human services.

In this book we attempt to build an administrative practice consistent with the values and goals which have historically framed the mission of human services. We believe we have molded an approach to administration which maintains that vision and also incorporates sound administrative principles permitting creative, democratic, and above all effective administration.

This book offers administrators, supervisory personnel, and others in our field an alternative to the edited readers or purely business-oriented texts on management. It focuses on the human service agency and develops a normative model of what administration must be if the agency is to develop to full potential its service to clients and the growth of its professional staff. The text proceeds by incorporating a "systems" stance into its administrative goals.

As educators we have been baffled by the scarcity of new texts on social work and human service administration. We believe this neglect is serious and that our field's administrators need to examine current management methods using a systematic approach attuned both to theory and practice. This type of "holistic" approach is not afforded by a collection of readings, no matter how well done.

The book is divided into three parts. Part I, "A Normative Approach to Administration," begins with a discussion of the unique role of human services in society: their historical mandate to guarantee effective assistance for people in need and ultimately to build a more just society. The normative approach of "management for just consequences" is the theme of the remainder of the book. Chapter 2 discusses the evolution of administrative principles and introduces the systems view of human service organizations provided in Chapter 3. Chapter 4 places the organization in environmental context, noting the dynamic potential of dealing proactively with both the external environment, in such areas as autonomy, fund raising, public relations, other organizations; and the internal environment, in relation to sexism, racism, and affirmative action.

Part II directs attention to a systematic view of the cyclical processes of management: motivation, planning, control, and organization of resources. Because human service organizations consist of people dealing with people, motivation is presented first in Chapter 5, which highlights the dynamic interaction that makes an organization succeed or fail.

The process and cycle of decision making is discussed in Chapter 6, which especially notes its pervasive application throughout the management cycle. This chapter stresses the need to aggressively seek out and systematize the information needed to make effective decisions. Chapter 7 discusses the cyclical steps in planning and links the process to the development of program plans and objectives, and the organization of structure and resources. Chapter 8 presents the need and the means for developing an ongoing monitoring and evaluation process under the rubric of positive control for accountability. Following the approach to control as a positive function, the concept of budgeting as both a planning and control system is introduced. Line-by-line, functional program and zero-based budgets are discussed. Chapter 10 emphasizes the importance of a proactive stance in the human services organization with respect to fund raising. To be effective, accountable, and autonomous, organizations must develop a systematic view of the funding process. Probably in no other area is the need to be proactive as acute as it is in the dynamic—even volatile—funding environment.

The last part of this book deals with three areas: convivial approaches, the creative organization, and the exceptional administrator. Chapter 11 introduces the concept of "conviviality,"—that is, the belief that a series of administrative tools exist that are not shrouded by extreme complexity and which lend themselves to easy adaptation and effective use by the human services administrator. This chapter describes in turn the "how-tos" of Management by Objectives (M.B.O.), Organizational Development (O.D.) techniques, and Program Evaluation and Review (PERT) as some particularly helpful tools. The Creative Organization (Chapter 12) explores organizational ecology and the administrative processes needed to help a human services organization reach its creative potential. The concepts of creativity and synergy, ways to unleash the talents of the staff group, the use of group dynamics, communication, and staff training, and the involvement of the client/patient/constituent dynamic are all considered with regard to the organization's functioning. The final chapter discusses "exceptionality," tying together the many concepts outlined throughout the book and asserting the administrator's need to be creative, caring, respectful, proactive, and future-oriented.

# part 1

---

# THE NORMATIVE SYSTEMS APPROACH

# CHAPTER 1

---

# a normative
# approach to
# administration

Administrative practice in the human services has unique qualities that are grounded in the experience, values, sanctions, skills, and goals of the organizations and people involved in that field. These factors have merged to create basic structural frameworks and communication patterns unlike other organizations. These patterns have been influenced by the field's historical missions, the nature of the services provided, the interpersonal, reciprocal relations of the clients and staff, and their visions of what life should be. Thus the administrations of the community-oriented settlement houses were usually less formal in their status relations than administration in the Charity Organization Society which preceded them and did not have the same community ties. Administration in public human service agencies tends to be more formal still due to legally mandated hierarchical positions.

## ADMINISTRATION FOR WHAT?

This question seems simple enough, and a range of straight-forward responses might include "getting the work of the agency done," "helping the worker do a better job," or "to be more effective," or "more efficient," "insuring accountable services," and so on. But why accomplish these tasks? Why do a better job? Why serve the client? Why undertake the responsibilities of administering a social agency? We would suggest that all of the activities of the agency, all the staff, the board, and the administrator must reflect the purposes for which all social welfare organizations were created. It must reflect the profession from which it evolved and to which it gives shape. The purpose of administration must be to support the major historical thrust of the profession. The commitment and tasks of the administrator should aim to increase the agency's ability to function in a manner that helps lead to a more "just society."

We believe the historical mission has been directed toward improving the quality of social relations through the development of individual and community responsibility. This would lead to the type of just society envisioned by Lukes[1] in which he stresses that "all people would be treated with respect and dignity and be entitled to freedom, autonomy, privacy and opportunities for human development."[2]

This view is in keeping with the American creed. As Robert K. Merton notes, the creed "asserts the indefeasible principle of the human right to full equity—the right of equitable access to justice, freedom and opportunity, irrespective of race or religion or ethnic origin. It proclaims further the universalist doctrine of the dignity of the individual, irrespective of the groups of which he is a part. It is a creed announcing full moral equities for all . . . viewed sociologically the creed is a set of values and precepts embedded in American culture, to which Americans are expected to conform."[3] It was out of this creed and the desire to see it reach fruition that the social work profession emerged.

Although historically set up with the hope that the need for the social agency would be short lived, this once minute part of our institutional life has become a ubiquitous Goliath. Services are planned and provided through complicated service networks that are often beyond the control of any one agency administrator. The degree of complexity is illustrated by the fact that the U.S. Bureau of the Census lists over eighty job titles under

1. Stephen Lukes, *Individualism* (New York: Harper & Row, Publishers, Inc., 1973).

2. For a more comprehensive development of these ideas, see Sonia and Paul Abels, *Doing Social Work: A Holistic View* (unpublished paper, Case Western Reserve University, School of Applied Social Sciences, December, 1978).

3. Robert K. Merton, "Discrimination and the American Creed," in *Discrimination and National Value,* ed. R. M. MacIver (New York: Harper & Row, Publishers, Inc., 1949).

4

the code of Social Worker, starting with "adoption worker" and ending with "welfare visitor." The ever-increasing range of concerns, fueled by increased demands for social justice, changing life styles, and the stress of technological advance, has strained the services of the agencies and complicated administrative responsibilities. Governmental regulations and demands for accountability have started to give the social agency a more traditional, bureaucratic management bent. Yet the social agency must find a way to cope with these demands and still maintain its own administrative modes.

We are certainly not the first to suggest that not all organizations are alike, and that the management of an organization needs to reflect its unique functions. Blau and Scott proposed a four category framework: 1) business concerns that benefit private owners, such as banks or General Motors; 2) commonweal organizations that benefit the general public, such as the police or post office; 3) mutual benefit associations benefiting the members of the organization; and 4) service organizations that benefit their clients, including hospitals and social welfare organizations.[4] Harshbarger notes that the nonservice organization's framework is basically output oriented and does not deal with the unique throughput factors, which in the human services would make for a vital difference in style. He notes that the human service organizations differ enough from other organizations that there exist "differing principles of both organizational change and human behavior in [such] organizations.[5]

The stewardship of organizations will vary with their funding, purposes, and auspices. One would not expect that the administrative procedures of a community youth center would parallel those of a junior high school—even when the ages served and the organization size may be similar. Nor would one expect that a private company like General Motors could maintain the same rigid controls over its employees as the U.S. Army might have over its staff, even though, again, the ages of the employees and size of the organization might be similar. The differences in these organizations demand idiosyncratic management approaches.

The adage "form follows function" suggests that the nature of organizational purpose should determine the structure and process of the administration set up to achieve those purposes. At the same time, little of the current literature suggests that administration in the human services differs from administration in industry, business, or government.

Historical pathways and/or reconstructive visions do, however, influence organizational style. The Charity Organization Society, for exam-

4. P. Blau and W. Scott, *Formal Organizations* (San Francisco: Chandler, 1962).
5. Dwight Harshbarger, "The Human Service Organization," in Harold Demone and Dwight Harshbarger, eds., *A Handbook of Human Service Organizations* (New York: Human Sciences Press, 1973).

ple, was an attempt to bring the giving of charity into a "scientifically" managed paradigm. These organizations were developed with an appropriate structure for operating under strong voluntary administrative leadership.[6] Their philosophy, as well as their differential assignments of volunteers and paid staff, set up a commitment to supervision as a control mechanism that still strongly influences agency practice and structure. The pattern of supervision has been maintained even though we have moved into professional control of the agency. Though new administrative perspectives are needed, these have to be "natural" to the profession if they are to gain acceptance.

In the human services the administrative beliefs seem to be that the management methods remain the same, regardless of needs and goals—a concept that warrants consideration, but is generally recognizable as fallacious. Rather than develop an administrative science appropriate to the human services, the field has turned to the professional manager, hoping that the value and beliefs of the human service will somehow be maintained.

When administrative structures and practices do not blend with the natural forces inherent in the helping professions serious problems are created for the organization. Studies have demonstrated that intraorganizational and interpersonal conflicts are created when agencies are administered without resolution of issues such as professional versus bureaucratic styles and values, or lack of client involvement in program design and service provision. These situations are explained away as deviant cases from the general administrative orientations. Rather than examining the differences by inquiry and comparison, or trying to develop views of administration grounded in human service practice, the differences are rationalized as being resolved when techniques or policies to accommodate them are established.

Drucker has noted that it is inappropriate for human service organizations to borrow from business or industrial organizations because of "important qualitative differences in the essential characteristics of these organizations." Among the differences which he identified are the intangibility of goals and objectives, criteria for determining efficiency, basis for budgetary allocations, determining the measurement of both outputs and outcomes, and the criteria for successful performance.[7]

We have not attempted to develop a new theory of administration in this book, but rather to ground our approach in the human services. We also believe that although administration in the human service agencies

6.   See, for example, S. Humphrey Gurteen, *A Handbook of Charity Organizations* (Buffalo, N.Y.: Courier Company, 1852).

7.   Peter Drucker, "On Managing the Public Service Institution," *The Public Interest* (Fall) 33:43–60. Quoted in Rosemary C. Serri and Yeheskel Hasenfield, eds., *The Management of Human Services* (New York: Columbia University Press, 1978), p. 11.

has many processes in common with administration in other organizations there are special attributes growing out of the special culture and needs of the clients, and the unique dedication of the social workers. This is reminiscent of Kluckhome's view that all people are like some other people; like all other people; and like no other person. Similarly, some aspects of social work administration will be like administration in any organization. For example, budgets have to be developed, staff hired, policies formulated. Yet there are also important differences. There has been some partial recognition of this in the literature. Friedlander notes:

> The practice of social agency administration is based upon the principles and techniques of administration in general, particularly of public administration and business management, but it is directed to the specific social work tasks of defining and solving human problems and satisfying human needs.[8]

We hold however, that the goals will also shape the process and that the profession's roots and values have led to a different administrative orientation—one conflicting with a pure market view. Increasingly research shows that environment helps shape behavior, and this is certainly true in the work place. Social work's practice context will shape the behavior of staff just as the environment itself is being shaped by staff and other factors in its environmental system.

## RESPECTFUL ADMINISTRATION

The historical vision of our profession is rooted in the desire to have the benefits of society available equally to all people, and for their respectful, dignified, and fair treatment. Although most agencies will not state their goals in such value-oriented terminology, most recognize that the people who come to them for help do so as a solution to problems that might not exist if their clients had equal access to funds, education, jobs, and services. Since insuring dignified, fair treatment of people is a major task of the human service professions it follows then that:

1. the agency policies of service should reflect that philosophy;
2. the agency processes of service should reflect that goal; and
3. the agency itself should reflect that orientation in its internal administrative processes.

All people are worthy of respect and need to be treated in a manner that insures their freedom and provides dignified, respectful consideration. This holds as concretely for staff as it does for clients. No one is *more*

---

8. Walter A. Friedlander, *Concepts and Methods of Social Work* (Englewood Cliffs, N.J.: Prentice-Hall, Inc., 1976), p. 160.

worthy or due *more* respect—not even the director. Human service administrators differ from other managers to the extent that they are concerned with having the consequences of their actions relate to the overall goals of a "just society" and their orientation, therefore, relates to a perception of agency service reflecting the major tasks of the profession. This includes:

1. helping people and institutions arrive at sound judgments regarding what ought to be (all things considered)*;
2. developing people's individual competence in keeping with those judgments; and
3. developing the agency's capacity to secure the services and social arrangements that support those judgments.

This reflects the historical efforts of the profession to build on a rational approach to individual change, while simultaneously continuing its tradition of reform. This latter task is what we refer to when we speak of securing social arrangements on behalf of individual competence. As Klosterman points out, the planning profession has been shaped by two similar traditions: 1. rationality and science, and 2. a movement to improve government and society.[9] The administrator must be concerned with restructuring those elements of society that he or she can influence toward these professional-societal goals.

The nature of the relationship between the professional social worker and the client is a contractual one.[10] In essence, the client engages himself with a person having a particular area of expertise and agrees to follow certain procedures in order to obtain certain rewards, such as insight, hope, ability to cope with problems, and so on.

The profession in turn has sought and at times received the sanction (contract) from society for the almost "exclusive right" to be the mediators concerned with the amelioration of social welfare problems. The profession in return for these exclusive rights has agreed to carry out its mandate in an ethical, rational, and effective manner, utilizing the most comprehensive knowledge and resources at its disposal. Thus the agency gets its sanction from society and its more immediate community to operate, and the agency administrator and board are the responsible parties mandated by the guarantee of that trust.

*Which means: all variables involved in the situation are taken into account including economic, psychological, sociological values and so on. (We call this a "holistic" view.)

9.   Richard E. Klosterman, "Foundations for Normative Planning," *Journal of the American Institute of Planners*, 44, no. 1 (1978), 37.

10.   For further discussion of the nature of the client-worker contracts, see, Charles E. Bidwell and Rebecca S. Freeland, "Authority and Control in Client-Servant Organizations," *Sociological Quarterly*, Vol. 4, no. 2, (1963); and Paul Abels, *The Social Work Contract: Playing it Straight* (unpublished paper presented at the Cleveland Chapter of the Group Services Section, March 23, 1967, Case Western Reserve University, School of Applied Social Sciences, Cleveland, Ohio).

In this book we shall attempt to provide administrators with insights and tools that will help them work with the board, community, and staff in the furtherance of the ends of administrative action that restructure service toward a "just society."

## what type of administration leads to a just community?

The melding of two distinct value-based professions, social work and management, into a "greater" profession, calls for: 1. synergistic approaches and convivial tools[11] and 2. a "normative administration" view of "what ought to be." A unique quality of administrational goals in the human services is the commitment to a vision of "what ought to be," if indeed we are ever to attain a just society. Administrators who truly believe in this vision will work to be role models striving toward that end. We view them as architects or designers who attempt to bring the agency into a "just community" design, where all plans and actions are within the "grand plan," with the administrator acting as a guide to that design and bearing the major responsibility for it.

*The purpose of administration is to provide the resources and structural and psychological supports necessary to insure that the agency will function in a manner leading to positive consequences for the client served and, ultimately, to a more just society.*[12]

## THE NORMATIVE APPROACH[13]

In order to further develop our view of what an effective human services administration needs to be, we must take the time now, thoughtfully, to reconstruct social work administration around the profession's historical focus of commitment to the improvement of human social arrangements and individual effectiveness.

11. Synergy is the pulling together of two or more elements into a single idea which is often better than either original element alone. The concept "convivial" has been selected by the authors to represent our belief that the tools to be used by human services administrators need to be basic and adaptable enough to be used in a relatively short period of time without painful cerebral struggles.

12. Chauncey Alexander notes the difference between administration and management: "Administration is viewed as focusing on efficiency—the direction and improvement of existing systems—while management is thought to encompass the additional responsibility of obtaining or redirecting resources and markets for new opportunities and thus to effectiveness." As Peter F. Drucker states: "Efficiency is concerned with doing things right. Effectiveness is doing the right things." *Management Tasks, Responsibilities, Practices* (N.Y.: Harper & Row, 1973), p. 45. Quoted in "Management of Human Service Organizations," *Encyclopedia of Social Work* (Washington, D.C.: NASW, 1977), p. 845. In our book we will use the terms interchangeably.

13. Based on the normative approach to social work practice advocated in "The Normative Model of Social Work," Samuel Richman, Sonia Abels and Paul Abels (unpublished paper presented at Cleveland, Ohio Chapter NASW, 1976).

We suggest that the normative model of social work administration makes its focus the planning for and realization of *what ought to be, all* things considered. Other administrative milieus are concerned with what ought to be only in a qualified or conditional sense. It is our concern with the societal context that leads to the importance of a "holistic" view, rather than a concern for what ought to be *if* we are to serve the clients' desires, or what ought to be *if* we are to serve the existing social norms or *if* we are to make a profit, or what ought to be *if* we want a military victory, or what ought to be *if* we want to succeed in court. Although this seems to contradict some of the suggested advocacy roles mandated to the practitioner in the past, it takes a more gestalt, or universal, view of the problem. We see this problem of the fragmented view emerging in the rights of mental patients area, various aspects of which include: the lawyers' advocacy of the clients' civil liberties, the psychiatrists' advocacy of the clients' need for help, the courts' advocacy of the patients' right to treatment, the community's advocacy of its right not to have half-way houses in the neighborhood, and so on. No one advocates for the whole person, taking the total situation into consideration.

If social work administration were reconstructed with a normative focus on what is good or desirable, *all* things considered, we think many role dilemmas built into nonnormative models, which come out of conflicts of interests due to role commitments to what ought to be conditionally, would not arise. We should try to see if these can be avoided by restructuring the role commitment so that the administrator's concerns are with the consequences of his or her administrative actions. An advocacy commitment to the client's claims, or the board's claims, or the funding source is a commitment to achieving what ought to be *if* the interest and claims of each of those groups alone are to be served. When the client's claims come into conflict with the legitimate interests of others, a dilemma arises because the hierarchical allegiance model of administrator-professional provides no way of dealing with the conflict. The administrative focus must be on a commitment to the best services to the client, not necessarily what the client states is wanted.

Normative administration provides a focus that often transcends these conflicts, for it builds decisions on what ought to be based on inquiry and evidence, and views as unprofessional all practice that has a prior commitment to a particular set of interests or other values. There will still be unresolved problems for staff and administrators, but not ones structured by the role itself.

This administrative mode is strongly oriented in a value base that suggests that staff, with sound administrative leadership, can develop the evidence, knowledge, and skill needed to function at the high level of morality required for a "just society." In addition, these values and processes are "natural" to the profession's values and in keeping with its mission.

The main obstacle to normative practice at this time is the lack of a normative cognitive base to support it. Management practice reflects the business-industrial literature. One of the reasons for this is that theories have not been developed out of actual social welfare experience. They are instead the general reflections of thoughtful people built upon the general human experience of other professional groups. These reflections have not had the benefit of well-documented, professionally-conducted work in actual social agencies, but have come from "management" cases. Unfortunately, the problem here is that the development of normative administration is a bootstrap operation. There is no way in which the cognitive base can develop for normative administrative practice except out of normative practices. Only knowledge established as currently adequate can be projected to future actual situations. Most research on management has grown out of the business-industry-military spheres and was appropriated for use by social agencies,[14] without having grown out of their own experience.

The dilemma is often magnified by the use of professional managers in the social agency—people who are not grounded in social welfare values. Note, for example, this view of his agency by the then Director of New York's Department of Social Services, a graduate of the Harvard Business School:

> I visualize the Department as a big paper factory . . . you put the client on the conveyor belt at the beginning and he/she gets off at the other end with a check or some other service. Social workers are fine . . . but these are problems that need real resources, real teeth. It's the biggest data processing show in town.[15]

Clearly the goals influencing his view of the department and people are more related to funneling people through his agency than to providing a *caring* service It is a factory assembly line and people are interchangeable parts—a machine model of administration. To move to a normative, human model, the reconstruction of social-work administration will require that administrators take on the additional roles of researchers and documenters. It will be important that they and their workers carefully note their prior reasoning that led to certain actions, their expectations of the results of their actions, and the actual results as far as they are able to determine them. For this to function properly they need to work with their peers—with other workers who have experience in similar situations *and* in dissimilar situations—to guard against idiosyncratic subject effects.

Our approach is a normal step for the social work administrator because it is in keeping with both the orientation of the helping mission, and with the concept and responsibility of the profession. In addition to

14.   See Murray Gruber, "Total Administration," *Social Work,* 19 (Sept. 1974): 625.
15.   Joseph Lelyvald, *New York Times,* Feb. 1, 1972, p. 16, Col. 3.

knowledge, it requires an ethical morality, as well as providing for an autonomous profession and public protection.

AGENCY MORALITY.  A normative focus provides a participatory role for administrators and staff in which they enter into a relationship of moral community with other people in society. Administrators in this model make their focus the common good—the discovery and achievement of which interests them no more or less than the other persons in the society. Nor do they enter into relationships in which others figure solely as *clients* to whom services are provided to help them deal with their problems. They view each problem as a part of the collective problems of the community in which they, as members of the community, have as much interest in as anyone else. Neither is the administrator a boss, with the staff merely his or her workers—they share the community concern and are all equally responsible to see that the agency's goals of client service are achieved. The relationship of the administrator with others in a moral community makes the administrator a full participant in the pursuit of a good society.

PROFESSIONAL AUTONOMY.  The professional association must create policies and structures that protect against hierarchical groups outside the profession, which frequently threaten the professional autonomy of the social worker and the administrator. Hierarchical accountability for practice puts it in the service of interests outside of the human services setting. Needless to say, the profession as a whole is accountable to society for the quality of its professional practice, and *practice must be at the current level of the art.* Funding sources that do not value social work of a professional quality will not support it, but such sources should not make the final determination of what constitutes professional practice. If we are to achieve a truly professional status in our work, we must not be compromised by political or economic pressures. It would be equally unprofessional for members of the education profession not to teach unpopular political or economic theories due to threats from political powers as it would be for members of the medical community to refuse to offer certain types of professional medical service due to similar political or economic pressures. It is no more a virtue for the social work profession to compromise its practice in the name of political "realism" than for any other profession to do so. Needless to say, a high level of unity regarding the focus of practice must be achieved if it is to be strong enough to stand up as a profession in protection of its own autonomy.

PROTECTION OF THE PUBLIC REQUIRES PUBLIC DOCUMENTATION.  The inclusion of peer accountability in protection of professional autonomy must be complemented by effective supports for high quality practice. Basically this requires strong collegial relationships. The normative-oriented administrator fosters a high peer-review standard within the operation of the agency. Effective review is review that actually succeeds in bringing out practice change.

Earlier we stressed the importance of basing administrative practice on knowledge grounded in practice, which requires that practitioners on all levels form a relationship like that of members of a scientific community. This involves documenting what one does in a way that strives to reach agreement with others, both on the account of the specific act and upon its general significance and explanation. These same cognitive standards, when carefully followed, become practice standards as well. Under these conditions, all practice moves upward in the direction of the best practice. It is hoped that poorer practice will not survive in the light of full public examination as better methods become known.

We are not proposing a new basis for administration that can bring out the unique qualities of social work administrators overnight. Rather, we advocate a long-term project that can make administration both an art and a science. Able documentation of actual work takes considerable experience and training. Current administrative case reports tend to be inadequate because they are not structured so as to permit others to check the reports against their own work. This failure in documentation quality is viciously circular. Because social work administrators lack well-documented material, it is difficult for them to articulate what they are doing in ways already found to be useful. The establishment of a genuinely valuable knowledge base will take years of reorientation in research and education, as well as administration.

Is it unrealistic to expect social work administrators to undertake the added task of documenting their administrative practice? We ought not to be frightened by the length of time nor the difficulty of the task, if moving in this direction will put us on a firm footing. We mustn't fail to learn all we can by bringing the most important matters of social work administration under cognitive controls. We will then truly have a scientific administration for human services that grows out of grounded human service research.

While we develop new approaches, we will have to use our current tools to function in the best possible way. We believe that these tools, discussed later in this book, can be enhanced by an underlying normative value base.

### steps to a normative stance
### in administration

The normative stance requires some value guidelines within which the new administrative mode functions. Such tentative guidelines are itemized below.

GOALS.    The goals of the administrative process are closely related to what the functions and purposes of the social agency "ought to be." In general terms these include 1. helping people arrive at sound judgments regarding what ought to be, 2. securing social arrangements and individual competence in conformity with such judgments. We feel that agencies should be interested in evolving sound, effective, moral solutions to the problems facing society and their clients, and that the administrator must offer leadership in these areas. Goals need to be seen in the context of a restructuring of society toward social justice.

***Principle** 1—Administrative actions should lead to just consequences.*

STRUCTURE OF SERVICE.   The structure and the patterning of the interactions within the agency, as well as its relations with other agencies, should be structured within a framework of democratic processes and moral behavior that insures dignity and respect for all people involved. It should also permit and encourage the minimizing of supervisor as expert while promoting the concept of agency as a "just" community. The hierarchical structure within the agency is of special concern. It has been shown to cause problems and should be minimized. Caudell's research demonstrated that participation in administrative conferences in a psychiatric hospital was strongly and positively associated with status on the clinical team. Furthermore topics introduced by nurses and lower status personnel were more likely to end inconclusively and lead to frustration.[16]

***Principle** 2—The agency structure should insure a democratic, minimally stratified environment.*

KNOWLEDGE BASE.   The major mode for the gathering of knowledge to be used in practice needs to be based on scientific inquiry— regardless of whether that practice is counseling, social change, supervision, or administration. The knowledge base must be grounded in human services practice, utilizing social science-management research as it appears applicable to and verifiable by our own grounded theory. Decisions need to be based on the availability of evidence, and the level of practice should be the "current state of the art." Power and status should not be the catalyst for a decision. Where there seems to be contradictory evidence, consultation is required.

***Principle** 3—Decisions needed to be based on rational inquiry.*

SYNERGISTIC PROCESSES.   Synergy is the melding of two elements into a greater unit. The establishment of a pattern of symmetrical, synergistic relationships, such as administrator-board, administrator-supervisor, supervisor-worker, worker-client, permits mutual problem solving without contest strategies. The problems are not differentiated and attached

16.   William Caudell, *The Psychiatric Hospital as a Small Society* (Cambridge, Mass.: Harvard University Press, 1958), pp. 231–65, 294–96.

to a particular individual or group, but, rather, seen as mutual concerns in which each plays a part, and with which the agency must deal as a totality. Current research indicates that neither technological change nor staff attitudinal change alone is enough to improve system effectiveness. The interaction between people and technology and among people themselves is what makes the organization more than just an aggregate of individual efforts. These interactions determine the degree of synergy and hence effectiveness that the organization will achieve.[17] Luchsinger notes that synergy takes place "when in combination the departments or various functions optimize one another so as to cause the whole to become more than the separate parts."[18] James Craig suggests that the organizational development field (O.D.) is developing out of synergistic principles and has been extremely effective in humanizing organizations.[19] The synergistic mode is meant to lead to "no lose" situations and "I win-you win" decisions.

**Principle**   *4—Agency social interactions within and among agencies need to be synergistic.*

MUTUAL AID DEVELOPMENT.   The administration has a continuing responsibility to encourage staff autonomy and to permit clients to develop their own self-help resources. Administration can promote the values and uses of self-help and also demonstrate the need for a public health-prevention view by developing and disseminating materials that can be used by the community in either self-help or worker-supported groups. Within the agency this would mean: 1. a flattening of hierarchical administrative practices and shared decision making; 2. ongoing staff development programs, including administrative leadership development, and 3. the development and support of interagency and community social networks.

**Principle**   *5—Administration should foster independence for staff and clients through mutual support and growth.*

ACCOUNTABILITY AND GROWTH.   Within the normative stance accountability is not necessarily to a hierarchical structure, but to peers, clients, and the moral community within which one functions. One must also scientifically evaluate one's work and give feedback to the broader

17.   William A. Pasmore and Donald C. King, "Understanding Organizational Change," *Journal of Applied Behavioral Science*, 14, no. 4 (1978), 466–67.

18.   V. F. Luchsinger and V. Thomas Dock, *The Systems Approach* (Dubuque, Iowa: Kendall/Hunt Publishing Company, 1975), p. 144.

19.   James H. Craig and Marge Craig, *Synergistic Power* (Berkeley, Calif.: Proactive Press, 1974), pp. 93–99.

professional community. The optimal result of all this can be an ethical approach to practice where any techniques not grounded in solid evidence are identified as such to the community. The major thrust for accountability is to the profession so as to provide the highest level of professional practice reflecting the current state of the art.[20]

The development of administrative practice knowledge that includes a knowledge of the appropriateness of objectives and consequences also has implications for accountability in social work. Its development makes accountability through the collective investigation of consequences a more ordinary part of practice and builds it into the development of professional knowledge. As a consequence there will be less dependence upon a hierarchical structure of social authority for accountability. Just as the individual scientist is generally accountable to the scientific community, so, too, the individual administrator will come to be generally accountable to his or her peers through his or her responsibility to contribute to the knowledge of consequences.

**Principle 6**—*The administrator promotes mutual accountability to insure the highest ethical level of practice.*

RECONSTRUCTIVE ORIENTATION. The administrator-synergist not only carries out, in a respectful manner, some of the traditional enabling administrative and development tasks long associated with the manager's role, but also assumes the task of architect and reconstructor so that just consequences can result within the agency and for the clients served, and the agency can evolve toward higher levels of functioning. Where the policies or practices of the agency or funding sources prevent practice which leads to "just consequences for people then the administrator must undertake reconstruction efforts to alter these procedures."

**Principle 7**—*The administrator is a guide.*

The administrator must help staff see the merits of a desired project. Rather than force a proposal's acceptance simply because he or she desires it, the vision of what it can offer the people served should be stressed. Instead of saying "Do as I tell you," the administrator should persuade with "Behold what might be!"[21]

20. Bertha Reynolds notes in speaking of the agency executive: "She is responsible in professional matters not to lay judgment but to the standards to which she and her professional colleagues subscribe, and which they jointly build." Bertha Reynolds, *Learning and Teaching in the Practice of Social Work* (New York: Russell and Russell, 1965), pp. 324–25.

21. "Guide" suggests a direction closer to the "Helmsmanship" of Cybernetics. Walter R. Fuchs notes that "Helmsmanship is unassuming and modest and does not behave as if it had done something wonderful." *Cybernetics for the Modern Mind* (New York: Macmillan, Inc., 1971), p. 18.

The major theme in the normative approaches which we hope administrators will reflect on is:

## management for just consequences

We are concerned with goal achievement, but want to go beyond the goals to their consequences. We are not satisfied with reaching a goal of getting five percent of the recipients off welfare unless the consequences for them are good ones. We must ask: "If the consequences may be bad, how can we modify them"?

The questions we are most concerned with as administrators are: 1. What modes of our practice will bring out the best in our staff's ability to work with people? 2. What practice promotes good consequences? 3. By what means can administrative behavior demonstrate the values we stand for as an agency and still offer high quality service? Clearly we believe that the actions of any administrator has impact on the *total* staff and, in time, the clients. The work of Stanton and Schwartz[22] clearly indicates that staff moods influence clients' moods, with the clients' reflecting the ups and downs of staff emotional confrontation. This systems view is an important part of our approach to administration. It recognizes the interrelatedness of our actions and alerts us to the idea that our actions may have unanticipated consequences.

In summary, the normative administrative approach stresses the interrelatedness of agency and community, worker and client, and administrator and staff. It holds that each is due respect and dignity as an individual. Our democratic morality must attempt to minimize the statuses and stratification and subsequent alienation that hierarchical organization often creates. This can be accomplished if people are treated with respect within the agency and synergetic processes are used that emphasize the just consequences of interpersonal action.

In the next section we will explore the systems view as a potential administrative tool. Its development as a way of understanding organizations and their place in a long historical process is traced in Chapter 3.

22.   Alfred H. Stanton and Morris S. Schwartz, *The Mental Hospital* (New York: Basic Books Inc., Publishers, 1954).

# CHAPTER 2

---

# the evolution of administrative principles

Organizations have been created by people to serve their needs; they are tools established to help them achieve certain goals. People have placed a great deal of trust in their organizations, assuming that, once established, they could continue (under guidance, of course) to fulfill the avowed purposes for which they were established. Periodically, however, we are reminded that these organizations are functioning in a manner that creates a number of problems not only for those to whom they are supposed to provide direct service, but for the general community as well. Some authors have questioned the "real" function of some of our institutions, maintaining that control, not treatment, is often the unstated but major purpose for many of them, or that survival or taking care of the organization often supplants the original service goals.[1]

---

1.  See, for example, Charles Perrow, "Demystifying Organizations," in *The Management of Human Services*, ed. Rosemary C. Sarri and Yeheskel Hasenfeld (New York: Columbia University Press, 1978).

Institutions designed to help prisoners evolve new life styles to make them active, acceptable members of society end up as merely "storehouses" where the life styles learned are often more criminal than those the prisoners had before entering. Some mental institutions aimed at restoring their patients' "mental health" often treat them as animals, objects to be used for research and self-aggrandizement. Many people who could be helped instead stagnate in the back wards of such institutions, or, if among the "lucky" ones, are in and out of a revolving door, receiving little but drug treatment and maintaining a continuing dependence on the institution.

The misery within our treatment institutions has been rediscovered periodically, and our shame absolved by a few newspaper headlines and study commissions. At times there is even some short-lived organizational restructuring, but too soon the violations of the human spirit are once more conveniently imposed on the "inmate" placed beyond closed doors for his or her own good. Although the disclosures are not new, the scientific study of these organizations, the exploration of what happens to the actors in the organization and the attempt to understand the "why" of the behavior is fairly new. There is a growing body of literature related to institutional behavior highlighted by Goffman's *Asylums*[2] and Polsky's *Cottage Six*.[3]

Perrow suggests that although stated organizational goals seem rational, we are often puzzled by the agency's lack of ability to reach its goals. The organizations really serve the interests of the social welfare elites and only marginally those of the clients. In his view, "we should expect little out of our organizations . . . they are part of the resources of other organizations."[4] Although this view may seem cynical, he suggests it might help us understand and develop new paradigms for organizational change.

The major objective of the human service professional, however, is not only to understand the why of the situation, but to understand it in order to act. These related professionals are generally committed to the helping field because of a belief in the concept of social justice—a society in which all of its citizens are treated with dignity and respect. A society in which people placing their trust in welfare and care-giving institutions can reasonably be assured that their trust is well founded. Though many professionals in the helping fields enter intending to do direct practice, and in fact may so do for a short period of time following their training, a large percentage soon find themselves in middle-management positions.

2.   Irving Goffman, *Asylums* (New York: Doubleday & Co., Inc., Anchor Books, 1961).

3.   Howard Polsky, *Cottage Six* (New York: Robert E. Krieger Pub. Co., 1977).

4.   Charles Perrow, "Demistifying Organizations," p. 118.

Although we have spoken of the organization, it is people and how they fit into it that sets the course for an organization's mission. The need to understand one's place and "who one is" as a human service administrator is felt by many professionals and we hope to clarify, if not codify, this need in our text. The organization is a design, the patterns of which have been set; but the administrator has the option of being either a manager who follows the design and imposes its restrictions, or one who works to improve that grand design.

The social agency and its network of community resources represents an extremely powerful force in society. Certainly the initiators of the profession were more certain of their ability to modify social forces by developing settlements, reform policies, and charitable societies to bring about desired changes. Often these prime movers were the agency executives.

Human service workers have continually maintained that they are mere pawns in the administrative power game. They have denied their power, and the impact that they have on others. Yet we believe that only a miniscule amount of their potential has been used. If this is true, and we believe that it is, then the power of the individual practitioner is substantial, and that of the administrator vast. An example of the power available to both parties is given by the following legal confrontation:

> Benny Max Parrish, a social worker for the Alameda County Welfare Department was dismissed for "insubordination" in 1963 for refusing to participate in a mass morning raid upon the homes of the county's welfare recipients. He sued for reinstatement and the case reached the Supreme Court of California.
>
> He maintained that "his superiors could not properly direct him to participate in an illegal activity and that he could not, therefore, be dismissed for declining to follow such directions."[5]
>
> The Welfare Director had not only ordered suspected fraud cases to be raided, but also nonsuspect homes in "order to provide a dramatic public demonstration of the Alameda County Welfare program and the low incidence of fraud."[6]
>
> Mr. Parrish's position was upheld by the court's findings with the following comment: "It is surely not beyond the competence of the Department to conduct appropriate investigations without violence to human dignity and within the confines of the Constitution."[7]

Thus we see the power of the director to invade the privacy of people's homes, to fire noncomplying workers, and to force others into illegal acts, to intimidate and to demoralize an agency. But the worker has

5.  *Parrish* v. *Civil Service Committee of the County of Alameda*, 425 2d 223, 57 Cal. Report 623.

6.  *Parrish*, Supra. 232.

7.  *Parrish*, Supra. 234.

III. Decisional Roles
   a. Entrepreneur
   b. Disturbance Handler
   c. Resource Allocator
   d. Negotiator

Patti then builds a paradigm showing how these roles are played out in three stages that he suggests are developmental in typical social service programs: design, implementation, and stabilization. Much of his helpful analysis is consistent with the situational leadership school view of group leadership as evolving out of a distribution of necessary tasks and their assumption by various people equipped to carry them out.

## THE PROFESSIONAL ROLE
## IN THE BUREAUCRACY

In the recent research on organizations, increasing attention has been given to another factor that modifies Weber's "ideal type": the professional employed within a bureaucracy. A general theme advanced by these studies is that the norms and values of the professional often do not coincide with those of others within administrative hierarchies of the organization. The result in many cases is role conflict for the professional.[20]

Greenwood suggests five basic factors for every profession: 1. systematic theory; 2. authority recognized by the clientele; 3. broad community structure and approval; 4. a code of ethics regulating practice; and 5. a professional culture sustained by formal professional association.[21]

It has been suggested that professionals and bureaucracies are incompatible, and that in principle, professional and bureaucratic codes are often mutually exclusive.[22] Barber states that one of the essential attributes of professional role is autonomy, or self-control by the professionals themselves with regard to the development and application of a body of knowledge. This is contrasted with the formal organization that requires coordination and superordinate control.[23]

Blau and Scott, in agreement with Barber, observed that although professional and bureaucratic modes of organization have some principles in common, they conflict over the principles of control.[24] Two

20. Andrew Billingsley, "Bureaucratic and Professional Orientation Patterns in Social Casework," *Social Service Review,* Vol. 38 (December 1967), 400–407.

21. Ernest Greenwood, "Attributes of a Profession," *Social Work,* Vol. 2 (July 1957), p. 45.

22. David Solomon, "Professional Persons in Bureaucratic Organizations," *Symposium on Prevention and Social Psychiatry* (Washington, D.C.: Walter Reed Army Institute of Research, 1958), p. 253.

23. Bernard Barber, "The Sociology of the Profession," *Daedalus,* Vol. 92 (Fall 1963).

24. Blau and Scott, p. 62.

sources of authority exist, therefore, when organizational discipline is based not only on position power—supported by formal sanctions and derived from the legal contract governing employment—but also on professional expertise that is enforced by collegial authority.

Role theory states that when the behaviors expected of an individual are inconsistent (one kind of role conflict), he or she will experience stress, become dissatisfied, and perform less effectively than if the expectations did not conflict.

A. D. Green offers an incisive commentary on this situation:

> The professional worker and the bureaucracy operate within different systems of authority and control, respond to different reference groups and different rewards, hold different attitudes toward service to the client, and make decisions on different bases. When responsible to both a profession and a bureaucracy, the individual finds himself confronted with two sets of mutually incompatible demands.[25]

Billingsley observed that the professional social worker was confronted with the following six conflicting situations:

1. Client needs vs. agency policies.
2. Client needs vs. professional standards.
3. Client needs vs. community expectations.
4. Agency policies vs. professional standards.
5. Agency policies vs. community expectations.
6. Professional standards vs. community expectations.[26]

Other reports depict adjustments social workers have made in their professional roles in order to simultaneously cope with the demands made by the agency and the clients.[27]

A consistent theme in all of these studies is that role occupiers had to make some choices to minimize role stress on the job. Some opted to identify primarily with the agency (the bureaucrat); others chose to focus primarily on the client (the professional); others attempted to find compromise stances wherein they could identify simultaneously with the agency and the clients. In the main, the stress was the greatest for those social workers who primarily identified with the clients, and their alternatives were either to make accommodations so as to become more closely identified with the agency, or to leave the agency.

25. A. D. Green, "Professional Social Worker in the Bureaucracy," *Social Service Review*, Vol. 40, No. 1 (1966), 71.

26. Billingsley, p. 403.

27. See: Ronald Miller and Lawrence Podell, *Role Conflict in Public Social Service*, (New York: State of New York, Office of Community Affairs); Neil A. Cohen, "The Public Welfare Department's Separation and its Impact on Role Conflict," (unpublished Ph.D. Dissertation, Case Western Reserve University, 1973).

Epstein attempted to study bureaucratic versus professional orientations among social workers and concluded: "a bureacratic orientation is conservatizing, a client orientation is radicalizing, and a professional orientation taken alone is neither conservatizing nor radicalizing."[28]

## THE ADMINISTRATIVE FUNCTION: HISTORICAL PERSPECTIVES

Although we could trace back some of the great thinkers in organizational theory to the building of the pyramids and beyond, western influence in organizational behavior had its roots in the late 1880s.

The more classical approach to administrative theory is exemplified by Henri Fayol, a French engineer and director of a steel and coal firm. In the 1880s he attempted to develop an approach to administration which could be applicable to all organizations. He was himself an administrator, and his approach was grounded in his own practice rather than on research. His view was that the functions of administration were:[29]

1. To plan: setting up forecasts and plans of action.
2. To organize: being concerned with the structure of the organization.
3. To command: setting the organization in motion.
4. To control: insuring the processes are moving according to the plan.
5. To coordinate: pulling the various parts of the organization together.

He believed that many people in the organization should participate in these administrative functions, and his ideas are generally accepted among modern managers. To aid in the understanding and dissemination of his doctrines, he developed fourteen important principles for administrators:[30]

1. There should be a division of labor, with different activities carried out by different people.
2. There should be a measure of authority inherent in managerial positions, and responsibility should be directly related to this authority.
3. There should be discipline throughout the organization maintained by good leadership, clear and fair agreements, and judicious penalties.
4. There should be a unity of command such that only one person exercises authority over the same man.

28.   Irwin Epstein, "Professional Role Orientation and Conflict Strategies," *Social Work* 15, no. 4 (October 1970), 92.

29.   Henri Fayol, *General and Industrial Management* (London: Sir Issac Pitman and Sons, 1949), pp. 19–42.

30.   Quoted and adapted from John B. Miner, *Management Theory* (New York: Macmillan, Inc., 1971), pp. 124–25.

5. There should be one person in charge of a group of activities having the same objective.

6. There should be continuing subordination of individual interests to those of the organization as a whole.

7. There should be a system of remuneration that is fair.

8. There should be a degree of centralization or decentralization of authority that is appropriate to existing circumstances.

9. There should be a scalar chain of authority and communication ranging from the highest to the lowest positions, except that horizontal communication should be encouraged where it is beneficial to the organization and where it is authorized by immediate superiors.

10. There should be material order such that each object is in its appointed place, and social order such that each individual is in his appointed place.

11. There should be equity in the treatment of individuals throughout the organization.

12. There should be, insofar as possible, stability of employment both in a given position and in the organization as a whole.

13. There should be every opportunity to exercise initiative at all levels in the organization. Initiative is both a means to satisfaction and a stimulant for motivation. As such, it is a great source of organizational strength in difficult times.

14. There should be constant encouragement of esprit de corps and harmony within the organization.

The development of the scientific management concept and the need for administrative planning can be traced back to the early 1900s in the work of Frederick Taylor. He assumed that workers were lazy and would not work without strong incentives. Therefore, a scientific management approach that required the organization to plan, organize, and control task performance was necessary. Taylor attempted to plan each worker's job, and offered careful research to assure that the best movements and tools would be used. He believed that there was one "best way," that certain people were suited for certain jobs, and that they needed to be found and trained for those assignments. In a sense he was carrying out Weber's ideas of role specialization. He also felt a number of foremen would be needed to maintain the proper rate of production. Rather than pay standard hourly rates, he believed in paying incentives to the workers for higher output.

Taylor was interested in research on work and developed a number of techniques for observation of work behavior, some which have come to be known as time studies. His approaches were successful and adapted by a number of concerns.

Following the initial success of his approach legislative hearings were held during which a number of questions were raised related to the "machinelike" image Taylor had of workers and their manipulations. Still his scientific management approach was a major breakthrough at the time, and contributed to making administration a scientific field of study.

The following excerpt from his famous book[31] illustrates part of his approach. In this example he relates how he has trained Schmidt, a pig iron handler, in the Taylor approach.

The task before us, then narrowed itself down to getting Schmidt to handle forty-seven tons of pig iron per day and making him glad to do it. This was done as follows: Schmidt was called out from among the gang of pig-iron handlers and talked to somewhat in this way:

"Schmidt, are you a high-priced man?"

"Oh yes, you do. What I want to know is whether you are a high-priced man or not."

"Vell, I don't know vat you mean."

"Oh, come now, you answer my questions. What I want to find out is whether you are a high-priced man or one of these cheap fellows here. What I want to find out is whether you want to earn $1.85 a day or whether you are satisfied with $1.15.

"Did I want $1.85 a day? Vot dot a high-priced man? Vell, yes, I was a high-priced man."

"Oh, you're aggravating me. Of course you want $1.85 a day—everyone wants it. You know perfectly well that that has very little to do with your being a high-priced man. For goodness' sake answer my questions, and don't waste any more of my time. Now come over here. You see that pile of pig iron?"

"Yes."

"You see that car?"

"Yes."

"Well, if you are a high-priced man, you will load that pig iron on that car tomorrow for $1.85. Now do wake up and answer my question. Tell me whether you are a high-priced man or not."

"Vell—did I get $1.85 for loading dot pig iron on dot car tomorrow?"

"Yes, of course you do, and you get $1.85 for loading a pile like that every day right through the year. That is what a high-priced man does, and you know it just as well as I do."

"Vell, dot's all right. I could load dot pig iron on the car tomorrow for $1.85, and I get it every day, don't I?"

"Certainly you do—certainly you do."

"Vell den, I was a high-priced man."

"Now, hold on, hold on. You know just as well as I do that a high-priced man has to do exactly as he's told from morning till night. You have seen this man here before, haven't you?"

"No, I never saw him."

"Well, if you are a high-priced man, you will do exactly as this man tells you tomorrow, from morning till night. When he tells you to pick up a pig and walk, you pick it up and you walk, and when he tells you to sit down and rest, you sit down. You do that right straight through the day. And what's more, no back talk. Now a high-priced man does just what he's told to do, and no back talk. Do you understand that? When this man tells you to walk, you walk; when he tells you to sit down, you sit down, and you don't talk back at him. Now you come on to work here tomorrow morning and I'll know before night whether you are really a high-priced man or not."

31.   Frederick Taylor, *Scientific Management* (New York: Harper & Row, Publishers, Inc., 1911).

> This seems to be rather rough talk. And indeed it would be if applied
> to an educated mechanic, or even an intelligent laborer. With a man of the
> mentally sluggish type of Schmidt, it is appropriate and not unkind, since it is
> effective in fixing his attention on the high wages which he wants and away
> from what, if it were called to his attention, he probably would consider
> impossibly hard work.[32]

It is interesting to note that Schmidt, on his $1.15 a day, had bought a small
plot of land and engaged in building himself a house before and after
work each day. Does this sound like a "sluggish" type?

Taylor's influence has spread into educational administration, operations management, behavior objectives, and management by objective.
The name "Scientific Management" has been discarded because of negative connotations exposed by labor unions and congressional investigation, but the repercussions remain.

Two other men of note should be included among the important
founding figures of administrative science. Luther Gulick and Lyndall
Urwick expanded on the work of Taylor and Fayol and cooperated in the
development of an edited text, *Papers on the Science of Administration*.[33] This
volume introduced their now famous concepts—generally known as
POSDCORB—which summarizes the duties of the chief administrator.
They are:

Planning
Organizing
Staffing
Directing
Co-ordinating
Reporting
Budgeting

One of Urwick's contributions was the concept of span of control
which states: that supervisors can supervise directly the work of no more
than five, or six subordinates. He also recognized and suggested that
people need to have the authority to carry out their assigned tasks,
maintaining: the administrator must hold people accountable for delegated activities, but must also give them the authority to discharge that
responsibility.

These early administrative thinkers were concerned with efficiency
and their impact was outstanding, but other, more holistic views of the
administrative functions were being developed concurrently.

Mary Parker Follett, one of the first women to be recognized as an
administrative theorist, was also active in community work, political

32.  Taylor, pp. 57–60.
33.  Luther Gulick and Lyndall Urwick, *Papers on the Science of Administration* (New
York: New York Institute of Public Administration, Columbia University Press, 1937).

science, economics, and social work. Her background may have helped her appreciate the social and psychological themes inherent in administration. She did not avoid dealing with the role of power, but emphasized as well creative problem solving, and melded these basic contributions with an emphasis on democratic procedures. Not only did she acknowledge the psychological and social factors in management, but early on recognized the importance of viewing the organization as a system.[34]

Hers was a pluralistic view of administration, maintaining that employees and representative councils should have a strong say in governing organizations. Follett realized that if administration was to be seen as a professional endeavor, it had to be of service. Not only was production a function of business, but, she said, it "[gives] an opportunity for individual development through the better organization of human relationships. . . . The process of production is as important for the welfare of society as the product of production."[35]

She developed four principles for an "active" view of organization. They are:

1. Coordination by direct contact among the responsible people concerned.
2. Coordination in the early stages.
3. Coordination as a reciprocal relating of all the features in a situation.
4. Coordination as a continuing process.

She saw these as the basis "upon which any enduring smoothly-operating organization must rest."[36]

Her contribution to problem solving is highlighted by her emphasis on "constructive conflict"—an attempt to resolve problems not by power, appeasement, or compromise, but by integrating the ideas into a greater whole. This concept is at the root of ideas of synergy that will be developed in a future chapter. Her major contribution was to take a dynamic view of management in which change was basic.

### the Hawthorne studies:
### Mayo and Roethlisberger

The famous series of Hawthorne studies opened another important phase in administrative theory development. These management studies were carried out by Elton Mayo and Fritz J. Roethlisberger in the late 1920s, and the results published in the 1930s.[37]

34.   Henry C. Metcalf and Lyndall Urwick, eds., *Dynamic Administration: The Collected Papers of Mary Parker Follett* (New York: Harper & Row Publishers, Inc., 1942).

35   Metcalf and Urwick, p. 32.

36.   Metcalf and Urwick, p. 23.

37.   See: Fritz J. Roethlisberger and William J. Dickson, *Management and the Worker* (Cambridge, Mass.: Harvard University Press, 1939).

The study started out to explore the impact of working conditions, such as lighting, on productivity. It became apparent to the researchers that their observations and interest increased production, as did the looser supervision of the workers. That is, increased attention seemed to increase production. The researchers were led to conclude that humane treatment of workers increased production. This was one of the founding projects leading to the Human Relations Movement in management. In addition, it can be viewed as the formation of systems thinking in the management arena.

Before proceeding further it is important to point out the historical significance of the Hawthorne studies for administrative thinking. Not only was the Human Relations Movement rooted in its outcomes, but the primacy of the role of the work group, and the impact of the informal structure as a normative force, were firmly established.

There is no question, however, that this movement was helped by the pioneering efforts of Follett and the concurrent work of Chester Barnard. These thinkers started what might be considered the worker-person orientation to sound administrative practice, as opposed to management-control paradigms.


### Chester Barnard


As president of the New Jersey Bell Telephone Company, Barnard's ideas on organizational theory carried a great deal of weight. He was interested in formal organization as "a co-operative system"—a "system of consciously coordinated activities or forces of two or more persons."[38] We might see Barnard, then, as one of the first systems-oriented administrators. He recognized the importance of communication in the administrative process.

Barnard also recognized the nature of informal organizations—a less consciously coordinated group. He recognized the importance of the informal organization as way of maintaining the personality of the individual in the face of certain effects of formal organization which tend to disintegrate the personality. As Gross notes, "This is indeed a far cry from those principles of Taylor's scientific management, which if effectively carried out, would destroy the individual's sense and reduce him to the status of machine."[39]

38.   Chester J. Barnard, *The Functions of the Executive* (Cambridge, Mass: Harvard University Press, 1938), 73.

39.   Bertram M. Gross, *Organizations and their Managing* (New York: The Free Press, 1968), p. 87.

## McGregor and his colleagues

Douglas McGregor's *The Human Side of Enterprise* introduced the concept of X and Y management styles into the administration literature. McGregor recognized the inherent conflict existing between the needs of the organization and the needs of the individual. In exploring what manner of administration would best help the individual adapt or fit into the organization, he opposed the more authoritarian style he labeled "X" and proposed a more humanistic attitude—the "Y" approach (Fig. 2-3). His attempt was to dichotomize some of the administrative styles into two distinct groups at extreme ends of the spectrum.[40] A number of studies related to personality types and their impact on the organization have been based on McGregor's approach. His work has also been closely linked with Maslow's self-actualization concepts, since the "Y" type manager would see the worker's need to grow and actualize himself. In fact, he based some of his principles on the work of Maslow, stating that management by direction and control "fails because direction and control are useless methods of motivating people whose psychological and safety needs are reasonably satisfied and whose social, egotistic and self-fulfillment needs are predominant."[41]

One can assess and predict the management approach of a public welfare administrator from the orientation of clients' needs as expressed in the statement below. As an aid, the reader might want to re-examine a few of McGregor's X–Y comparisons (see Fig. 2-3) in light of this welfare official's statement:

> Society stands in the same relation to them (welfare recipients) as that of parent to child . . . [J]ust as the child is expected to attend classes, so also the "child adult" must be expected to meet his responsibilities to the community. In short, "social uplifting"— even if begun on the adult level—cannot expect to meet with success unless it is combined with a certain amount of social disciplining—just as it is on the pre-adult level.[42]

Of course, any dichotomy tends to oversimplify the situation and in critiquing the X–Y approach, Drucker notes:

> The motivation, the drive, the impulse lies outside them. But this is not compatible with either Theory X or Theory Y. It implies that it is not human

40.   Douglas McGregor, *The Human Side of Enterprise* (New York: McGraw-Hill Book Company, 1960).

41.   Quoted in George E. Berkley, *The Administrative Revolution* (Englewood Cliffs, N.J.: Prentice-Hall, Inc., 1971), p. 16.

42.   Alan D. Wade, "The Guaranteed Minimum Income: Social Work's Challenge and Opportunity," *Social Work,* 12, no. 1 (Jan. 1967), 98.

**FIGURE 2-3**  *Two Sets of Assumptions About People*[43]

| TRADITIONAL (X) | POTENTIAL (Y) |
|---|---|
| People are naturally lazy; they prefer to do nothing | People are naturally active; they set goals and enjoy striving. |
| People work mostly for money and status rewards. | People seek many satisfactions in work: pride in achievement; enjoyment of process; sense of contribution; pleasure in association; stimulation of new challenges, etc. |
| The main force keeping people productive in their work is fear of being demoted or fired. | The main force keeping people productive in their work is desire to achieve their personal and social goals. |
| People remain children grown larger; they are naturally dependent on leaders. | People normally mature beyond childhood; they aspire to independence, self-fulfillment, responsibility. |
| People expect and depend on direction from above; they do not want to think for themselves. | People close to the situation see and feel what is needed and are capable of self-direction. |
| People need supervisors who will watch them closely enough to be able to praise good work and reprimand errors. | People who understand and care about what they are doing can devise and improve their own methods of doing work. |
| People have little concern beyond their immediate, material interests. | People need the sense that they are respected as capable of assuming responsibility and self-correction. |
| | People seek to give meaning to their lives by identifying with nations, communities, churches, unions, companies, and causes. |

nature, but the structure of job and work, that in effect, determines how people will act and what management they will require.

We also now know that individuals can acquire the habit of achievement, but can also acquire the habit of defeat. This again is not compatible with either the Theory X or the Theory Y of human nature.[44]

The "Y" approach is more compatible with the contextual approach which suggests we must view people in their total situation.

43.   Adapted from Douglas McGregor, *The Human Side of Enterprise* (New York: McGraw-Hill Book Company, 1961), and lecture by Goodwin Watson at National Training Laboratories, Ken Executive Conference, 1961, Bethel, Maine.

44.   Peter F. Drucker, *Management: Tasks Responsibilities Practice* (New York: Harper & Row, 1974).

Chris Argyris's work augmented that of McGregor's. He suggested that the work people do needs to be made more significant for them, and therefore more satisfying, if workers are to do their best. The talents of people must be cultivated through upgrading of jobs. He sees this as one of the most important emphases in leadership training.[45]

Other forces in the human relations approach in management have been the T. Group and Awareness Group, which have been on the scene since the mid 1940s. Having its origins in the fields of education and social work, this movement held that small groups, made up of managers and workers, educators and professionals, could help each other open the channels of communication. Increased awareness of their own and others motivations can lead to more open communications.[46] This group, generally influenced by Lewin, Argyris, and Likert, takes a broad view of administrative leadership, and advocates distributing power and involving the community. They stress democracy within organizations.

Much of the emerging emphasis on human relations in administration is not new to administrators of social work agencies. In 1961 Trecker defined administration as "a process of working with people in ways that release and relate their energies so that they use all available resources to accomplish a purpose.[47]

The importance of the work place to people and the growth of alienation led many people to feel that a more open and aware communication process, both for training purposes and individual growth, could help the work place become a "temporary community." The popularity of the T. Group movement has led to other self-awareness groups, some bordering on "cults."

It is important to note that many of these developments owe their origins to the pioneer work of Moreno in *Psychodrama and Sociodrama*,[48] Grace Coyle in group work, and Neva Boyd in the play movement. A number of current administrative approaches have also grown out of the therapeutic field of gestalt therapy and transactional analysis.[49]

The final group of administrative thinkers we will deal with are involved in decision theory. The development of game analysis, simulations, models, and perhaps most significant, computer and mathematical models for decision making, has opened up new areas of study.

45. Chris Argyris, *Increasing Leadership Effectiveness* (New York: John Wiley and Sons, 1976).

46. See, for example, Rensis Likert, *New Patterns of Management* (New York: McGraw Hill Book Company, 1961).

47. Harleigh Trecker, *Administration* (New York: Association Press, 1961), p. 14.

48. Jacob Moreno, *Who Shall Survive?* (New York: Beacon House, 1953); Grace Coyle, *Group Work with American Youth* (New York: Harper & Row, Publishers, Inc., 1948).

49. See, for example, Eric Berne, *The Structure and Dynamics of Organizations and Groups* (New York: Ballantine, 1973), and Fritz Perls, *The Gestalt Approach* (New York: Bantour, 1973).

Pioneered by Norbert Weiner's cybernetics,[50] computer decision theory has been championed by Herbert Simon, whose *Administrative Behavior* is a classic study of the decision making process.[51] Simon's analysis of the means-ends chain clearly establishes the interrelatedness of ideas and actions. It is an important view in analyzing the organization in system terms. In a subsequent work with James March, Simon attempts to formulate a hypothesis related to organizational relationships and aimed at developing a theoretical base for organizational behavior.[52]

## THE ETHICAL IMPERATIVE

The evolution of administrative theory seems to have progressed— albeit in a rather staggering progression—from management as an elite autocracy that maintained control over the life of the worker, and which viewed the worker as a tool which *it* had to get the best of, to a view in which the basic humanity of both worker and manager are recognized. Management has moved from getting things done, no matter how, to working with people.

> Whenever and wherever possible the executive's authority should be diffused and decentralized in such a way that its force seldom emerges from him alone. While the skillful administrator in social work therefore is guided by his board and while he sees to it that the opinions and recommendations of his staff have full weight, he is cognizant at all times that his ultimate authority derives from the needs of the community. Thus his authority is more correctly a mandate that flows through him in the nature of a moral obligation, couched within legal and moral limitations, but nevertheless compelling in its pressure. This type of authority and its use stands in direct contrast, therefore, to that generally referred to as "dictatorship" and which usually represents the desire of an individual to dominate any situation in which he finds himself.[53]

The development of the settlement movement had also highlighted the concept of more egalitarian use of authority. The greatness of a person like Jane Addams kept her in the forefront of the movement, but Christopher Lasch notes the influence a *setting* like Hull House had on administrative development.

50.   Norbert Weiner, *The Human Use of Human Beings* (New York: Avon Books, 1967).

51.   Herbert Simon, *Administrative Behavior* (New York: Macmillan, Inc., 1957).

52.   James March and Herbert Simon, *Organizations* (New York: John Wiley & Sons, Inc., 1958).

53.   Leonard W. Mayo, *Social Work Yearbook, 1945* (New York: Russell Sage Foundation, 1945), p. 18.

For many Hull House residents, especially for the women, the settlement became a training ground for new professional careers as experts and administrators in government, industry and the university.[54]

These early administrative pioneers were instrumental in keeping us to a more moral type of administration and their continuing influence is reflected in a universal shift taking place in management.

This latter view suggests that in a situation where one person has a position of relative authority and may make decisions which affect other's lives, the imbalance of power creates interpersonal problems for both. This concern was discussed fully in Selznick's description of his endeavor to bring about "macro change" in a large geographic area of our country. He relates the administrative-moral problems a large government project presents to administrators and communities.[55]

Some way needs to be worked out to minimize this conflict and, at the same time, enhance the accomplishment of the task. Important ethical questions have been raised as to the right of any one person to control and manage the lives of others. Certainly Taylor's work is often used as an example of manipulation and over-control. In his framework, the administrator was the authority and was to use his power to the fullest.[56]

The proper use of authority is one of the basic issues facing the administrator of a social welfare agency. The roots of administration in our profession bear proud testimony to its constant focus on analysis. Mayo notes:

> In the moral or ethical sense, as well as in the practical and legal, the first use of authority in an agency is to determine and define its main functions and how they shall be carried out. Any definition of function must also include a determination of scope (that is, where the functions begin and end) and their relation to similar and supplementary functions (that is, agencies) in the community. The second use of authority is to establish operating policies and the means whereby policies may be modified or new ones formed as occasions demand. The third is to set up procedures or the detailed steps necessary to the carrying out of policies.[57]

One sees the roots of our professions' democratic principles in Mayo's efforts to keep the lines of communication open to all staff.

Is it possible to maximize both for good human relations and task accomplishment? The answer is probably a clear "No" if taken in the short

54. Christopher Lasch, *The Social Thought of Jane Addams* (New York: The Bobbs Merrill Co., Inc., 1965), p. 80.

55. Philip Selznick, *TVA and the Grass Roots* (New York: Harper & Row, Publishers, Inc., 1949).

56. Frederick Taylor, *Scientific Management* (New York: Harper & Row, Publishers, Inc., 1911).

57. Mayo, p. 15.

run. In the long run, however, there is growing evidence that job production and turnover is related to worker satisfaction, and worker satisfaction is related to the proper treatment of human beings.

One of the first and, perhaps, most influential works on productivity was related to the Lippitt and White studies on leadership styles.[58] Their work on democratic, autocratic, and laissez-faire styles showed that although tight autocratic management might initially result in high production, in the long run, democratic management styles enabled staff to produce on their own and maintain high productivity levels without intense supervision.

What is the problem that keeps cropping up in all the administrative studies? Why do many theorists feel uneasy with the concept of management? Basically, it seems related to *the right of one person to control another*— to expect work from another person under one's authority. It seems to be paradoxical to control free men in our democratic society. Thomas A. Cowan points out:[59]

> In our course of an analysis of the nature of the mind, the philosopher Hegel calls attention to a deep paradox which attends all human effort. I might risk putting it somewhat as follows: By dint of superior effort, by a stroke of good fortune, or perhaps by the exercise of chicanery, one man becomes boss over another. From the point of view of the boss this looks like a happy or at any rate a superior position; the "worker" is an inferior. But then a peculiar thing happens. Time and again, the boss begins to deteriorate as a human being, and the worker gains in moral stature. Apparently, what dignifies human effort is the work itself. The loafer, the shirker, the time-saver, be he boss or subordinate, pays for his dereliction in moral degeneration.

Cowan is concerned primarily with administration of other scientists. He recognizes the dilemma of the necessity to have administrators.

> Let us in imagination abolish all scientific administration for the moment. There results a random assemblage of unrelated single scientists. What happens is that each becomes his own administrator. Each creates a monster which allows the scientist no freedom whatever. It is precisely this horrendous system of constraints that forces the scientist to associate with his fellows and to try to rationalize the division of labor by means of administration.

His solution is to suggest the following administrative tasks.

> I think much of what an administrator must do for a scientist is to treat him as a unique human being in sore need of a multitude of services to enable him to practice his art. I put this need, which I call a need for the proper feeling life,

58.   Ronald Lippitt, et al., *The Dynamics of Planned Change* (New York: Harcourt Brace Jovanovich, Inc., 1955).

59.   Thomas A. Cowan, "Paradoxes of Science Administration," *Science*, vol. 177, pp. 964–67.

even prior to any function which the administrator may exercise as an adjudicator. Obviously, when human beings come into conflict, whether they are scientists or just citizens, they need law and a judge to settle disputes and apportion scarce goods. But an administrator is not primarily a ministrator, and what he ministers to is the feeling life of the scientists he has undertaken to care for.

In conclusion he suggests:

His role is to create an environment that nourishes scientific creativity.[60]

We might suggest that this is not too far afield from our view of what an administrator in the human services field needs to do. Practitioners are scientists who need the freedom to practice and pursue their knowledge. A role of the administrator is *to provide staff with resources and supports that help them carry out the agency purposes creatively, effectively, and in a self-dignifying manner.*

This can occur when the agency leadership keeps in mind not only the agency purposes, but the fact that interactions with staff must lead to consequences which are similarly in keeping with those purposes. Administration theory has currently evolved far enough to recognize the need for "a just organization," but it also faces the necessity of dealing with a growing emphasis on technological and bureaucratic-legislative mandates. One of these technological developments emerging from the "new scientific management" is "systems" analysis—a process we will discuss in the next chapter.

A systems-normative approach to administration is, in our view, the next step in the historical development of administrative thinking. First, the systems view recognizes the interrelatedness of people and their actions. It establishes the bond that exists among all organizations and people whether or not they heretofore recognized that bond. People shape organizations, but organizations shape people as well. Therefore, however small a negative administrative act may seem, its implications for all parties involved reverberate and spread like the proverbial pebble tossed into a pool.

Secondly, the normative view helps people examine what should be—if we were to have an agency in which good consequences are the keynote. It reaffirms people's confidence in their organizations and gives them a clear position and a guide for their actions emphasizing not only the achievement of goals, but goals which themselves have consequences for social justice. The result will be synergistic in that what's good for the organization will truly be good for society, for there will be no dichotomy.

Organizations are still being modified; they are moving on an

60. Cowan, "Paradoxes," p. 967.

evolutionary tract which runs concurrent with society's own evolutionary strides. As people find new, "higher" ways to relate to each other, they will mold their agencies in their new image, but there will always be a lag in the agency's ability to keep pace and to reconstruct itself because of the complexities involved.

The ability to maintain the agency's normative service-reconstructive stance will be an important task and responsibility of the human service administrator. One objective of the subsequent portions of this book is to provide some of the modes of inquiry and practice by which this can be achieved.

# CHAPTER 3

---

# holistic administration: the systems view

Having provided our philosophical framework for what human services administration "ought" to be like, we will now undertake to suggest a design for administrative action.

The basic motif is provided by the concept of "systems"—a way of looking at the world that helps the administrator better understand the interrelatedness of the phenomena under consideration. From that base we will explore agency linkages and supportive organizational networks.

The final portions of the chapter discuss how decisions concerning change can be assessed and how change can be undertaken within the framework of a normative systems approach.

## SYSTEMS

An emerging development in management theory is the establishment of "system" as the basic integrating unit for organizational analysis and understanding. It is the cornerstone of the "New Scientific Management" and an influential concept in current approaches to helping in the human services.[1]

"Time after time, the system is the solution," "hypes" recent advertisements by the Bell System. The statement is accompanied by a visual presentation of some corporation problem that was resolved by a current technological advance enhanced by the systems thinking that the telephone company was able to provide. Just as often however, but in less public contexts, we are likely to hear people say that the problem is the "system." "The System Fails and an Abused Child Dies," flashes in half-inch letters in the *New York Times*. Obviously the term system is being used in differing ways. The first use suggests an integrated organization working toward the achievement of some responsible goal: the solution of your problem. The second and third refer to a large, amorphous power that controls "things," and usually carries a negative connotation implying a rigid ordering of bureaucratic procedures interfering with other, sensible ones.

Although it is clear that "system" may have many meanings, we will try to establish its use in this book as the unification and integration of parts of a complex organization into a unitary structure aimed at achieving specific goals.

The following "case," which is a partially fictionalized version of a doctors' strike in California, exemplifies some of the consequences of systems at work. We will examine a number of the ways the idea of systems is used, and we will work with the reader to sift out some of the fundamental elements and values in the development of a systems approach to administration.

> Following a threatened increase in rates of over 327 percent on their malpractice insurance, sixty surgeons at four Los Angeles hospitals went on strike. Although there had been doctors' strikes in New York and Chicago earlier in the year, this was one of the first on the west coast.
>
> By the end of a week the administrator of Hospital *P* had to lay off aids and a number of support employees in two of the surgical wards. Some of the aids went to the state employment service and began collecting unemployment insurance. Others were able to find employment at another institution.
>
> The social service workers were asked to contact all the people who had been scheduled for surgery and make changes. Within one week everything other than emergency surgery was postponed. Mrs. A., a school teacher who had planned to be admitted for corrective surgery and had arranged with her principal to be off work for two weeks, had to change her scheduled time off. Other workers were involved with comforting some outpatients who were concerned that they would not receive their needed surgery or treatment. The head of social services at a staff meeting helped his staff look at

---

1.   Rino Patti , "The New Scientific Management: Systems Management for Social Welfare," *Public Welfare*, 33, no. 2, (Spring 1975), and Catherine A. McWilliams, "Systems Analysis Can Solve Nursing Management Problems," *Supervisor Nurse*, 10, no. 2 (May 1980), p. 17.

some of the stress the postponement of surgery might put on their case load.

The switchboard was crowded with calls from people who wanted to know if *all* doctors were out on strike. They were reassured that about 80 percent of the usual hospital functions were still being carried out.

In the meantime the state legislature met to work on legislation to alleviate some of the financial stress on the physicians. The local press became very involved in covering the strike and there was also national television coverage for two evenings. By the end of the first week, "Governor Edmund G. Brown, Jr. and State Legislative leaders said that they had agreed on a new proposal that might end the slowdown."[2]

We might continue by hypothesizing some of the impact on the patients, the doctors, the workers—employed and unemployed—as well as on their families. There was pressure on the administrator in his deliberations with the hospital board, the committees, and the staff. How much authority did he really have? We could examine the need to alter other systems. For example, a news article reports that "Dr. Richard Jurmain, a cardiologist and spokesman for the striking doctors . . . contended that solution of the problem requires fundamental changes in the legal system."[3] What did Dr. Jurmain mean by "system"? The legal code, the bar association, the courts, the law schools, the relation between lawyer and client, or the democratic system? Even if he had been more specific, the problem of setting boundaries around a system is a serious one. The interaction of these subsystems on each other makes rigid boundaries into fragile constructs that are soon destroyed by the reality of human action.

In our example, if the state legislature (a system) had acted sooner to pass emergency legislation, it might have avoided the series of problems. Similarly, fewer large damage awards in malpractice cases might have minimized the rise in malpractice insurance rates. Social workers urging patients to demand their rights might also have led to more law suits. Self-help groups have offered alternative health "systems." These groups, too, might alter restrictive administrative demands placed on the patients. Once more we see that there is an interrelatedness of various groups, units, and structures—all of which are called systems.

Can an understanding of systems theory help administrators function more adequately, perhaps avoid some problems, and offer better services? Practitioners and writers in almost every discipline have come to recognize the value of a systems approach at least as a way to perceive the interrelationship of the part under study to its environment.

Ludwig Von Bertalanffy, generally accepted as the father of modern "general systems theory," developed system principles within the context of biological theory, but acknowledges their subsequent application to other fields, including social work.

2.  Robert Lindsay, *New York Times,* January 30, 1976, p. 11, col. 1.
3.  Ibid.

The present writer has stated a number of "system principles," partly in the context of biological theory . . . However . . . the main principles offered such as wholeness, sum, centralization, differentiation, leading part, closed and open system, finality, equifinality, growth in time, relative growth, competition, have been used in manifold ways, (e.g., general definition of social types of growth; systems engineering, social work.)[4]

Herein lies one of the first cautions to be made in thinking about system theory; superimposing the concepts from other mechanical and natural systems onto "man" and "social systems" can be problematic.[5] The human as an open system has the capabilities to alter goals and control system inputs and outputs in ways impossible for nonhuman systems. Another difficulty grows out of determining the limits of a system—where to draw the boundaries of the social system, for both analysis and practice. For example, each category in Chart I can be considered an open system.

This brief outline, however, will suffice to bring us face to face with a beginning concept of systems and system thinking. Basically, one event (in this case a decision to increase insurance rates) will have far-reaching impacts on other systems, individuals, and social structures.

## WHAT IS A SYSTEM?

What do we mean by system? Simply stated, we suggest that *a system is a set of bounded, interacting parts that are coordinated in order to accomplish a goal.* An open social system is a grouping of people who exist within conceptual or physical boundaries (community, classroom, profession) and whose interactions with each other over time matter. Other definitions are: "An organizing whole unit which includes the interactions of its interdependent component parts and its relationship to the environment,"[6] and "A system is an organized complex or whole; an assemblage or combination of things or parts forming a complex whole, connotes plan, method, order and arrangement."[7]

Social systems are always open in that they can be affected by environmental forces. They can change and in fact must change over time in order to survive.

The agency and its relations with others can also be seen as a system of interacting systems.

4.   Ludwig Von Bertalanffy, "General Systems Theory: A Critical Review," in *Modern Systems Research for the Behavioral Scientist,* ed. Walter Buckley (Chicago: Aldine Publishing Co., 1968), p. 15.

5.   For a critical view, see: Robert D. Leighneuger, Jr., "Systems Theory," *Journal of Sociology and Social Welfare,* 4, no. 4 (July 1978).

6.   Walter Buckley, *Sociology and Modern Systems Theory* (Englewood Cliffs, N.J.: Prentice-Hall, Inc., 1967), p. 28.

7.   Vincent P. Luchsinger and V. Thomas Dock, *The Systems Approach* (Dubuque, Iowa: Kendall/Hunt Publishing Company, 1975), p. 142.

A System:  An agency as those things within the walls or, for example, two or more of the combinations illustrated below are an interacting system if viewed linearly.

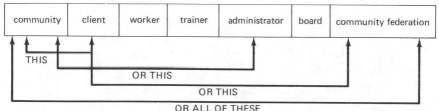

One problem is that at times the system may be not the answer, but the problem. Although one leading system analyst suggests that "Systems are made up of sets of components that work together for the overall objective of the whole,"[8] there are certain situations where this is not completely clear and where parties to the interaction may not have the same apparent goals, such as clients and worker in a welfare department, prisoners and guards, and so forth. The goals of the parts may not be the same, or the goals may be confused. The system may founder under those circumstances and become a nonsystem.[9] We mean, of course, that the coordination of the parts toward primary goals is not such that they can work together synergistically.

When the parts are working toward a common goal it is possible to visualize the open system by schematic presentation in Figure 3-1.

**FIGURE 3-1**  *A General Systems Model*

(Environment)

INPUTS | THROUGHPUTS (PROCESS) | OUTPUTS

Guidance Mechanism

FEEDBACK
(Positive or negative.)

POSITIVE FEEDBACK:  Things are fine, continue with the same inputs.

NEGATIVE FEEDBACK:  Things are bad, change the inputs or the process

8.  C. West Churchman, *The Systems Approach* (New York: Dell Publishing Co., Inc., 1969), p. 11.

9.  See Paul Abels, "The Managers are Coming. The Managers are Coming," *Public Welfare*, 31, no. 4 (Fall 1973), 13.

Feedback from the environment—such as critical comments from clients, the community, or other professionals—can also act as inputs to the system. Usually it is the negative feedback that stimulates the guidance mechanism to initiate changes in the actions of the system. The proactive organization will often set up its own means of assessing the need for change, and thus minimize the amount of negative feedback from outside sources. The more open the organization is to outside concerns, the less likely it is to receive unpleasant surprises from them.

**FIGURE 3-2**   *Example: The Hospital Strike*

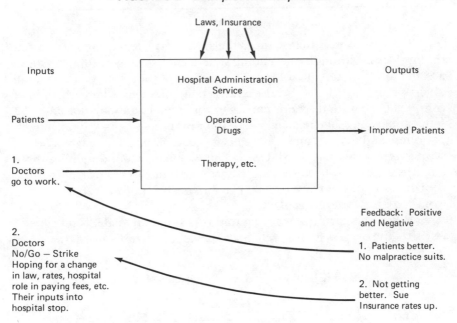

This example is naturally a simplified look at the terrain. We might expand our view a bit to a more complex analysis.

Even the expanded hospital system shown here is a simplification of all the inputs that impact upon the system and with which the administration must cope. Try to imagine, for example, all the other systems that must be involved if a new hospital ward is needed. The complexities are not only exacerbated by the number of organizations that are involved with the hospital, but by each of those organization's own subsystems "set."

As we have seen, various human arrangements can be viewed as systems. Generally speaking, all human systems are open; that is, they can be modified by various forces, and react to their environments in self-directed attempts to adapt, rather than perform as do physical systems, such as fixed electrical circuits.

**FIGURE 3-3** *An Expanded Hospital System*

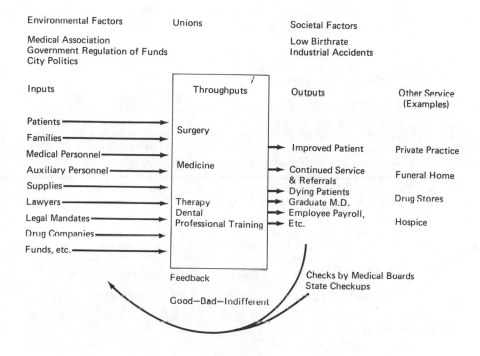

Environmental Factors      Unions      Societal Factors

Medical Association                       Low Birthrate
Government Regulation of Funds      Industrial Accidents
City Politics

| Inputs | Throughputs | Outputs | Other Service (Examples) |
|---|---|---|---|
| Patients | Surgery | Improved Patient | Private Practice |
| Families | | | |
| Medical Personnel | Medicine | Continued Service & Referrals | Funeral Home |
| Auxiliary Personnel | | Dying Patients | |
| Supplies | | Graduate M.D. | Drug Stores |
| Lawyers | Therapy | Employee Payroll, | |
| Legal Mandates | Dental | Etc. | Hospice |
| Drug Companies | Professional Training | | |
| Funds, etc. | | | |

Feedback                  Checks by Medical Boards
                              State Checkups
Good—Bad—Indifferent

## the value of systems thinking to administrators

There are some important benefits to the administrator from utilizing a systems view in a more formal manner:

1. It helps him or her get a glimpse of the bigger picture. It can prevent the administrator from assuming that the solution or problem exists only in one small area. It helps give a more interactive perspective of the situation and its interface within the agency context.

2. It helps administrators understand that altering one unit of a system usually has repercussions for other units in the system, or for other systems in the community. With practice, the administrator is soon able to make some quick assessments regarding the consequences to other parts or to the larger system by a change in one part.

3. It may help the administrator see what parts of systems aren't working well.

4. It helps the administrator see what other systems or portions of the environment may be worthy of consideration then and/or before subsequent actions, and to see what other people and/or organizations need to be involved in the change.

5. The systems view helps an administrator think in an interactional mode, offering the potential of the gestalt or total picture while helping him or her to understand the interdependence of people. One report, discussing the reasons for crisis in middle management notes:

> Above all, there is no managerial philosophy. There is no systematic procedure whereby a manager learns to think in a conceptually different way from a worker.[10]

6. It may even offer clues to how the administrator can be more effective. Most important, it prevents an administrator from isolating him- or herself from some of the "nasty" things going on in the agency or the environment, because he or she understands that, like it or not, an administrator's actions or interactions impact upon the system. Not only is silence acquiescence, but the administrator's style of management training and decision making will either modify the system or help sustain it as is.

7. It may offer them alternatives for action. If, for example, it is decided that change in one portion of the system is not feasible, then a decision to modify another part of the system may have important consequences for the "real" target. Bypassing a trouble spot and dealing with an interfacing portion of the system may prove just as effective as a head-on confrontation.

Patti's caution that "[t]he utility of systems management technology for social welfare should be questioned because of its generally simplistic view of the relationship between the organization and its commitment"[11] might be important to note here.

An example of how a systems or ecological view can expand our range of services to people was demonstrated in an article by Edgar H. Auerswald, who compared two agencies, one utilizing a team approach and the other a systems model for helping.[12] The latter approach fosters a much more open inquiry process because inputs come from various communities, thus assuring a much broader data base from which to make decisions.

> A further example demonstrating the systems view can be constructed from an actual New York City Welfare Department experience. Imagine the following scene. It takes place in New York City outside a welfare office. The time is 7:00 A.M., and although the office does not open until 8:30, the line started forming at 6:30. Since this has been occurring each day for the past few weeks, and the neighbors have been complaining about the noise, there are now two or three police officers attempting to keep the line quiet. Their

10.   John Darnton, "Middle Management in City Government Held to be in Crisis," *New York Times*, September 23, 1975, p. 33, col. 2.

11.   Rino Patti, "The New Scientific Management: Management for Social Welfare," *Public Welfare*, 33, no. 2 (Spring 1975), 29.

12.   Edgar A. Auerswald, "Interdisciplinary Versus Ecological Approach," *Family Process*, 7, no. 2 (September 1968), 202–15.

presence makes those waiting edgy. By 8:30 there are almost one hundred people shoving to enter as the doors open. The doors are closed at 10:30. A woman who was denied service is angered over a new regulation and, having endured a four hour wait, demands to see a supervisor. The social worker tells her she will have to call to make an appointment. She starts to scream and then hits the worker. Other clients stand by and watch. The work continues. A railing is installed to keep the clients three feet from the workers. The next day the welfare rights group pickets the agency.[13]

Who or what is the system here? Is it the client and worker? The policy makers and the staff? Is it the community and the agency? The neighbors? Should the woman in prison still be counted as part of the system? Does the Welfare Department have any responsibility to her? Will the judge be concerned with her family? Could a better-trained staff have prevented the problem? Let's just view these interacting systems by reference to the Figure 3-4.

Of course, the chart presents an oversimplified analysis because in all of these systems other factors, such as culture, politics, publicity, and so on, will also play a strong part in the decision.

As Garrett Hardin has pointed out, it is impossible to do one thing, because every action has unforseen consequences. We must look at the

**FIGURE 3-4**  *A Client System Network*

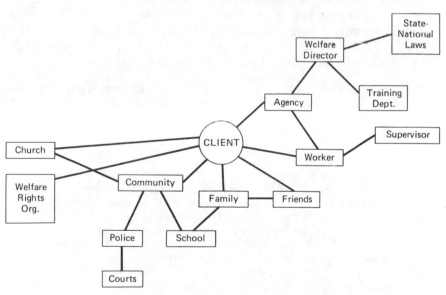

13.   This incident was adapted from a story in the *New York Times*, March 7, 1978. In September 1978, the Cleveland Metropolitan Housing Authority announced vacant apartments. Over three thousand people lined up and waited, some for three days. The C.M.H.A. said it didn't expect so many people.

possible repercussions of our actions. This means that any single change in the system will modify other parts of the system, at least temporarily.

> We can never do merely one thing. Wishing to kill insects, we may put an end to the singing of birds. Wishing to "get there faster" we insult our lungs with smoke.[14]

A change in regulations has impact on the staff, the client, the community, the police, and so forth. But proper staff training and understanding of the changes or of worker-client relationships can make for different, more positive consequences. By attempting to anticipate these developments we can more adequately take advantage of systems thinking. When representatives of systems that may be affected by the decision are consulted, more information is available upon which to base a sound decision.

It is important to remember that although the boundaries of the action system are often more closely defined—i.e., the worker and the client, the worker and his/her supervisor, executive team, and the agency—and the significant rules procedures may be clear, some "systems" still do not seem to fit the crucial requirements as human system. For example, the teacher and the class are a system where: 1. people within the system are working toward a common goal; 2. there is a clarity of effort; and 3. the goals—the learning of the material—has a chance of being achieved. Where the goals are not common, however, we have a "nonsystem situation." We know that in some systems with which we are familiar—prisoners and guards, probation officers and probationers, and clients and workers, for example—all the actors' objectives are not the same objectives.

> This, then, gives us our first clue in recognizing features of a welfare nonsystem; no one is clear about what the overall objectives are, or as we shall see, different parts of the nonsystem are working towards different objectives. To qualify, a nonsystem:
>
> · must be consistently unsuccessful;
> · must be comprised of interacting parts with different goals;
> · must be comprised of parts in interaction who would prefer not to have to interact with each other, (for example, welfare clients and caseworkers, doctors and patients, guards and prisoners);
> · must have boundaries which it is constantly trying to expand even though it cannot handle the problems now confronting it (for example, social workers as politicians, doctors not permitting other professions to use the term psychotherapy, and psychologists as community change agents);
> · must be centrally controlled by extremely conservative forces, such as the A.M.A. or punitive prison officials.

14. Garrett Hardin, "The Cybernetics of Competition: A biologist's view of society," in *Modern Systems Research for Behavioral Scientist,* ed. W. Buckley (Chicago: Aldine Publishing Co., 1968) pp. 449–59.

The actors in the nonsystem have to perform tasks they would rather not perform. Examples which come to mind are the need of the caseworker to declare certain people ineligible for funds, to have to ask people to leave their homes because of urban renewal, or to move aged people to new nursing homes.[15]

We would hold then, that even though boundaries may be loose, communication imperfect, and resources (inputs) hard to come by, where the goals are commonly held by all parts of the system, there is still a chance of success.

We have to use systems theory as a tool for understanding, but cannot expect the tool to perform as it might in the natural sciences. It can be most successful when modified to the needs of the field using it and when linked to a value base supporting the basic tenets of that field—in our situation, the provision of a service that has "good" consequences for people.

## THE SERVICE SYSTEM

In order to orient ourselves to the administrative area as an interrelated part of the total agency system, we must view the administrator in the context of the agency service system. We cannot understand the administrative function without realizing that the context is the environment that will shape that functioning. The service system, then, would involve the interrelationships among the client, community, the service agency, the administrator, and the board of advisors or commissioners.

### the elements of the agency system

The gestalt of agency encompasses the idea of a totality working on behalf of others. All the parts are oriented toward the provision of a service.

THE CLIENT OR CLIENT SYSTEM.    This element of the system generally refers to the person, group, or community segment generally seen as the target of help or change. Until recently, although the client was seen as central, the importance of recognizing that the client was a basic portion of the agency system was ignored. Participatory programs and constructive confrontation with clients should be part of the entire approach to service planning and delivery. In some agencies the clients are the agency or the system—for example, Alcoholics Anonymous, Recovery, Synanon.

THE COMMUNITY.    Clients do not exist in a vacuum. They are

---

15.    Abels, "The Managers are Coming," 1973, p. 14.

influenced to a great extent by the community. Their view of the agency determines their willingness to accept help from that particular agency. Often the staff development program will call for interpreting community life and needs to other staff members. Community resources will be used to help teach, and often community people will be employed as staff. These people will bring their biases to the agency, and be a vital source of information. For the sake of simplification we will incorporate several groups under the general title of community. Administrators need to maintain important, helpful contacts with many parts of the community, including: the family of the client, the school of a child, and the work place of the alcoholic.

THE SERVICE AGENT.   This term refers to the individual who works directly with the client—whether caseworker, group worker, community worker, generalist, paraprofessional, or untrained worker.

It is important that workers recognize and accept the fact that they are indeed part of the system. At times they may not like what the system does and act as if they were not part of it. But the client usually sees them as clearly belonging to the system.

PROGRAM HEAD OR DEPARTMENT DIRECTOR.   These are primarily administrative functionaries who may or may not be supervisors, branch directors, or even directors of subunits. These roles are often referred to as middle management, and they act not only as role models, teachers, and administrators, but often as mediators between the service agent and administration.

EXECUTIVE.   The agency director and the administrator.

BOARD OR PLANNING BODY.   The agents responsible for the overall functioning of the agency. They generally delegate the workings of the agency to a paid director, but play an important role in policy development, fund raising, and as community liaison.

STAFF.   These are office and maintenance people and miscellaneous other staff, such as business managers, budget and publicity personnel, who make up the organization or agency. In an agency working in a therapeutic milieu, these staff play an important role in promoting the health of the clients.

THE AGENCY.   All organizations can be viewed as interrelated groups of people bound by common goals and in constant communication with each other. The agency is a complex organization that may employ numerous people, many with specialized skills, who provide effective service—the major reason for the agency's existence.

In order to organize themselves for service, complex organizations generally form chains of command and control, define areas of responsibilities, and attempt to assess effectiveness. These structural chains are usually set up as bureaucratic hierarchies.

THE EXECUTIVE-MANAGEMENT BODY.   The organism that serves as the control center is in a position to make decisions determining the processes taking place within that system. In nonhuman systems, such as heating units, the thermostat (temperature) may trigger other parts to operate. In some nonphysical systems, such as butterflies or humans, the brain acts as the control center, and regulates the functioning of many other parts. Most other open formal systems—social systems—also have central control mechanisms for decision making. In a family it may be a parent, both parents, or even "voting" agreements.

In a community it might be the mayor, the legislature, or other bodies. These "decision-making elites" in any system make choices based on some goal-issue signals to the performing units, and respond to signals fed back by the performing units.

In the human being, for example, it is unlikely that an arm might object to being controlled by the brain. In social systems, however, a part may indeed object to and resist instructions to act in a certain way.

Many of the cases one sees in a family service agency are a result of a "guidance center"—parent—feeling that a child is not listening; or one spouse believing that he or she is the guidance center complaining that the other spouse doesn't do his or her share. In agencies, a common gripe is often that some staff don't get records in or do as they are told.

### the administrative guidance center

In the social agency, a great deal of the control or guidance either comes from the administrative office or is within its purview. To the degree that this office is open to rational advice, consultation, democratic decision-making processes, and involvement of all units of the system, the system is considered open and just. When all people have an equal opportunity to make decisions, or the decisions are on behalf of all people, we might say the system is more open or more pluralistic.

The administrator must understand that his or her contribution will influence the total system. Administrators have sought to insure that their actions are relatively objective and do not reflect only the idiosyncratic thinking of the administrator. Advisory committees, executive committees, "kitchen cabinets," "town meetings," surveys, and trial balloons are just a few ways in which to encourage inputs from staff. Social science research has shown that where people have had an input into a decision they are more likely to support it—even if they don't particularly like it—than if their opinions were not sought.

### the agency bias

It is natural to postulate that not only would the experience of the workers and the nature of the service influence agency style of administration, supervision, and staff training, but the setting would provide a backdrop for action and be seen as both environment and as a force that influences behavior.

Social service-related agencies can expect to reflect the historical value system and societal grounding of social welfare. We can assume that this value system will be reflected in the approaches to administration taken by a social work-oriented administrator. In turn, the resistance that a nonsocial work-oriented administrator will encounter will be due in part to the social work staff's insistence on their historically incorporated value system. This is not to suggest that only those trained in social work should be used as administrators. What is suggested, however, is that the value system of concern for people and social justice must be incorporated into the nonsocial work value repertoire.

This carry over of the social work value system into the management-administration arena has created conflict, produced accusations of a nonscientific approach to management, and, more recently, fostered the incorporation of management "types" into traditional social welfare administration slots. More recently, schools preparing leadership-level staff for the human services have undertaken to meld two distinct disciplines—coming from different value-ethical systems, a different science base, and perhaps even a different motivational-personality orientation—into a "new human" administrative gestalt. We would suggest this is an extremely difficult and frustrating task, particularly without a solid normative orientation and the proper use of synergistic methods. The synergistic melding of these two disciplines, if it can be achieved, will result from taking the best of both to create something even better. If each has its own bias about what it can offer the other, how can the bias be overcome?

Gregory Bateson points out that in the thermostat, a fairly closed system that can respond only to temperature, there is a bias set by someone, in this case someone outside the system.[16] The bias is the temperature to which the thermostat responds. If the bias is 72, any temperature below or above that activates the thermostat either to turn on or turn off. This bias is deterministic, narrow, limiting and not open to negotiation—only to the information: "temperature is not 72 degrees." This "not" is a negative feedback to which it responds, but it cannot decide on its own that the temperature should be 73.

Who sets the bias in an agency that is an open system? The bias may be viewed as the way things get done within the agency: its culture—those things to which the agency system will respond and those ways in which it has been taught to respond. Although many factors influence the bias—laws, customs, or the board of directors—modifications of these influences are possible by all the "humans" in the system, either by intentional efforts or by "human error."

16.  Gregory Bateson, *Steps to an Ecology of the Mind* (New York: Ballantine Books, Inc., 1972), pp. 309–37.

Because of the nature of the position and our culturally influenced views of authority, the administrator is the most influential person in any attempt to alter the bias of the agency. What he or she supports has positive "vibes" and is more easily accepted. Things he or she opposes create added difficulties for acceptance within the agency. Often the director assigns other people to help modify the agency bias.

In staff-development programs, the person who is in the most "crucial" position to set the bias or, if you will, to change the bias, is the training director. The reasons are threefold:

1. The power of the teaching-learning situation.
2. The "Modeling Potential."
3. The pool of knowledge under the administrator's control.

This suggests that the administrator, through sound educational programs, can influence the bias of the agency toward a "just community." The total agency system can join in the developing of goals, providing appropriate resources (as their talents permit), and insuring that the service is provided. With such support the administrator can fulfill his or her function of enabling staff to achieve the agency goals. The result is a reciprocal, synergistic solution.

### the system in the community

It is easier to define the community of a settlement house, neighborhood law office, or hospital than it is to define the "community" served by a county welfare department. The focus for the administrator, however, remains the same. Serving the community and acknowledging the interrelationship between community and agency that goes beyond the direct chain of worker-service-client.

Many environmental forces from external client-political-societal systems will operate upon the internal agency systems and have consequences for the agency services. These include availability of funds, the tax rate, unemployment, the condition of the city, the political climate, competition from other agencies, the state of the art, and so forth. However, the community perception is that the agency is not outside but, rather, part of the community. They need each other and are intertwined.

The ability to react creatively to the systemic-environmental pulls and pushes will be related in part to agency resources and community support, but to a great extent, it will be the agency function—its contract with society—which helps it withstand "unreasonable" influence from self-serving groups or individuals. It is the contract that helps staff focus on the "real" reason for its existence and to interpret it to the community. This does not mean that at times seemingly "unreasonable" demands that go beyond the contract may not indeed be reasonable, and call for a reassessment of agency service or the development of other agencies. It is possible, and probably likely, that the community will recognize its needs long before the agency has formalized a program to meet them.

We have seen this occur frequently, in for example, programs where parents have pressed for education of retarded or handicapped children. Thus, while the administrator needs to educate the community, he or she must at the same time maintain an agency willing to be educated. This type of feedback helps the agency provide immediately necessary services.

### systems alone are not the answer

It has been noted that system analysis has traditionally been considered a useful device in situations with single centers of ultimate authority.[17] The welfare system is a complex maze of organizations with conflicting, competing goals and centers of power. This may explain the difficulties encountered in the attempt to alter the welfare system to any great degree by use of a systems approach, and for the failure of the war on poverty. In order to coordinate these divergent views new methods of coordination and communications were deemed necessary. There was an "assumption that information is the crux of the welfare problem."[18] Rather than solving social problems, they have been redefined and made amenable to computer treatment. "Thus, as an instrument of public policy making, techniques of system analysis often encourages emphasis on the wrong questions and provides answers to the more dangerous for having been achieved through a 'scientific' or rational means . . . it does not represent a strategy likely to resolve the welfare problem even if its promises were fulfilled."[19]

Does it seem paradoxical after lauding the values of a systems approach to now emphasize its shortcomings? On the contrary, our view holds that systems analysis can be most effective when it is grounded in a strong moral base as reflected by the normative approach outlined in Chapter I. Its effectiveness is increased when its holostic view also incorporates a process for selecting action or change mechanisms. Thus we suggest a multifaceted approach to administrative action.

### a framework for administrative action

The following list summarizes our basic view of administration.

1. Normative Value Perspective.
2. Systems Analysis.

17.   Charles W. Williams, *Analysis of U.S. Welfare Concepts and Systems, Present and Future* (Menlo Park, Calif.: Stanford Research Institute, 1973), p. 52.

18.   Williams, p. 54.

19.   Williams, pp. 61–62.

3. Supportive Networks.
4. Field Theory.
5. Engagement in Action.

The normative perspective provides a special view of both the hoped for and actual consequences of our actions. Systems thinking offers a method for analysis of the total situation. Field theory offers a way of pinpointing the actions needed and a way to modify the problem, and the supportive network and engagement are ways of enhancing the change and supporting continued results. It is the melding of these five elements by competent people that provides the basis for increased potential effectiveness in the area of social welfare, a human concern that has proven to be the most difficult to comprehend and modify.

## SOCIAL NETWORKS

Often the agency is not in a position to offer the total range of services that might be needed to resolve a particular problem. It is almost certainly unable to deal with the entire range of supportive services frequently needed to stabilize the change. We have not as yet dealt with the relationship among systems that see themselves as autonomous units. As the illustration below strongly illustrates, systems can also set limits for themselves that inhibit service to people. The importance of interorganizational ties, linkages, or social networks must be recognized.[20]

In discussing one administrator's attempt to help a severely retarded young man, Ronald Sullivan reported:

> Wilbert Rosa is a severely retarded, 40-year-old patient in the psychiatric division of Bellevue Hospital Center, and everyone involved in his case agrees that he does not belong in a psychiatric ward, that he has regressed there and that he is endangered by acute psychotics who might take advantage of his docility and helplessness.
>
> Moreover, hospital officials contend that the $50,610 in Medicaid funds that has been spent to keep Mr. Rosa in Bellevue since his admission there in February would pay for at least three and a half years of specialized care in a facility for the retarded that might even improve his condition.
>
> But getting Mr. Rosa transferred has been a losing bureaucratic struggle as Harriet Sym, a young administrator at Bellevue, has found out.
>
> Miss Sym's principal responsibility is to justify to state Medicaid authorities the care Bellevue gives to poor psychiatric patients. Her efforts in behalf of Mr. Rosa began when Medicaid officials said that he did not belong in Bellevue and that they would no longer pay for his care there. That was in March.
>
> Since Mr. Rosa had lived in Staten Island with his brother's family, Miss

---

20. We will use the term social network rather than systems network in order to recognize that often a single person—a friend, a boss, or an autonomous worker—plays a vital role in the network.

Sym tried a nursing home there. But state Medicaid officials said that a nursing home was no place for him either.

"I then tried the state's Manhattan Psychiatric Center," she said, "but they only take you if you're psychotic."

She wrote next to the Manhattan and Brooklyn Development Services for the mentally retarded, agencies of the State Department of Mental Hygiene. She said she had never received a reply but had been told when she had called later that she should try Willowbrook since Mr. Rosa had come from Staten Island.

But Willowbrook was being closed, and Miss Sym was advised by officials there to try elsewhere, for instance, one suggested, Manhattan Developmental Services.

During June, Miss Sym tried the state mental retardation office at the World Trade Center where she was advised to start looking for private residential centers for Mr. Rosa.

All the while, she said, Medicaid officials kept threatening to cut off reimbursement funds for Mr. Rosa's Bellevue care.

"I tried the state's Metropolitan Placement Unit," she said. "They were very nice, but couldn't help. They said call United Cerebral Palsy," but Mr. Rosa did not have that disease so he did not qualify for help there.

Another call went to the Association for the Help of Retarded Children, but Mr. Rosa lost out again because he is not a child . . .[21]

Not only were the agencies unable or unwilling to work together in a manner which would be helpful to this client, but the other community supports were lacking. There were no social networks involved or known that could be mobilized to help Mr. Rosa.

The family was not able to take care of him because he could not work or feed himself, and agencies where he might have learned these skills were not available to him. Increasingly, alternative "systems"—halfway houses, self-help groups, and supportive networks—are being developed to help people who "fall between the cracks" or are ill-served by traditional institutions.

It is common knowledge that institutions, even the best, carry negative consequences for children, staff, and families. Within a network perspective, the practitioner's focus is shifting towards developing networks to maintain children outside the institution, and away from primary attempts to improve institutional life. As is evident from reports of knowledgeable group workers, even the most prestigious children's institutions are *structurally* unable to provide children with qualitative life experiences.

Sarason describes networks as "informal associations of individuals, one major purpose of which is to help its members explore and pursue ways by which they could use each other in mutually productive ways."[22]

21.   Ronald Sullivan, "Bellevue Administrator Tries to Help a Man No One Seems to Want," *New York Times*, Oct. 30, 1977, p. 59, col. 3.

22.   Seymore Sarason, *Human Services and Network Resources* (San Francisco: Josse-Bass, Inc., Publishers, 1977), p. 91.

Social network is both a concept and a description of reality. Unlike a small group or system, every unit in a network does not necessarily interact with other units. Thus, in one study that examined how women found abortionists, each person contacted a person who knew a person and so on. Every person in the network is known or can be contacted through other people. Some are high-density networks where individual friends are also friends of each other, while others are low density. There are no clear boundaries in a network. The lines of communication extend in many directions and the levels of complexity exceed that seen in small groups or systems. There is a growing use of networks in organizational analysis.[23]

Networks are open, members do not necessarily share common aims, a distinctive subculture, or geography and new members may be encountered at any time. Network concepts allow the description of the actual complexity of social phenomena and differ from systems concepts that tend to simplify the complexity of phenomena. This complexity includes the reality of both direct and indirect interactions occurring on a large scale between focal individuals or families, or between individuals or families of diverse social categories (i.e. sex, race, or economic class). The network categories and variables are not predetermined.

Collins reports on the support of networks for day-care services when the social work professional maintained contact with approximately 50 families.[24] Speck, in examining dropouts' networks, found the networks were weighed heavily with other youths, who used each other for support more often than they used their kin.[25]

Moreno's and Jennings's writings illustrated the importance of social networks and the work involved in strengthening and in supporting these structures. Jennings, in her classic book, *Leadership and Isolation*, focused on children's institutions and the presence of the institutions' internal networks,[26] as did Polsky in *Cottage Six*.[27] Moreno's book, *Who Shall Survive?*, broadly implied that those who could count on strong networks would be the survivors.[28] The idea of survivors has similarities to the work done by Epstein on survivors of concentration camps. She speaks to the quality of the relationships that maintained people's hope and commitment to life within the horror of the camps.[29] Administrators need to help

23. Noel Tichy and Charles Fombrum, "Network Analysis in Organizational Settings," *Human Relations*, 32, no. 11 (1979), 923.

24. A. H. Collins, "The Day-Care Neighbor Service," *Community Mental Health*, vol. 5 (1969), pp. 219–224.

25. R. V. Speck, "Psychotherapy of the Social Network of a Schizophrenic Family," *Family Process*, vol. 32, no. 11 (1979).

26. Jennings, *Leadership and Isolation* (New York: Longman, Inc., 1954).

27. Howard Polsky, *Cottage Six* (New York: Russel Sage Foundation, 1962).

28. Jacob L. Moreno, *Who Shall Survive?* (New York: Beacon House, 1953).

29. Helen Epstein, *Children of the Holocaust* (New York: G.P. Putnam's Sons, 1979).

their staff view people as just such complicated networks of relationships. This focuses attention on the concreteness of people's lives.

Sonia Abels notes that the individual's social network is most likely to provide the necessary climate and ongoing supports. Networks that are extensive and complex serve as counteracting forces to the authority-control aspects of our social institutions and their accompanying neglect of people. Networks strengthen the means by which human development, equality, and democratic participation evolve. The agency can help develop these social networks to aid in the survival of the client much as it needs organizational networks to insure its own survival.[30]

### field theory

The administrator often needs a way to assess potential for change within the system. Next in our program for normative administration, we will examine Kurt Lewin's "Field Theory," which provides a systems perspective, clues for action, and a proven potential for success.

Lewin's field force analysis offers a theory-action oriented approach to change.[31] It permits one to view all the parts of the system, including external forces, on a linear plane. Lewin held that:

1. Any social situation could be perceived as being in a state of equilibrium or balance at any point in time, and that the nature of that equilibrium could be assessed. Current staff functioning, for example, is held in equilibrium by the number of opposing forces that are equal in total strength.

2. Certain forces are at work that promote learning and doing in a new way (change). These are the driving forces: a desire to do a good job, recognition, potential for growth, supervision, attending classes, an open mind.

3. Certain forces are at work which retard change. These are the restraining forces: Heavy job load, busy supervisor, fear of the new, stereotyping, or traditional patterns of behavior. For example, some supervisors may view peer group supervision as an attack on their merit. This is a restraining force that would need to be eliminated.

4. In addition, there are certain blocks that are neutral but still influence the worker: building size, budget, and laws, for instance.

Theoretically, if the current level of functioning is in balance, an alteration in either the driving or restraining forces should alter that

30. Sonia Abels and Paul Abels, "Group Works-Contextual Purposes," *Social Work with Groups*, vol. 3, no. 3 (Winter 1980).

31. Kurt Lewin, "Group Decision and Social Change" in *Readings in Social Psychology*, ed. Eleanor Maccoby and Theodore Newcomb (New York: Holt, Rinehart & Winston, 1952), p. 469.

balance. The addition of another driving force, or the elimination of a restraining force should help the supervisory group move closer to the goals of improved practice. Lewin suggests specific steps in the process.[32]

1. Unfreezing the current behavior. This may be done through confrontation, change of space (culture island), presenting new facts.
2. Moving to a new level, preferably closer to the desired level.
3. Refreezing the behavior at the new level. Find ways of supporting those changes that have been accomplished. (We will examine the concept of social networks as just such support systems later in this chapter.)
4. Repeat the process.

A force field analysis can be developed over a period of months in an agency analysis, or it can be done in five minutes prior to meeting with a client. It helps maintain a focus on the tasks to be done. By maintaining a "point of concentration" that helps focus on the specific portion of the problem to be solved, even large problems can be broken down and dealt with. This point of concentration must be maintained by all the group members during the problem solving.[33]

Lewin's approach was an attempt at re-education that impacted people at three levels: the cognitive level, the value sphere, and the action level. He based his re-education process on ten principles that were applicable to individual and organizational change.[34]

Donald Klein uses Lewin's approach in his work on community mental health and demonstrates how community analysis and action evolves out of that framework.[35]

## A CASE EXAMPLE

We might examine a hypothetical situation of an agency attempt to establish a residence for retarded young adults in a suburban community.[36]

Although the limited experiences with group homes have been

32. Kurt Lewin, p. 472.

33. Viola Spolin, *Improvisations for the Theatre* (Evanston, Ill.: Northwestern University Press, 1963).

34. Kenneth D. Benne, "The Process of Re-Education," *Group and Organizational Studies,* vol. 1 (March 1976), pp. 26–42.

35. Donald Klein, *Community Dynamics and Mental Health* (New York: John Wiley & Sons, Inc., 1968), p. 35.

36. A more complete description of this problem is presented in Hattie Butler, Tom Holland and Paul Abels, "Engaging Communities in Change Strategies for Developing Neighborhood Residential Programs" (unpublished paper presented at American Association on Mental Deficiency Conference, Toronto, June 1974).

generally encouraging, a number of problems have arisen which impede the more extensive use of such patterns.

Among the basic problems confronting the further use of group homes are two expressions of the age-old prejudices against the retarded: 1. restrictive zoning ordinances and community groups biased against the handicapped, and 2. the unavailability or inaccessibility of a range of common human service programs for the retarded.

An examination of the various individuals and systems that the agency might have to deal with are suggested by the following "systems net."

**TABLE 3-1** *The Systems Net of Neighborhood Residential Services: A Sample Coverage\**

| *City* | *Neighborhood-Community* | *Private* |
|---|---|---|
| Zoning Board (1) | Neighbors (1) | Lawyers (1) |
| Planning Commission (1) | Neighborhood | Social Service |
| City Hall (1) | Association (1) | Agencies (2) |
| Building Department (1) | Community Groups (1) | Parents' Councils (2) |
| Health Department (2) | Real Estate Offices (2) | Funding Agencies (3) |
| Fire Department (2) | Press (3) | |
| City Council (1) | The Area Council Member | Courts (3) |
| | Agency Developing Community Residences | |
| Trustees and Contacts (1) | People Needing Service | Professional Groups (2) |

The numbers in parentheses following the participants reflect relative degree of involvement:
\*Major actors in the systems net
1. Most frequent involvement
2. Less frequent involvement
3. Occasional involvement

For visual clarity the connecting lines in the net have been omitted. The connections, nature, and importance of each group will differ with communities.

### community change in field force perspective

Some social science theory helps us perceive change transactions as a totality, a system, or gestalt. Lewin's Field Force approach is one such theory (see p. 64).

> 1. We must have a thorough knowledge and a fairly accurate understanding of the current situation and ecology of the neighborhood or community in which a residence is to be located. This composite represents a *field* made up of forces influential in determining whether or not the desired change will occur.

2. Certain forces that promote change are at work. These are the *driving forces* and are made up of the change agent, the agency that is developing community residences, and their allies.
3. Certain forces that retard change are at work. These are the *restraining forces* and are likely to be the irrational fears of neighborhood residents or restrictive zoning ordinances.

To create change within a community, the number or intensity of the driving forces must be increased enough to eliminate or weaken the restraining forces. A change in any of these may alter the equilibrium of the force field.

The interactional forces mainly reflect the patterns of interaction and communication among the various groups in the community systems net. The degree to which these groups are knowledgeable about and comfortable with one another will influence their ability to achieve change.

In this complex there were three levels of interaction to be considered: 1. the level of interaction within the action agency; 2. the interaction between the change agents and other agencies; and 3. the interaction among change agents and neighborhoods and community groups.

Comparable relations with other agencies need to be worked out.

**FIGURE 3-5**   *The Force Field of Neighborhood Residential Services: A Sample Coverage The Involvement Phase*

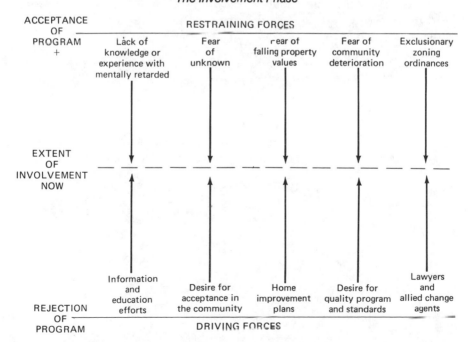

This interorganizational work becomes a vital step in the modification and development of the original agency strategy.

A similar format could be used to analyze an individual client's need, a community's efforts to mobilize itself for a rent strike, or an agency's ability to develop a team approach to service. It can be done in a short time—ten to fifteen minutes—or, in the case of a community, such a survey might require several months' research. The following might be used as a quick assessment of an agency's ability to work as a team: *What are some of the factors in our agency that would help or hinder us in working as a team?*

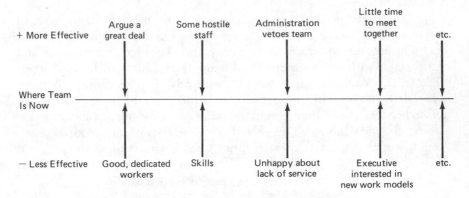

Assuming the above analysis was undertaken by the administration, and the decision is made to modify the situation, some assessment would still be required as to:

1. which force to work on;
2. who should do it;
3. when it should be done; and
4. anticipated consequences for parts of the system.

This process might be repeated with some of the other forces so that three or four alternatives become available. We know, of course, that often

**FIGURE 3-6**  *The Holistic View*

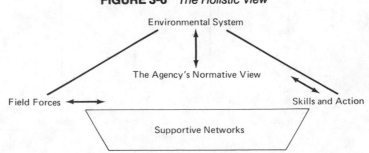

the process of examination and inquiry will itself bring about change because of the involvements and/or new understandings. It can also mobilize resistances to change.

## SUMMARY

Thus we have come through the five steps in administrative action: normative value perspective, systems thinking, supportive networks, field theory, and action. Each is important in that each provides an added dimension that can improve our chances to make sound judgments and move toward positive actions.

What we have provided in the latter part of this chapter is a model for analysis and inquiry, rather than a process model with specified steps to take for change. We will discuss specific techniques in this book. We believe, however, that for now it would be best to avoid any preset model that would only serve to restrict the creative thinking and action of the administrator. The emergent administration process provides a number of process models. We will review some of these in the next chapter.

# CHAPTER 4

---

# the agency
# in its contextual
# environment

Due to the context within which every organization exists, events occurring outside the organization have varying degrees of consequences for its functioning.

An earlier chapter discussed the dynamic quality of the external environment of human service organizations. Such a quality makes it necessary for administrators to understand the context of their practices— those elements of the environment that actually or potentially affect the organization. This chapter will look at these elements and discuss their relationship to the agency in terms of agency dependency, fund raising, public relations and interorganizational relations.

## THE QUEST FOR AUTONOMY

Like the individual, an organization strives to grow and to function as an autonomous unit, free to work toward chosen goals with a minimum of constraint; and, just as it impacts with the individual, the very dynamic and, at times, volatile quality of the external environment affects the care-giving organization. Cuts in funding, changes in political leadership, governmental policy changes, demographic changes, and community attitudes all serve to point out the dependent nature of an organization. Complete independence—that is, no relationship with the external environment—is impossible for any care-giving organization. The intimate relationship of services to people to organizational purposes precludes such independence. Further, the organizational administrator finds that in order to render services and provide organizational maintenance a knowledge of the external environment and its potential effects is very necessary—hence the dependency.

All too often, however, this dependency is played out reactively. Changes in the environment provoke crisis management techniques that often make for poor results: less work, and, most important, poorer service. There is a need to be proactive rather than reactive—that is, to try to sense or project what might happen and to plan for the implications of such changes for the organization. Further, in true proactivity, an attempt to positively influence the environment's elements should be made through assertive, organized behavior.

The administrator must be aware, however, that this attempt to influence the environment will in fact start a chain reaction with new environmental responses calling for additional agency responses. Thus, there is a continual interaction between agency and environment. For example, a decision by one agency to add a service for drug addicts brought forth reactions from neighborhood groups who felt it would hurt the community. Meetings with the community uncovered a lack of youth facilities, a service the agency offered. This balance was successful until the popular program started to attract youth from other communities to the area, causing parents to become concerned. Once again community meetings were held and expanded services in the form of "canteens" and "coffee houses" in other communities were initiated. The interactive growth process continued as community people began to see the need to reemphasize youth activities throughout the city.

Challenges to the autonomy of the agency can be seen as opportunities for service and growth. In the normative sense, the administrator should attempt to transform these environmental forces into positive changes that will benefit service delivery.

There are a number of important elements in the typical care-giving organization's environment. Each of these elements has a continuing influence upon the organization's ability to effectively meet its goals and objectives. A brief commentary on each element follows.

OVERALL COMMUNITY VALUES AND NEEDS.  Any care-giving organization depends on community support for its existence. This sense of community auspices—whether active support, toleration, or resistance—

is an extremely important environmental element for the organization. Active support is manifested by, for example, increased funding, increased referrals, a positive disposition toward increased services, and the like. At present, programs for the aged and for children are enjoying this active support, whereas only a decade ago, negative values and apathy tended to downplay the need for such programs. Toleration usually means neutrality or mixed values in the face of which programs do not grow. For instance, public attitudes/values toward pretrial, supervised prisoner release programs range from positive support for rehabilitation to demands for full incarceration of offenders. Programs are always in the business of mere survival—especially when community values are opposed to them. An example would be the resistance of neighborhood groups to halfway houses and detention centers. Examples of changing attitudes are shown in the ups and downs of child- and spouse-abuse programs. A short time ago, social taboos made a complete denial of the need for such programs the norm. Now, due to changing attitudes about the rights of children and spouses, such programs enjoy a healthy existence. Only when values change can the ever-present needs be faced, identified, and acted upon.

NEEDS/EXPECTATIONS OF CLIENTS/PATIENTS/CONSTITUENTS. Increasingly, care-giving organizations are recognizing the rights of the people they serve. This "quiet" revolution—or evolution—has served to change the relationship between the "served" and the "server" resulting in a number of organizational changes. These include: decentralization of services; outreach programs; development of programs that take into account the "personal acceptability" factor as opposed to mere geographic/financial accessibility; increased consumer involvement in boards, advisory committees, task forces, program committees, and so on; staff changes; ombudsman programs, and the like. All have served to heighten the relationship between organization and consumer.

SOCIOECONOMIC TRENDS. Changing demographic patterns, income levels, competitive financing and dollar availability, and absentee industrial/corporate ownership all serve to influence organizations and point out the need to forecast such trends and proactively plan for potential effects. For example, if there is a taxpayer revolt (e.g. the California "Proposition 13"), what is the potential effect upon public, private, and quasi-public organizations?

GOVERNMENTAL ACTIONS. In this period of increased governmental activity in the human services field, a number of relationships must be considered. These include: public-private agency relationships, community block grants, general and special revenue sharing, Title XX, the use of accountability measures, regionalization of service areas, catchment areas and levels of decision-making control, shifts to program and prototype zero-based budgeting, affirmative action compliance, and the like. All such relationships must be faced. The rapid sequencing of changes in governmental actions point out the need, once again, for proactive, rather than reactive activity on the part of care-giving organizational leadership.

POLITICAL FORCES.   Every care-giving organization, whether public or private, must be more cognizant of the actual/potential political forces operating in its environment. Under the "New Federalism," local officials have more control and/or veto power over the use of funding and, therefore, must be looked upon as elements to be made sympathetically disposed towards the organization. The positive use of influence by key contacts and advocates has become a necessary activity for administrators. This is especially important in attempting to obtain legislative and/or administrative support for changes in laws, benefits, and eligibility and for financial changes.

PLANNING BOARDS.   A major innovation of the past decade has been the creation of planning boards of a regional and/or categorical nature. Depending on the nature of the care-giving organization, it may have to deal with a number of public or private planning boards. A tentative listing reflects this growth: Health Systems Agencies (formerly Comprehensive Health Planning Agencies); Area Services to the Aging; Regional Councils on Alcoholism; Health and Welfare Planning Agencies (either independent private agencies or affiliated with the United Way); Sectarian Planning Agencies/Divisions; Regional Coordinating Agencies (serving huge geographical/county areas); Area Housing Plans; Municipal, County, and State Planning Agencies, and the like. Each of these agencies can and do have an effect upon individual organizations by various means (e.g. A−95 Review). In the view of the planning agency such effects (for example, amount of funding, size of organization, type of service, type of client/constituency, and the like), are designed to coordinate the means of service delivery in a rational, meaningful manner. Autonomy may be threatened but, on the other hand, such bodies can also be made responsive to both rational (planned) and nonrational (influence) activities. Once again, only the assertive, proactive organization will continue to exist and carry out its functions.

FUNDING BODIES.   Care-giving organizations respond to from one to many funding bodies. Many private organizations receive support from federated financing bodies—United Way, Urban Leagues, Jewish Federations, Catholic Charities, and so forth—and public organizations—municipal, county, regional, state, and federal (e.g. Title XX). Public agencies often come under the same types of public-funding auspices. Such funding bodies have a great deal of impact upon the ability of an organization to meet its objectives. The administrator who ignores the need to take active steps to positively influence funding bodies and budget committees can expect to receive diminshing support over a period of time. Funding bodies warrant increased periods of administrative analysis and planned for activities designed to affect them, rather than the reverse.

OTHER ORGANIZATIONS. Care-giving organizations can also relate to other groups including: similar organizations (e.g. child-care organizations); action/education groupings (community/neighborhood congresses and coalitions, consumer advocate groups, League of Women Voters, and so on) and others, such as service clubs, civic clubs, cultural, fraternal, and ethnic organizations. Such groups can serve as positive—though not necessarily financial—supporters of the care-giving organization by helping to mobilize support for its goals and objectives.

SUMMARY. In the normative sense, the administrator of the care-giving organization needs to proactively analyze the external environment and its many elements, such as those noted above. In this manner, he or she will initiate a proactive plan for dealing with the environment rather than simply reacting to such elements, which often yields deleterious results.

### fund raising

This important factor in the survival of the agency will be fully discussed in a chapter of its own. It is important to note it briefly here to highlight its impact.

Probably the sense of proactively dealing with the environment as a state of dependency is manifested nowhere more clearly than in the area of financial dependency. No organization, public or private, can afford not to be continually sensing and forecasting actual and potential sources of financial support. The government, at all levels, has assumed many charitable functions. This has resulted in increasing the complexity of the "how" of financing organizations, and increasing competition for the scarce but vital amount of available funds. Programs begun in times of easier fund raising are often forced to compromise and to seek funding regardless of the effect on organizational goals and services. When survival becomes the primary and services the secondary goal, organizations literally lose their reason for being.

### public relations

In light of their ever-changing external environments and their need to mobilize constituencies, attract financial support, develop overall community support, and effectively deliver services, care-giving organizations must take the time and effort to develop a planned program of public relations.

Kotler and Zaltman strongly support the need for a planned public relations effort by care-giving organizations and introduce the concept of social marketing as a necessary endeavor. They define social marketing as "the design, implementation and control of programs seeking to increase the acceptability of a social idea or practice in a target groups(s)."[1] This is an all too often neglected area of organizational activity.

Systems theory and exchange theory serve to highlight this need. The systems approach denotes the importance of importing inputs from the system's external environment (such as people being served, staff, finances, capital, and so on) and translating them into services as outputs. This exchange with the external environment is a feature of the open system, and the more viable the exchange is kept, the more the system is nurtured and developed. The concept of exchange introduces the aspect of "quid pro quo," that is, that parties or organizations will enter into a mutual relationship if both parties realize that each has something of value to offer to the other. This is at the heart of the existence of the care-giving organization: that society will offer backing and financial support to such an organization because of the exchange value placed on delivery of needed services, fostering of well-being, and the like. However, there must be a continual renewal of this exchange relationship and it cannot be taken for granted. Many a funding source has been lost because an organization did not give positive feedback about its expenditure of monies and meeting of goals and objectives. Similarly, the loss of memberships, as alluded to earlier, was a loss of constituency in that organizations did not maintain their exchange relationship with key supporters.

Each of the elements in a care-giving organization's environment, may be viewed as a target for change or renewal. Kotler presents the concept of markets and publics in relation to nonprofit organizations and his discussion has merit for the administrator. He defines market as "a distinct group of people and/or organizations that have resources which they want to exchange, or might conceivably exchange, for distinct benefits."[2] Using this concept, the administrator can begin to analyze elements in the organization's environment with regard to their actual and potential support. This returns to the previous discussion on proactivity, of moving out of the agency to positively predispose environmental elements—markets—towards agency support.

Another helpful concept is Kotler's use of "publics" in relation to nonprofit organizations. He defines a public as "a distinct group of people and/or organizations that have an actual or a potential interest and/or

1. Philip Kotler and Gerald Zaltman, "Social Marketing: An Approach to Planned Social Change," *Journal of Marketing* (July 1971), 3–12.

2. Philip Kotler, *Marketing for Nonprofit Organizations* (Englewood Cliffs, N.J.: Prentice-Hall, Inc., 1975), p. 22.

impact on an organization."[3] He further classifies three types of publics on the basis of level of involvement with the organization: "a reciprocal public is a public that is interested in the organization, with the organization also interested in them. A sought public is a public that the organization is interested in, but that is not necessarily interested in the organization. An unwelcome public is a public that is interested in the organization, but in whom the organization is not interested."[4] The key elements in the organization's environment as discussed earlier can be classified according to these categories.

For example, the overall community could be viewed as both a reciprocal and sought public. Similarly, clients, patients, and constituents can be seen as both reciprocal and sought publics (in the exchange of service for contributions, as well as in the organization's need for its consumers—otherwise there would be no reason for its existence). Governmental bodies, political forces, planning boards, and funding bodies can be classified as any one or all three types of public depending upon the relationships between the care-giving organization and such bodies. At times, care-giving organizations perceive public and private funding bodies as bordering on being unwelcome publics.

The human service organization, then, should actively explore its external environment and analyze the types of public actually and potentially critical to its service effectiveness and maintenance. These publics should be viewed as marketing targets figuring in planned public relations programs.

Public relations aims at shaping and changing other people's and organizations' values, beliefs, attitudes, and behaviors. As an influencing tactic, it is directed towards two areas: general and specific. The general area asks the question: "What does everyone need to know about the organization, and what media will be effective (radio, T. V., newspaper, brochures, pamphlets, and so forth)?" The specific area asks: "What does a particular person/group/organization need to know in order to be favorably predisposed toward the organization, and what content and medium will be effective (brochure, personal contact, and so forth)?" The former implies a rational approach, while the latter is more amenable to a nonrational one. This will be elaborated upon in the section on inter-organizational relations.

Both of these approaches call for a planned activity moving from research to action to selective communication. Research involves an analysis of the general or special groups of people towards whom the public relations program is directed. This includes analyzing opinions and attitudes regarding the human service organization's goals, objectives,

3.   Kotler, p. 17.
4.   Kotler, p. 20.

personnel, and so on. The action step is the selection by the human services organization of a change desired in the present state of affairs (negative opinions, lack of consensus or organizational goals, apathy, and so on). Selective communication involves approaching the general or special publics in such a way as to influence them positively. This could involve one or more public relations techniques depending on the public-action-communication continuum, such as advertising, brochures, pamphlets, radio, television, newspapers, lobbying, handbooks, periodicals, speeches, agency tours, special events, personal contacts, and many others.

In short, in the spirit of proactivity, the care-giving organization should design a public relations program to persuade various publics to become its supporters. This calls for a strong year-round public relations program to insure a diversified support base and an adequate public understanding of the organization's objectives.

### interorganizational relations

We have been focusing on the relationship of the human service organization to its environment, pinpointing the sense of dependency and the need to be proactively involved with external publics regarding fund raising and public relations. By now it should be clear that all human service organizations are parts of the environment of other organizations. In systems terms, for existence and growth the organization must continually interact with its environment and maintain a steady equilibrium. Increasingly in human service organizations the boundaries between organizations will become less rigid and more permeable. Kast and Rosenweig point out that "one of the most dramatic trends in the future will be the development of systems-oriented approaches which can deal with broad social problems on a total rather than a piecemeal basis. In many ways, the development of wide-boundary organizations will be similar to the evaluation of the business corporate firm which has been so successful in the production of goods or services."[5]

The alphabet soup of comprehensive planning organizations (H.S.A.'s, R.T.A.'s, R.P.A., R.C.A.'s, and so on) have increasingly pressured human service organizations to expand their boundaries. Additional pressures in this trend to more permeable, more open, and expanded boundaries have come from catchment area formation, public-private purchases of services, intersystem linkages, joint packaging of funding proposals on the part of public and private organizations, goal elaboration, and the like.

The net result of such environmental pressures is to emphasize the

5.  Fremont E. Kast and James E. Rosenzweig, *Organization and Management* (New York: McGraw-Hill Book Company, 1970), p. 593.

need for human service organizations to be proactive with their environment. The field of interorganizational theory is only recently becoming a focal point for study, but it does highlight the increasing necessity for attempts to influence critical "other organizations."

A key concept is that of *interface*, which can be viewed simply as the area of contact between one system (organization) and another. This area is where the major interaction of organizations takes place and where formal and informal lines of communication exist. These may include, for example, referral of cases from one organization to another, budget committee meetings between funding bodies and recipient organizations, joint agency planning councils or committees, and so on.

It is important to the human services organization that its interface with other organizations be positive—that is a movement from sought to reciprocal publics, and/or a reduction of the strain placed on the organization by an unwelcome public. The key for many organizations, then, is to exert a positive influence so that another organization(s) becomes predisposed to act favorably towards it. Since key decision-makers set organizational policy, this activity in essence becomes one of influencing leaders.

We noted in an earlier section that there are two approaches to persuading people—the generalized approach and the special approach—and that both are related to content and media. In the general approach, we noted, one seeks to discover what everyone needs to know about a desired organizational goal and then determines how best to reach everyone (T. V., radio, newspaper releases, speeches, and so on). The specialized approach deals with determining what special person(s) and/or organization(s) needs to know about a desired organizational goal and developing a specialized approach to reach that person or group (i.e., getting on an agenda, personal and/or key contacts, and the like).

This special approach, dealing with key persons in specific publics, involves the use of persuasion/motivation. In short, it requires analytical action on the part of organizational leadership in three areas: sense of need, "net costs," and key people. Sense of need relates to analyzing how one's own needs can be made congruent with another person(s) and/or organization(s) needs (i.e., appealing to their interest, interpretation, community loyalty, or whatever). "Net costs" refers to the simple axiom that an individual acts in one way or another depending upon how he or she perceives the action in relation to personal or organizational benefit or loss (i.e., is the action seen as beneficial to self-esteem, social esteem, personal solidarity, and so on). Key people refers to the fact that in any organization certain people have the ability to influence other decision-makers and/or the entire organization. Often their ability is associated with one or more roles: the advisor to the key decision-maker (one who has developed personal credibility over time); the negotiator (one who finds the terms that other key leaders can and will agree upon); or the publicist (one who tries to create public opinion favorable to certain ventures).

It follows that in dealing with external publics, as in interorganizational relationship building, such publics should be analyzed in a positive sense and that influence is a necessary ingredient in organizational life.

### board-staff-committee relationships

The focal point for many staff members—their major source of identification—is most often their agency. It may make up the bulk of their lives. Thus, they may be unrealistic about the agency. On the other hand, the board's major responsibilities frequently lie elsewhere. Therefore the board can bring a more critical view to the agency, but also may shape its environment, acting as an important link to other networks and agencies.

Integral to the ability of a human services organization to render effective services are the relationships among the key members of organization board and/or advisory committee, organizational staff members, and members of organizational committees. These relationships are the substance upon which organizational plans are developed, problems are solved, and activities are carried out. When such relationships are unbalanced, the organization operates ineffectively, has low morale, and stands in danger of losing the support of its immediate public. In the case of a public agency, when there is a strong board of directors or advisory board coupled with a weak executive staff, the result is usually an ineffective organization characterized by high staff turnover. When there is a strong executive staff coupled with a weak board of directors, the result usually is poor accountability, one-sided decisions, and poor board attendance. With organizational committees there are two possible faults: the "rubber stamp" committee that merely gives *pro forma* endorsements of decisions already made, or the "long–drawn-out" committee that deals only with process and rarely arrives at a final decision.

Such ineffectiveness of relationships is depicted in Figure 4-1 below. This triangle calls attention to the one-way communication aspect of board, staff, and committee relationships. A board that sees itself only as a controlling body will not be open to the positive and alternative opinions of staff and committees regarding organizational policies, goals, and activities. A staff that looks upon itself only as an advisor of boards and committees does not really take responsibility for its recommendations. If it does not try to positively influence action taken on its recommendations then it is sterile in its professional activity. Finally, the committee that only receives and reports advice is not assuming its obligations as an active arm of the organization.

**FIGURE 4-1** *Effective Organizational Relationships*

The normative sense of such relationships implies a constant inter-change of ideas, mutual exchange of information from within and without the organization, and a continual feedback process. It is based upon mutual respect among the three parties. This more healthy relationship is depicted in Figure 4-2. Here the shaded area portrays the interface among the three parties where particular attitudes, values, and infor-mation are brought to the relationship by each group and serve to influence how decisions are shaped, rendered, and implemented. The full and open mutually-directed communication enhances the decision making by offering more complete alternatives for consideration. For example, both board members and committees can interpret community attitudes and information vital to the process of deciding to change or add to organizational service delivery. Concurrently, staff can bring its expertise concerning community needs and monies available for service delivery to bear on the same issue. The positive interchange of such information should result in a much richer decision-making process.

For an effective organization, all three groups must bring a sense of mutual respect to their active involvement in the grey area of inter-

**FIGURE 4-2** *Effective Organizational Relationships*

relationships. Each party must also have a sense of its own purposes, as indicated in the following discussion.

Briefly stated, the board of directors of a private human services organization or an accountability body in the public organization, commission, or comparable body, is charged with the following general purposes: to assure citizen participation; to assure an effective administration of the organization (ultimate responsibility reposes in the board of directors, but implementation is delegated to the director); and to assure continuity of the organization's programs. These purposes are played out through the establishment of general organizational goals and policies, and in the overseeing and validation of organizational operations. A particular point here is that the board plays a two-sided interpretive role in validation: validating the organization to the general community and other key publics, such as funding bodies and planning bodies; and validating community concerns to staff, thus influencing staff activities.

Generally, committees in human service organizations are organized instrumentalities of the board of directors (this does not prevent staff committees from dealing with particular issues), that is to say, a committee assists the board in carrying out its functions. In human service organizations, two types of committees are common: the ad hoc or special purpose committee that is designed to work on a particular problem, issue, activity and so forth within a particular time frame; and the standing committee that generally relates to matters of continuing responsibility, such as a personnel or program committee. Committees are omnipresent in the human service field and, ideally, are the means to involve lay and professional leadership in the process of organizational operations.

Staff, as an integral part of the organizational endeavor, brings professional expertise in such areas as planning, organization of resources, evaluation of alternatives, coordination, and so forth to boards and committees. The interchange of this professional expertise and lay experience, along with validation and interpretation, becomes the heart of the effective organization.

In sum, the ideal state of affairs is the mature relationship of boards, committees, and staff working in concert and with mutual respect to enhance organizational programs and services.

## DISCRIMINATORY ENVIRONMENTAL FORCES

We are all shaped by our environment—often without being aware of the nature of that shaping. This chapter has taken a systems approach to the relationship of a human service organization to its environment in terms of the intertwining relationships of dependence, fund raising, public relations and interorganizational relations. Stratification and discrimination are aspects of our society that shape agency actions. The administrator ought to emphasize the need for ethical, proactive behavior on the part of the organization toward its environment as opposed to reactive or destructive activities.

Although we are taught in schools of social work about the hidden dimensions of sexism and racism, some of these problems have become institutionalized in our own profession, and the administrator needs to be aware and "self-aware" of these problems. The roots of discrimination in social work are deep.

### sexism in social work[6]

The legal and moral pressures to conform to the requirements of affirmative action have been supported by the activities of various minority groups on behalf of themselves. The structure of the profession itself has been a factor in forcing a closer look at the plight of women in social work.

From the beginning, women have comprised between 60 and 90 percent of the profession, estimates averaging around 70 percent. Various studies have shown both salary and position discrimination. Knapman, looking at the entry and subsequent promotion comparison of 132 MSW's, 77 female and 55 male, pointed up some of the inequities, as Tables 4-1 and 4-2 show.[7]

### women in administrative positions

Sonia Abels points out that "social work manpower is predominately women's power. Women make up sixty percent of the profession. . . . Since the profession's inception, the belief that women are the most appropriate persons to carry out personal services has remained constant."[8]

The Charity Organization Societies, which legitimized and substantiated the professionalization of social work, sanctioned women as service deliverers. Seventy-five percent of all "friendly visitors" were women and ninety percent of the Boards of Directors were male.[9]

---

6.   We are dealing more fully here with women rather than other minority groups not because we feel that their problems are more severe, but because women make up such a large proportion of staff in the field. The problems of other minority groups are at least as severe. Furthermore the problems for other minority members who are also women are no doubt compounded.

7.   Shirley Kuchak Knapman, "Sex Discrimination in Family Agencies," *Social Work*, 22, no. 6 (November 1977), 462–63.

8.   Sonia L. Abels, "Women and Social Work: A Historical Critique," *Social Development Issues* (Winter 1978), p. 4.

9.   Abels, p. 6.

**TABLE 4-1**  *Initial and Current Position Levels of MSW Social Workers†*

| Sex of Respondent | Initial Position Level[a] | | | | Current Position Level[b] | | | |
|---|---|---|---|---|---|---|---|---|
| | 1 | 2 | 3 | 4 | 1 | 2 | 3 | 4 |
| Female | 75 | 1 | 0 | 0 | 52 | 13 | 10 | 1 |
| Male | 45 | 5 | 2 | 0 | 27 | 5 | 6 | 14 |

†Knapman, p. 463.
[a]$x^2 = 9.31$, df $= 2$, p $.01$.
[b]$x^2 = 20.28$, df $= 2$, p $.001$.

**TABLE 4-2**  *Average Current Salaries and Average Rate of Increase for Females and Males in Small and Large Communities*\*

| Sex of Respondent | Number | Average Current Salary | Average Rate of Increase |
|---|---|---|---|
| Female | | | |
| All females | 56 | $11,154.40 | 19.54 |
| Small communities | 8 | 12,436.99 | 11.92 |
| Large communities | 48 | 10,922.25 | 21.07 |
| Male | | | |
| All males | 50 | 12,140.84 | 27.16 |
| Small communities | 19 | 13,804.31 | 18.52 |
| Large communities | 31 | 11,178.95 | 36.40 |

\*Knapman, p. 464.

In 1969, another appraisal showed that forty-three percent of female social workers performed some administrative tasks, compared to fifty-eight percent for men, but a closer appraisal reveals that the women more frequently held lower level administrative jobs. Whereas twenty-five percent of the men listed direct service as their main job functions, forty-three percent of female workers did so. When we note that the median annual salary for male administrators was $13,000.00 to $13,999.00, compared to a median salary of $9,000.00 to $9,900.00 for female administrators, the lower income level for women in general becomes obvious.[10] In addition, women holding similar positions as men often make a smaller salary.

Although social work has often been considered a "woman's" job, Chafetz notes that "men remain dominant in that traditional occupation and invade 'women's occupation' at the highest levels."[11]

10. Janet Saltzman Chafetz, "Women in Social Work," *Social Work* (September 1972), p. 14.
11. Chafetz, p. 18.

Friedman points out that there was a time when most hospital administrators were women: "Well into the twentieth century, female nurses or members of religious orders were frequently found in charge of hospitals." In 1979 she found only 1,331 women among the 10,895 nominees of the American College of Hospital Administrators.[12]

Women rightfully feel oppressed when they are qualified to perform administrative positions but are relegated to direct service, or when they do not receive salaries appropriate to their tasks.

A more general feeling that only women can provide the best service to women pervades some women's movements, and has manifested itself in courses, articles, and advertisements promoting feminist therapy.[13] Interestingly the consciousness raising of feminist groups has led to a similar, though more narrow, approach for men.

Beyond changes for women staff, one important additional benefit has been a heightened awareness of the problems of women clients in our society. Staff and administrators are more aware of the problems facing a working mother or wife, or a mature woman seeking a career. Their uphill struggles have been presented, documented, and subjected to analysis and policy planning.[14]

### racism and discrimination

Discrimination takes many forms. It may be directed against the aged, the handicapped, various religious groups, or others seen as deviant. Although social work is a profession dedicated to equality and justice, it is part of a society and influenced, often subtly, by its values and processes. To say that discrimination exists in agencies is not to judge them, but to help administrators become more aware of how they are influenced by the cultural context.

"Racism may be described as a system of attitudes and beliefs, behaviors and practices, and laws and policies that are predicated on a negative evaluation of the minority group."[15] We might suggest further that racism is a part of our way of life; it has been institutionalized in the patterns of American life. "Institutional racism exists when the structure and operation of institutions are determined by racial criteria and results

12.   Emily Friedman, "Women CEOs: they're good for the field, but is it good for them?" *Hospitals* (Feb. 1, 1980), p. 62.

13.   Susan Amelia Thomas, "Theory and Practice in Feminist Therapy," *Social Work*, 22, no. 6 (November 1977), 447.

14.   Miriam Dinnerman, "Catch 23: Women, Work and Welfare," *Social Work*, 22, no. 6 (November 1977), 472.

15.   *Black Perspectives on Social Work Education* (New York: Council on Social Work Education, 1974), p. 4.

in unequal access to the protection, benefits, opportunities and rewards of society."[16]

Many groups have felt this discrimination and have spoken to it. There have been attempts in our profession to modify racism in social service organizations. However, it has been said that "the pervasiveness of racism in American society in many events and covert ways makes the achievement of the goal of integrating black content into the social work curriculum difficult indeed."[17] After a great deal of soul searching and particularly through the concerted efforts of minority members, the profession has been able to deal with some of the elements of racism, sexism, and agism in its own organizational life. The National Association of Social Workers, which has long seen the elimination of racism as one of its major goals, made some of the following pronouncements in its recent delegate assembly resolution.

> The policy of the National Association of Social Workers shall be to work towards the building of an open society in which social and racial differences are accepted and respected and within which individual and institutionalized racism will not be encouraged, supported or tolerated. . . .
> It is the responsibility of NASW members to look into their own practice and in the agencies where they work for specific ways to attack racism where it exists . . . [within the Profession and to:]
> (1) Continue to strive for full representation of minorities at all levels of leadership and employment—policy formulation, administration, supervision and direct service—in social work and in NASW. (2) Implement the concepts of affirmative action in all facets of practice, education, and professional development, at both voluntary and paid levels of service.[18]

No doubt other bodies within the human services range have taken similar important steps to eliminte discrimination and inequality within their own organizations. The Association of Black Social Workers has worked hard in this area, as has the Council on Social Work Education.

Often leadership in this area has come from students, through national groups or at the local level through their schools of social work. Some of their stands have reflected the belief that the student is often treated with the same disregard as more commonly recognized minority groups.

In his attempts to alert social work educators to the concerns and needs of the Puerto Rican community, Betances notes the error in drawing negative distinctions between Puerto Ricans and others by saying, "Efforts to eliminate institutionalized racism, which is such a destructive

16. *Black Perspectives*, p. 4.
17. *Black Task Force Report* (New York: Council on Social Work Education, 1973), p. 7.
18. *NASW News*, "Delegate Assembly Actions," 25, no. 1, (Jan. 1980), 27.

force in the lives of young Puerto Ricans, are undermined by this sort of perspective . . .".[19] Garcia notes the prejudice against aged Chicanos.[20]

Statements from other minority groups call for increased minority enrollment in schools of social work and in the makeup of faculties.[21] The growing awareness by groups that they not only need to speak up for themselves but have an obligation to do so has helped bring their situation into public view.

Yet most evidence shows that the vast majority of people are still callous to the needs of minority groups. Most recently we have observed the lack of concern of many planners of programs and facilities to the plight of the handicapped and the aged. It would appear that there is still a long way to go. When it comes to new buildings and new programs, however, it is clear that the leadership in the decision-making process is in the hands of the administrator. This is an area in which administrative power should be used.

### affirmative action

Nothing is more basic to the success of the lengthy struggle to eliminate discrimination from American life than the effort to establish equal access to occupations and career opportunities. The Civil Rights Act of 1964 was a clear statement of the national desire to end discriminatory treatment of minorities and women in the job market. The implementation of this Act has proved exceedingly difficult and has provoked intense debate about the methods used to eliminate discriminatory practices. Presently, "the controversy is centered around the concept of 'affirmative action,' a term that in a broad sense encompasses any measure, beyond simple termination of a discriminatory practice, adopted to correct or compensate for past or present discrimination or to prevent discrimination from recurring in the future."[22] The question is whether certain actions exceed what is required to establish equal opportunity for minorities and women, thereby succeeding at the expense of others.

19. Samuel Betances, "Race and the Mainland Puerto Rican: A Review of the Sociological Literature," in *Puerto Rican Curriculum Development Workshop: A Report,* ed. Angel P. Campos (New York: Council on Social Work Education, 1974), p. 63.

20. Alejandro Garcia, *Factors Affecting the Economic Status of Elderly Chicanos* (unpublished paper presented at NCSW, New York, May 1974).

21. See for example: Marta Sotomayor and Philip D. Ortego y Garsca, eds., *Chicano Content and Social Work Education* (New York: Council on Social Work Education, 1975), John E. Mackey, ed., *American Indian Task Force Report* (New York: Council on Social Work Education, 1972), and Magdalina Miranda, ed., *Puerto Rican Task Force Report* (New York: Council on Social Work Education, 1973).

22. United States Commission on Civil Rights, Statement on *Affirmative Action* (Clearinghouse Publication, Publication 54, Washington, D.C.: U.S. Government Promoting Office), October, 1977, p. 2.

Normatively speaking, human service organizations should and must be involved in supporting affirmative action in organizations other than their own regardless of the controversy. Affirmative actions in the case of such organizations calls to mind the earlier discussions of proaction versus reaction. It is not enough for human service organizations to react favorably to the dictates of the 1964 law by eliminating discriminatory practices. Rather, human service organizations should proactively define and implement positive action steps to remedy discriminatory problems, as well as increase opportunities for minorities and women at all levels of the human service organization's work force. This calls for result-oriented programs in the areas of recruitment, hiring, training opportunities, promotion, seniority and job classifications, working conditions, equal pay and even the termination process. Such results-oriented programs require affirmative action plans. In the normative sense, this is a potential means to involve a committee—jointly composed of administration, staff, and board members—to be responsible for development and implementation of affirmative action procedures.

## SUMMARY

This chapter discussed the need of the administrator to proactively deal with key elements in the organization's contextual environment. The interaction of the external and internal environments modifies the behavior of all the participants in the organization's activities. Self awareness as well as an understanding of the impact of discriminatory forces are critical for the administrator interested in managing an organization in a "just manner."

# part 2

## THE MANAGEMENT CYCLE

## INTRODUCTION

If there is a base for a necessary role-set of activities associated with administrators, it is the responsibility for arriving at effective decisions in a range of areas. These include organizational objectives such as: how do we build our organizational structure; how do I motivate my supervisors; what kind of evaluation mechanism do I utilize; where do we obtain funding; who should be the new unit director; when should we begin and end our financial campaign; and so on. These questions fall within both the decision role of the administrator and the four key management functions of planning, organizing, controlling, and motivating. The relationship between decision making and each of these four functions is one of necessity. One does not plan without having made some earlier decisions about the why and how of planning. Similarly, one does not organize resources, implement a control and evaluation process, nor initiate a motivation or promotion process without having made conscious decisions to undertake such activities. Tersine supports this view by pointing out that the manager "makes decisions in establishing objectives; he/she makes planning decisions, organizing decisions, motivating decisions and controlling decisions."*

Decision making, then, is both common to and an integral part of the four key management processes. Complementary to the crucial base of decision making is the need for skills in dealing with human resources. The best administrative structures, planned programs, service delivery implementations, budgeting and evaluation techniques all depend upon decisions made in light of the human factor. If personnel are unknowledgable, unskilled, or unwilling, even the best decisions and actions are doomed to failure.

Consistent with our systems orientation, we know that the aforementioned four key management processes interact with each other— each affects and is affected by the others. They often occur simultaneously, but are also continuous, dynamic processes. They are cyclical in nature. When interactively operating efficiently and effectively, they serve to convert a care-giving organization's input into outputs in keeping with the avowed purposes of the agency.

Figure 1 illustrates the cyclical nature of these processes and their dependency upon solid decision making.

*Richard J. Tersine, "Organization Decision Theory—A Synthesis," *Management Planning*, 21, no. 18 (July, August, 1972), 74.

**FIGURE 1**  *The Functional Cycle of Management*

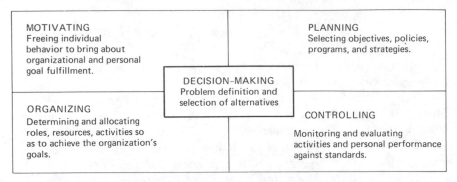

The four processes can be described as follows:

PLANNING PROCESS.   Analyzing with all staff levels, pertinent information from the past and present, as well as predicting the most likely future developments, so that a course of action may be formulated to enable an organization to attain its stated objectives.

ORGANIZING PROCESS.   Creating the formal series of role structures and responsible relationships which are most likely to enable the organization to attain its stated objectives.

CONTROLLING PROCESS.   Creating a fair and equitable process of monitoring, measuring, correcting, and evaluating tools to assure the organization's ability to attain its stated objective.

MOTIVATING PROCESS.   Examining and establishing reward systems in keeping with human needs.

Central to each of these processes is the internal process of:

DECISION MAKING.   The rational-evidential choosing from alternatives in order to best attain the organization's stated objectives.

Each process is both social and technical in nature—social in the sense that human care organizations, in order to operate, require social interaction of human resources; and technical in that a series of functions, activities, and events must occur in order to accomplish the care-giving objectives.

A systems framework can be helpful in understanding these processes. By use of an input, throughput, and output perspective we can view each of these processes in an integrative way. Figure 2 illustrates an interpretation of the framework in systems terms, which include:

PLANNING.   Formulation of the organization's objectives and assessment of the organization's inputs (e.g., what specific resources, manpower, capital, time, etc. are needed to accomplish these objectives).

ORGANIZATION.   The utilization of the organization's throughput processes (placement, deployment of human resources and activities) to

**FIGURE 2** *Key Management Processes in Systems Terms*

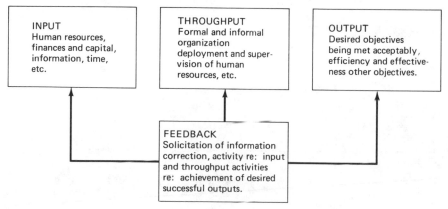

most effectively and efficiently attain the organization's goal—that is, to build the bridge between acquisition and use of resources so that they are used rationally to achieve desired outputs.

MOTIVATION. The employment of human resources technology within the throughput process so as to enable people simultaneously to fulfill the organization's and, as much as possible, their own desired outputs.

CONTROL. The planned feedback activity that initally sets up standards of successful performance, then evaluates and measures performance and initiates corrective mechanisms if the feedback is negative.

Once again, underlying each of these functional processes, is:

DECISION MAKING. Determination of: the organization's objectives; methods and strategies of achievement; selection and procurement of inputs (resources) necessary to attain these objectives; throughput mechanisms (organization and motivation of resources); and feedback (monitoring and evaluation) on input and output activities determining whether or not if they have contributed to the attainment of desired outputs.

Following this introduction to the cycle of management functional processes, each chapter of Part II will focus on one process in depth. The first two chapters examine the concepts of motivation and decision making as integral to carrying out the remaining processes, discussed in the succeeding chapters.

# CHAPTER 5

---

# motivation

**WORKER MOTIVATION
AND SATISFACTION:
MEETING HUMAN NEEDS**

The demise of the work ethic has been forecast regularly during the past few years and has intensified since the publication of the Federal government's report, *Work in America*.[1] The reduction of productivity, strikes, sabotage, and other indicators of worker alienation have focused the nations' attention on work incentives and work motivation. Changing times have called forth not only new understandings of worker motivation, but ways of dealing with it. "The stick of the traditional approach to managing worker and working was hunger and fear. Traditionally, all but a handful of men in every society lived at the very margin of subsistence

---

1. U.S. Department of Health, Education and Welfare, *Work in America* (Cambridge, Mass.: MIT Press, 1973).

and in imminent threat of starvation. . . . The basic fact—unpalatable but inescapable—is that the traditional Theory X approach to managing, that is, the carrot-and-stick way, no longer works."[2]

There have been numerous studies concerning worker motivation, satisfaction, and productivity. These studies have produced some findings contrary to the earlier belief that a worker's satisfaction with his or her employment was related primarily to salary.

Blauner found that marked differences exist in work attitudes and expectations from one occupational level to another and that the "principal source of job satisfaction is autonomy and independence on the job."[3] Herzberg found that "the principal sources of satisfaction [were] achievement, recognition, the work itself, responsibility or advancement." He also reported that the amount of salary itself is not a source of job satisfaction, but that "low salaries, or those considered unfair, are a source of job dissatisfaction."[4]

Herzberg hypothesized that the opposite of dissatisfaction is not satisfaction, but simply no dissatisfaction, and that the absence of satisfaction, again, is not dissatisfaction, but no satisfaction. His postulation of these sets of factors as being different in character, separate, and discrete caused the theory to be called the Herzberg "Two-factor Theory of Job Satisfaction." A listing of the basic factors—which he called "satisfiers" and dissatisfiers"—may illustrate the substantive differences in their character, though not necessarily in the order of importance within each set of factors.

| | |
|---|---|
| Satisfiers: | Achievement |
| | Recognition |
| | Responsibility |
| | Work itself |
| | Growth |
| | Advancement |
| Dissatisfiers: | Working conditions |
| | Policies and administrative practices |
| | Supervision |
| | Interpersonal relations |
| | Salary (all forms of financial compensation) |
| | Status |
| | Job security |
| | Personal life |

2.  Peter F. Drucker, *Management: Tasks, Practices and Responsibilities* (New York: Harper & Row, Pub., 1974), p. 235.

3.  Robert Blauner, "Extent of Satisfaction: A Review of General Research," in *Psychology in Administration,* by Timothy W. Costello and Sheldon S. Zalkind (Englewood Cliffs, N.J.: Prentice-Hall, Inc., 1963), p. 84.

4.  Frederick Herzberg et al., *Job Attitudes: Reviews of Research and Opinion* (Psychological Service of Pittsburgh, Pennsylvania, 1957), p. 95.

Further analysis of the responses suggests that the satisfiers are all integral to the performance of the job, and therefore are referred to as job-*content* factors; whereas the dissatisfiers have to do with the environment surrounding of the job itself, and thus are referred to as job-*context* factors. Herzberg called the satisfiers "motivators" and the dissatisfiers "hygiene factors," since they serve merely to support the climate for the job-content or motivating factors; therefore, the theory is often called the motivation-hygiene theory of job satisfaction. He also referred to the dissatisfiers as "replenishment needs" (they also go back to zero), since they must always be provided for, but their importance is realized only when they are inadequate or absent. The motivators are called "growth needs," since they are the work elements that provide the real motivation in this theory of job satisfaction. Generally speaking, the dissatisfiers, or hygiene factors, represent the lower-level needs on Maslow's hierarchy (discussed below), and the satisfiers, or motivators, are roughly analogous to the upper levels of the hierarchy—esteem and self-actualization.[5] Work is only one part of the life system for people and its importance in their total life picture is being increasingly minimized.

Satisfaction can be defined as "a psychological judgment made by the individual regarding his evaluation of his feeling about his job."[6]

Many studies report similar findings. In essence, wages, which are generally ranked by administrators as one of the major factors in job satisfaction, are rarely rated among the top three satisfiers by staff. People seem to want to work where they have some opportunity to control their work situation and where they have some degree of independence. They seem also to seek achievement, recognition, responsibility, and the opportunity for advancement. These might be considered as the mental-health, or ego-building, aspects of the job. Herzberg's "hygenic" factors only tend to prevent dissatisfaction and poor job performance. The secondary factors, the "motivators," lead to "self-actualization" or "self-realization."

In social work the nature of the job itself can often provide satisfaction in the areas defined as motivators. Responses from social workers have often indicated that there is a great deal of satisfaction in helping people, and that the work itself is rewarding. We have to examine more closely, however, whether rewards such as achievement, recognition, and advancement are attained by the agency-trained worker on the same basis as they are attained by the professional, by the staff person as they are by the executive. The job must offer all workers a certain amount of stimula-

5.   Frederick Herzberg, Bernard Mausner, and Barbara B. Sydeman, *The Motivation to Work* (New York: John Wiley & Sons, Inc., 1962). A few authors differ: see, for example, Clair F. Vough, *Productivity* (New York: Amacom, 1979), p. 14. Vough suggests that higher wages are the major items of importance, basing his conclusions on personal managerial experience at I.B.M.

6.   Paul Abels, "The Agency-Trained Worker: The Sub-Professional in Professionally Oriented Group Service Agencies" (unpublished Ph.D. dissertation, University of Chicago, 1967).

tion and opportunity if they are to try themselves in new activities and with new tasks.

Lack of interest in the content of the worker assignment has also been a source of dissatisfaction in social work and, in one study, proved to be the major reason given for leaving a staff position. The paradox, of course, is that despite people's complaints about work, nonwork due to retirement acts as a haunting and stressful threat. Recent legislative alterations in the retirement age point this up.

Worker satisfaction as an important factor in worker morale, job attitudes, and worker turnover has been studied by a number of investigators. Pearlin, in discussing organizations, states: "In order to retain its staff and to maintain itself as an on-going institution, [an organization] must gear itself not only for the attainment of the ends for which it was established, but also for the satisfaction of the diverse aspirations and opportunities sought by its members."[7] Collins and Geutzkow point out that there are a number of terms that have been used interchangeably with satisfaction: "A highly satisfied person have high morale and the satisfied worker has job satisfaction or favorable job attitudes. . . . Most researchers define satisfaction as a judgment of a subjective state of feeling or evaluation."[8]

Management studies, such as the Hawthorne series, began to alert psychologists to the realization that people respond to other than financial rewards. One of the major influences in our current recognition that man does not live by bread alone came from the work of Abraham Maslow, whose development of the concept "hierarchy of needs" has led to what is known as the "new" movement in understanding human behavior.[9]

Maslow holds that "the human being is motivated by a number of basic needs which are species-wide, apparently unchanging and genetic or instinctual in origin." As Figure 5-1 shows, these needs, beginning with physiological states, proceed to a quest for self-actualization. Self-actualization, a term first used by Kurt Goldstein, suggests that people must find a sense of self-fulfillment, but that this is most often achieved when other basic needs—physiological, safety, love and esteem—have been met.

Maslow suggests that when those needs are unsatisfied, they create tensions in the person so that a solution is sought. When the needs are met (i.e., hunger satisfied), that need no longer creates a tension and its potency as a motivating force is lost until the person is again hungry. In the meantime, the person can be motivated by other needs.

According to Maslow's later work, managers have the responsibility

7.   Leonard I. Pearlin, "Alienation from Work: A Study of Nursing Personnel," *American Sociological Review*, 27, no. 3 (June 1962), 320.

8.   Barry Collins and Harold Guetchow, *A Social Psychology of Group Process* (New York: John Wiley & Sons, Inc., 1964), p. 189.

9.   Abraham Maslow, "A Theory of Human Motivation," *Psychological Review*, 50 (1943), 370–96.

**FIGURE 5-1**  *Maslow's Hierarchy of Needs*

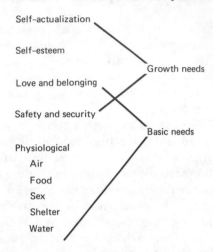

to create a climate in which the human potential can be actualized.[10] Reviews of the literature do not show consistent support for his theories, but certain parts of Maslow's work have been generally accepted.[11]

### the press to competence

Providing the opportunity to grow and make discoveries is part of an approach which holds that the human being has a natural bent toward discovery and learning, and that we should make use of these natural tendencies by placing the learning experience within the hands of the students to a greater extent. This natural thrust toward growth takes us into the "wilds" of motivation—an immense topic only touched on in this discussion. However, some of the ideas of theorists who have seen this "will to learn" as an intrinsic motive should be mentioned. Bruner speaks to this point and lists four intrinsic motives for learning: curiosity, competence (accomplishment), identification, and reciprocity. "The early helplessness of man, for example, seems to be accompanied by propelling curiosity about the environment and by much self-reinforcing activity seemingly designed to achieve competence in that environment."[12]

10. Abraham Maslow, *Eupsychian Management* (Homewood, Illinois: Richard D. Irwin, 1965), pp. 3–5.

11. For a review of the literature see: Mahmond A. Wahba and Lawrence G. Bridwell, "Maslow Reconsidered. A Review of Research on The Need Hierarchy Theory," in *Motivation and Work Behavior*, ed. Richard M. Steers and Lyman W. Porter, (New York: McGraw-Hill Book Company, Inc., 1979), pp. 47–55.

12. Jerome S. Bruner, *Toward a Theory of Instruction* (Cambridge, Mass.: Harvard University Press, 1966), pp. 113–28.

White discusses competence motivation quite fully in his brilliant work on motivation. He writes:

> The thesis is then proposed that all of these behaviors (visual explorations, grasping, crawling and walking, attention . . . , language and thinking . . . , and producing effective changes in the environment) have a common biological significance; they all form part of the process whereby the animal or child learns to interact with his environment. The word competence is chosen as suitable to indicate this common property.[13]

Efforts to make use of these natural tendencies have led to the development of the discovery or inquiry "models" of learning. "Inquiry has been defined as the controlled use of interaction in the pursuit of meaning."[14] Building on the work of Dewey, the proponents of inquiry and discovery suggest that it is natural to want to learn, particularly about things that catch one's fancy, or which are needed to gain competence. Suchman states: "It can be argued that free inquiry is the most naturalistic form of learning behavior."[15]

The reader should note the similarities in the belief in intrinsic human motivations and McGregor's "Y" person. This humanistic school interweaves many divergent fields—management, education, planning, and social work. It should also be noted that Drucker feels the debate of "X" and "Y" is largely "a sham battle." The question the manager needs to ask is not, "Which theory of human nature is right?" The question is, "What is the reality of my situation and how can I discharge my task of managing worker and working in today's situation?"[16] This is more of a contextual view that takes into consideration the nature of the environment and times, as well as the worker. A normative view would add another dimension: "How can I move within this situation to 'what ought to be' under the circumstances in which I find myself?"

An individualized look at the worker is important in any consideration of motivation. Although we can make generalized assumptions, clearly the concept, "different strokes for different folks," summarizes the manager's dilemma. It is important to note, however, that we believe that most workers would like to do a good job and consider themselves competent, but that many things can get in the way of that basic motivation.

Faced with continued frustration, lack of rewards, and failures, most people soon take the easy way out for fear of still more rebuffs. The

13.  R. W. White, "Motivation Reconsidered," *Psychological Review,* vol. 66, no. 5 (1969).

14.  J. Richard Suchman, "The Pursuit of Meaning: Models for the Study of Inquiry," in *Behavioral Science Frontiers in Education,* ed. Eli M. Bower and William J. Hollister (New York: John Wiley & Sons, Inc., 1967), p. 484.

15.  J. Richard Suchman, p 484.

16.  Peter Drucker, *Management,* p. 235.

manager must be able to look past the surface hostility, boredom, passivity, or abrasiveness to assess whether in fact a worker's motivation can be rekindled. Most of us, no matter how altruistic, will retreat in the face of continued rebuffs and lack of rewarding work experiences. The human services worker may be particularly vulnerable because of the nature of the work.

We know that the time it takes to train a skilled, sensitive, helpful caseworker is not weeks, months, or even a year. The people in need of help should not be deprived of the helping skills of an experienced caseworker and be presented with a novice. The administrator needs to search out ways to assist workers ranging from a vacation to change in case load to picking up the "case that broke the camel's back" him or herself. The problem is where to start. The model we suggest is a variation of the Lewin Force-Field Approach, previously discussed (p. 64). Although generally applicable to the assessment of a wide range of problems, we would use it on a microlevel in this situation.

There are three major stress-reducing mechanisms available within the agency: the preventive, ameliorative, and self-help approaches.

1. The *preventive* approach calls for a restructuring of agency services to recognize the danger in concentrated exposure to stress-plus transactions. Built-in vacations, timeouts, supervision, and alternative case loads are all ways to restructure the environmental force.

At times restructuring of agency practice may counteract burnout-stress. For example, a worker could carry fewer cases or less difficult cases. More frequent breaks or vacations, or "timeouts" when a worker could do a less strenuous task, such as writing a report, also support preventive modes. Sometimes longer "timeouts" are necessary (e.g., returning to school for a course or a conference).

Where stress is related to a gap between needed knowledge and current ability, courses, formal supervisory assignments, or self-learning may help resolve the stress. Similarly, a workshop on dealing with stress might reduce the stress, or prepare practitioners, supervisors, or administrators to minimize it within their own agencies.

2. Availability of peer groups and/or a colleague to help the worker in times of unusual stress when psychological supports are necessary provides an *ameliorative* mode of stress management.

Emphasis on this latter mode, of course, will lead to dealing with stress when a great deal of the damage may have already been done. Emphasis on the preventive mode will leave the worker in jeopardy if the structural supports have not sufficed. There must be a balance between the two. In addition, the worker must know him or herself. That can take an awfully long time. Honest, sensitive feedback from one's peers can often shorten that time.

Maslach, notes, as have others who have studied in this area, that the availability of formal or informal programs where professionals can get together to discuss problems and get advice and support is another way of helping workers cope with stress. When there is a sympathetic ear, there is usually an outpouring of expression of stress and concern, and the "burnout rates are lower for those professionals who actively express, analyze and share their personal feelings with their colleagues."[17]

> 3. The growing awareness that individuals can increase their own abilities to control their minds and bodies through *self-help* techniques such as meditation, logs, biofeedback, and diet, has led to "holistic" approaches to stress reduction. Although these are used experimentally with clients, they pay off for helpers, too.

The Progoff "log" and Girodo's self-talk technique also may be seen as self-supervisory techniques that can act as mechanisms for growth and self-analysis.

Dr. Herbert Freudenberger, who has done extensive work in the area of staff burnout, suggests that exercise, running, or any activity that tires a person out, thereby inducing sleep may help alleviate some of the results of stress.[18] Others have suggested that a change of diet might help. The ecological or holistic view of health is seen as a significant factor in stress management.

The worker who is also going through a high stress situation in his or her personal life may be more vulnerable to stress on the job as well. The work of Holmes suggests that competent workers usually able to handle transactional stress may accumulate a "cumulative overdose" because of too many stressful situations within a shortened time span. They may be "swamped" by the overload of private and work-related stress.

Staff burnout has been a major concern in the mental health professions for a number of years. There is movement toward a new approach focusing on the helper's more direct involvement with clients. New programs to confront life's brutality, such as rape crisis centers and centers for battered children and adults, have been developed. In addition, there is a growing realization that problems are more difficult to resolve than was thought to be true in earlier times. These factors, combined with attacks from funding sources and the community, exacerbate professional vulnerability and lower the helper's tolerance for stress. The major solution

---

17. Cristina Maslach, "Burned Out," *Human Behavior*, 5, no. 9 (Sept. 1976), 20.

18. Herbert J. Freudenburger, *The Staff Burn-Out Syndrome* (Wash., D.C.: Drug Abuse Council, Inc., 1975), p. 15.

seems to be not to turn inward or away from the client, but toward one's own peers—a self-help group within which one can learn better to cope with the stress. The wise administrator can help establish a climate supportive of motivated workers by providing the rewards, stimulation, and agency supports that make for growth situations rather than overwhelming stress.

### maintaining worker productivity

Human service staff leave their jobs for the same reasons as their peers in industry and business. That money is rarely the prime concern was shown in a study on staff turnover done for the National Federation of Settlements. Vinter found that the reasons given for leaving were, in order of frequency: (1) work content, (2) staff relations, and (3) personal reasons.[19]

However, staff who do not leave agencies when they are dissatisfied can pose considerable problems for themselves and the agency. Bernard Levenson notes that "[e]mployees who do not have the economic leverage or the physical vitality to start anew may resign themselves to the fact that they have reached a point of no return. . . . Aware that they must remain on the job despite blocked mobility they gradually lose interest in their work and settle down to a minimum level of performance."[20]

Maintaining high productivity is a major concern of the administrator and staff motivation is a major responsibility. The carrot and the stick no longer is an effective management technique. In a search for alternatives, Drucker turns to a comparative analysis of situations that do seem effective. He examines three success stories:

1. Japan's use of "continuous training." Every employee, often up to and including top managers, keeps on training as a regular part of his or her job until retirement. The focus is on the working of the plant rather than the job of this or that person.
2. The Zeiss Optical Works introduced continuous training and now seeks feedback from the workers, and offers a money back to workers system for scholarships, housing, and emergency protection.
3. I.B.M. trains its staff for broadened responsibilities and maximizes jobs, and involves all staff levels in design and planning. It also has innovative ways for establishing productivity. "Each worker develops with his/her own foreman, his/her own rates of production."

19.    Robert D. Vinter, "Report of the Personnel Turnover Study," in *The Round Table* (New York: National Federation of Settlements, May–June 1957), p. 1.

20.    Bernard Levenson, "Bureaucratic Succession" in *Complex Organization,* ed. Amitai Etzioni (New York: Holt, Rinehart & Winston, 1961), p. 369.

Drucker suggests that the basic principle of work is the emphasis on "organizing responsibility."[21]

Social agencies are work intensive and often the workers' responsibilities are broad and not easily delimited. Where responsibilities are clearly perceived by the workers and others, job satisfaction becomes more likely. Similarly, when workers feel they have opportunities to expand their tasks they tend to be more satisfied. Vinter suggests that "[s]ettlements may reduce turnover due to work content dissatisfactions by three related approaches: first, limiting excessive demands on staff; second, increasing opportunities for exercise of professional skills; third, providing more adequately for proportional opportunities."[22]

Abels, in his study of worker satisfaction, set up a model closely related to the normative approach, and then compared agencies' operations to the model. Not only were workers more satisfied with their jobs in agencies operating closer to the model, but a year later, a follow-up showed that the turnover rate was statistically significantly less.[23]

Research shows that although job satisfaction does not clearly lead to better job performance,[24] job dissatisfaction does lead to absenteeism and turnover,[25] and absenteeism and turnover may have a very direct influence on the organizations effectiveness. Although the cost of turnover for low-level jobs has been estimated at $2,000 a person,[26] in some welfare organizations the cost has been estimated as high as $5,000.[27] In terms of service to clients the cost is even more difficult to measure.

One area in which the administrator can affect motivation is through efforts to make the job more meaningful. There are three dimensions that contribute to this: 1. skill variety; 2. task identity (a whole or complete piece of work) and 3. task significance.[28] In the human services, although much of the meaningfulness is in the nature of service itself, job enrichment is still possible.

In order to enhance the management cycle, the administrator must understand the motivating forces inherent in the whole agency staff, which includes the administrator. These motivations are related to three

21. Peter F. Drucker, *Management*, p. 248.

22. Vinter, "Personnel Turnover Study," p. 5.

23. Abels, "The Agency-Trained Worker," 1967.

24. V. H. Vroom, *Work and Motivation* (New York: John Wiley & Sons, 1964), p. 64.

25. *Work in America*, p. 83.

26. Edward E. Lawler, "Satisfaction and Behavior," in *Motivation and Work Behavior*, ed. Richard Steers and Lyman Porter (New York: McGraw Hill, 1975), p. 300.

27. *Closing the Gap in Social Work Manpower* (Washington, D.C.: U.S. Department of Health, Education and Welfare, 1965), p. 73.

28. Steers, p. 408.

levels of goals within the agency: organizational, work group, and individual. As the administrators involve themselves in the planning process and day-to-day decision making in the agency, these needs/goals chains become the underpinnings of administrative action.

There is also a growing amount of evidence that job redesigning and flexible hours planned and organized by the staff members themselves lead to higher motivation, increased productivity, and satisfaction.[29]

The process of management by objectives permits members of the organization to work together as they identify common goals and coordinate efforts to achieve them. This process of examining directions for the future, when melded with aspirations toward just consequences, sets a tone for the agency in which agency achievement leads to a synergistic outcome of community achievement as well. This sense of accomplishment of worthwhile ends increases the feeling of actualization among the staff and guides future planning decisions.

29.   See, for example, Gary Gappert, *Post-Affluent America* (New York: New Viewpoints, 1979), pp. 150–56 and Paul Dicks, *The Future of the Workplace* (New York: Weybright & Talley, 1975), pp. 41–84, 209–80.

# CHAPTER 6

---

# decision making

## INTRODUCTION

This chapter examines administrative decision making as a basic tool and activity undergirding the cycle of the planning, organization, control, and motivation functions. Systems concepts serve as a framework to place such concepts in perspective.

It has been said: "Not to make a decision is to make a decision." The insight to be derived from this, as applied to care-giving organizations, is that the tempting tendency to put off a formal decision as much as possible—sometimes in the hope that the problem will just go away—is not really avoiding anything. However, the need to respond to both external and internal demands and pressures calls for more conscious decision-making activity as a means of coping positively with such pressures. Often, the administrator must react to these pressures at a time of conflict or crisis, but is still subject to fulfilling administrative responsibilities in an efficient manner. A basic premise, for instance, is that all plans are decisions, but not all decisions are planned. Too much reliance on unplanned decisions is inefficient, demoralizing, and ineffective. It says something about the motivation and attitude of the administrator who engages in such reactive, rather than planned, activity in all situations. The concept of decision making is an expression of the effort to respond rationally to what is sometimes a nonrational or irrational world.

Regardless of position in the administrative hierarchy, people must make decisions. For example, the caseworker's decision to pursue a new counseling strategy, the supervisory decision of how to delegate a series of cases, the program director's decision to go with one type of program rather than another, and the executive director's decision (in concert with a board or advisory committee) to expand or cutback the number of programs a particular agency is offering—all represent the responsibility for making decisions. Thus, we find that the pervasiveness and continuity of the decision-making process is clearly evident throughout a care-giving organization.

DECISION MAKING DEFINED.   Most authors are in fairly close consensus about the definition of decision making. For example, Ives defined decision making as "a rational attempt to consider quantitative and qualitative means in the selection of alternative courses of action."[1] Loomb and Levey define decision making as "the conclusion of a process by which one chooses among available alternatives for the purpose of achieving a set of desired objectives;"[2] Cleland and King, in a novel approach, focus upon the decision maker as "an entity, either an individual or group, who is dissatisfied with some existing state or with the prospect of a future state and who possesses the desire and authority to initiate actions designed to alter this state."[3] In short, at its most basic, decision making is the choosing from alternatives in order to best attain the organization's stated objectives. It involves, for example, the administrator choosing among various programs of service delivery, various means of funding, various staff utilization patterns, various evaluation methodologies, and the like.


## THE DECISION-MAKING PROCESS

The decision-making process is technical in that it incorporates a number of activities—from a simple beginning to an increasing awareness of the fact that a decision must be made to an assessment of alternative solutions to action implementation.

1.   Brian D. Ives, "Decision Theory and the Practicing Manager," *Business Horizons*, 16, no. 38 (June 1973), 38.
2.   D. Loomba and Samuel Levey, *Health Care Administration* (Philadelphia: J. B. Lippincott Company, 1973), p. 169.
3.   David I. Cleland and William R. King, *Systems Analysis and Project Management* (New York: McGraw-Hill Book Company, 1968), p. 20.

Many authors describe the process as a series of steps. For instance, Samuel Elion describes the mental process that a decision maker goes through before arriving at a conclusion:

> First there is an information input, say from some data processing machinery. This is followed by an analysis of the information material with the purpose of ascertaining its validity and discriminating between its significant parts. The analysis leads to the specification of performance measures, which provide the basis for determining how a particular course of action is to be judged, and then to the construction of a model in order to describe the behavior of the system for which the manager is asked to make a decision.
>
> In a productive-marketing system, for example, the measures of performance may include profit, mean level and/or variance of plant utilization, level of meeting customer demand, and so on. Thus, any given courses of action, whether they represent existing policies or whether they are hypothetical propositions for new policies, can be described by arrays of the measures of performance that are thought to be most relevant.
>
> A set of alternatives (or "strategies" in the language of the theory of games) is enumerated and predictions are then made regarding the possible outcomes in the light of their respective measures of performance is set up and finally the selection (called here resolution) is made.[4]

An alternative, but similar view, is systematic decision-making cycle of activities such as depicted in Figure 6-1.

In the cyclical process, it becomes more clear that the steps in the cycle are dependent upon each other but are interrelated, rather than

**FIGURE 6-1** *The Decision-Making Cycle*

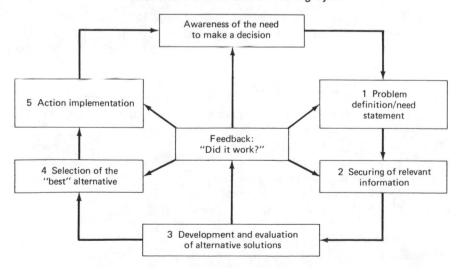

4. Samuel Elion, "What is a Decision?" *Management Science,* 16, no. 4 (December 1969), quoted in Samuel Levey and N. Paul Loomba, *Health Care Administration* (Philadelphia: J. B. Lippincott Company, 1973), pp. 206–207.

necessarily sequential. One or more of the steps may be occurring simultaneously—depending upon where each one enters into the process (e.g., need statement and information securing). Each activity is important, but one or more, at a particular point in time, may command full attention.

### the cyclical steps in the decision-making process

The normative process of decision making, in light of Figure 6-1, may be outlined in practical terms helpful to the administrator of a care-giving organization. First, the administrator must be cognizant of the fact that a decision must be made. If the decision maker is not dissatisfied with the present or potential state of affairs, then a conscious decision to change will not be forthcoming. The implication to be drawn from an administrator's satisfaction is that a formal or informal decision has been made to maintain the status quo. However, once the administrator becomes aware that something is not quite right (in both the intellectual and emotive sense) dissatisfaction sets in, and systematic decision-making activity is initiated. Given the sense of dissatisfaction and the knowledge that something must be done, the following steps can support rational change.

**Step** 1—*Problem Definition/Need Statement*

The major focus for the ensuing decision is formulated in this step, which provides the direction for the whole decision-making process. The aim is to define the activity one hopes to accomplish within a reasonable amount of time and with reasonable additional resources. Stemming from dissatisfaction, it serves to identify the current condition as compared to the desired condition in light of objectives. This identification process is assisted by a systematic effort to obtain answers to as many of the following questions as possible:

1. What is the deviation between what currently is and what should be?
2. Where does this deviation occur?
3. When does the deviation occur?
4. What is the extent of the deviation?

Given the information about the deviation, the decision maker can formulate a problem statement. For example: "Outreach workers are frustrated because they are not able to give mothers who need medical care adequate help or information."

Problems can be translated into needs simply by focusing upon the necessity to effect a change as in the statement: "Outreach workers need to become familiar with basic criteria and procedures."

**Step** 2—*Securing of Relevant Information*

This involves the search activity designed to acquire relevant internal and external information. It requires knowledge of past experience, data related to what should be and what is, information from other similar organizations, the use of records, observation and the like—all screened for relationship to the problem and/or activities in question. This information is necessary and must be gathered and assembled in order to evaluate potential solutions. A concomitant of this step is the arrangement of the data into specifications for performance measures. That is, in light of objective-seeking activities, one can identify a series of choice criteria against which alternative courses of action are to be judged. This involves designing a model for expected solution outcomes containing objective and subjective criteria that will enable a decision maker to evaluate various alternatives. One must note here that in setting criteria the decision maker must be fully cognizant of constraints within which the final decision must rest (e.g., time, manpower, monetary constraints, and so on).

**Step** 3—*Development and Evaluation of Alternative Solutions*

In light of objectives to be met, and in consideration of potential and actual constraints, the decision maker must now develop a series of alternative courses of action. This involves the assembling of a range of alternatives in such a way that comparisons can be made. Through the utilization of the aforementioned choice criteria, the decision maker attempts to detail: 1) the advantages and disadvantages of each alternative and 2) the predictions of the extent to which each alternative might succeed. We must note that the rational objective analysis of an alternative must be weighed against a subjective, often political, one in order to obtain a complete comparison.

**Step** 4—*Selection of the "Best" Alternative*

The actual selection of a "best" alternative is based upon: an assembling of the alternative courses of action; the assessment of their relative objective and subjective advantages and disadvantages according to solid criteria; and a rational prediction of the potential success of each of the alternative courses of action. Once again we stress the normative view—

that in the field of human services, a strong commitment to ethical considerations, as well as more pragmatic ones, must be present in selecting alternative action courses.

## Step 5—*Action Implementation*

Many theorists include this step as a necessary part of the decision making process, reasoning that the previous steps all lead to action, which should not be divorced from analysis. This calls for the commitment of the decision maker and the organization to effecting the "best" solution. It involves the allocation of available resources, organizing them, and sequencing the activities necessary to bring about successful resolution.

## Step 6—*Feedback*

The final step requires a two-pronged approach. First, monitoring the continuous assessment for the purpose of assuring the most efficient and effective use of resources; and evaluation, the final analysis of whether the selected course of action was successful in meeting its objectives.

## AN EXAMPLE OF THE CYCLE

An example from the field of organizational fund raising will help to portray the decision-making cycle.

Critical to the delivery of human services and organizational maintenance is financial support. Private agencies and organizations, especially those without tax bases, devote much of their energies to fund-raising projects and membership campaigns.

Throughout this fund-raising process, the need to make decisions on the part of the organization's professional and lay leadership is imperative. Many questions must be answered, such as: What is the best campaign structure at this time? Who is the right person to solicit a particular gift? Where in our campaign team will we utilize the independent worker? When shall we have our kick-off? How can we overcome negative publicity? That these questions call for decisive and effective action is undisputed. What is needed is a planned process for decision making based upon the key factor of information. The following example addresses itself to this decision-making process by applying the six basic steps.

Elements such as those contained in the above questions are present in every decision problem. The key is to view their pertinence to the particular questions—fund raising decisions in this case—that must be answered. For each of these problem areas a decision must be made either individually or in concert with volunteers and/or staff. Throughout the process, the agency/organizational fund raiser must consider each of the decision-making steps in relation to a desired objective or set of objectives. Before concentrating on the final selection of a course of action, the decision activity as a whole must be considered. The fund raiser has several alternatives and his or her choice involves a comparison among these alternatives as well as the evaluation of their outcomes.

### problem/need

First, there is informational input. Data has shown that some of our contributors in the large gifts financial campaign division have substantially decreased their giving levels over the past two years—and that much of the decrease seems due to a poorly functioning campaign section in the large gifts division. The problem is a poorly functioning campaign section; the need is to develop a successful solicitation unit.

### securing of relevant information

Next, the informational material is analyzed to check its validity and distinguish between its significant and insignificant elements. This analysis leads first to the specification of performance measures, which provide how a particular course of action is to be judged, and then to the construction of a model to describe the behavior of the solicitation system for which the fund raiser is asked to make a decision. In this example, a deeper analysis shows that forty-five of the large givers who have cut back their contributions did so due to factors within the solicitation process. Other decreases were due to factors beyond our control (move-outs, retirements, illness, and so on). A measure of performance potential would be an increase of 50 to 75 percent in contributions from these 45 persons. This measure of performance seems appropriate because of our knowledge of their ability to give.

### development and evaluation
### of alternative solutions

Alternatives (strategies) are enumerated and predictions are then made regarding the possible outcomes of each alternative. Then, a criterion for comparing outcomes in the light of their respective measures of performance is established, and finally the selection is made.

In the example three alternatives were considered:

| Alternative 1 | vs. | Alternative 2 | vs. | Alternative 3 |
|---|---|---|---|---|
| Create a special unit for these 45 givers with emphasis on changed solicitors. | | Assign a special team for early solicitation but retain within the large gifts unit. | | Stay within the large gifts unit and stress improved solicitation. |
| Prediction 1 | | Prediction 2 | | Prediction 3 |
| Successful | | Most successful | | Least successful |
| Choice Criteria | | Choice Criteria | | Choice Criteria |
| Successful if additional 10 solicitors can be obtained; costly in terms of manpower, time, and communication. | | Successful if early solicitation manpower can be obtained; some costs in time, but effective. | | Successful if guaranteed improved solicitation; costly in time and motivation of previous solicitors with marginal effectiveness. |

### selection of the best alternative

Granted that no one alternative is the "ideal" alternative, this step focuses upon selection of the one that has the most advantages (in this case, best chance of success) and fewest disadvantages (smallest cost). Alternative two would be selected.

### action implementation

This step calls for the implementation of alternative two: picking training, and sending the special team out to solicit funds.

### feedback

On-going monitoring of the activities of this special team and final evaluation of the results of their solicitation efforts would be effected. These endeavors would address such questions as: How successful was this alternative? Should further action be taken? Is there a need for a resolicitation? and so forth.

We emphasize once again that the above-named decision-making activities are not unrelated and that the total process permeates the care-giving system. The decisions continually turn on the need for clear objectives and the inherent decision-making relationships. A fuller discussion of objectives is to be found in Chapter Ten. For the moment, it should be stressed that one may identify the input-throughput-output process of a care-giving system—but it's worthless unless the process is related to the objectives and goals of the system. The administrator must: consider the acquisition of inputs in light of their ability to help the organization achieve its goals and objectives; consider throughputs in light of whether the organization's process/activities are the most effective, efficient way of reaching the goals and objectives (that is, are there alternative activities that can be measured against each other for better results?); and consider the organization's output (did we miss our objectives; can we evaluate how effective we have been, etc.). Therefore a comprehensive decision-making process is needed that involves a systematic way of setting the objectives of the organization, making plans in order to achieve these objectives, allocating resources, implementing plans, and controlling and evaluating the system's performance. Each step of the decision-making process must be considered in light of the organization's goals and objectives.

This decision making process, as it applies to the field of human care service organizations, has been classically illustrated by Elkin and Cornick.[5] They contend that decisions are made continuously in the management process, and present a useful model identifying major decision areas, their interrelationships, and typical information requirements.

Elkin and Cornick[6] describe this process in terms of a circular systems model that identifies the major process stages—Objectives, Control, Input, Operations, Effective Output and Feedback—of which decisions must be made. These decisions are concerned with effectiveness, efficiency and quality. Elkin and Cornick define *effectiveness* as a measure of the degree to which a service reaches its objectives stated in terms of outcomes (impact of service upon target/goals) or in terms of output units (productivity); *quality* as the degree to which specific elements of input comply with standards[7] (i.e. type of training and ratio of input units, staff, to client units); and *efficiency* as a ratio of input units to client units[8] (number of counseling sessions per day). They discuss the key decision areas in light of effectiveness, quality and efficiency as follows:[9]

1. *Objectives*: Decisions about objectives have to be made first. These decisions determine the type of target and level of service rendered by the care-giving organization.

5. Robert Elkin and Delroy L. Cornick, "Utilizing Cost and Efficiency Studies in the Decision-Making Process in Health and Welfare," in *Social Work Administration,* ed. Harry A. Schatz (New York: Council on Social Work Education, 1970), pp. 364–371.

6. Ibid., p. 367

7. Ibid., p. 366

8. Ibid., p. 366

9. Ibid., p. 367–368.

2. *Control*: Decisions have to be made on levels of efficiency, quality and effectiveness to meet the specified objectives of the organization.

3. *Input*: Decisions have to be made on actual utilization of resources (staff, volunteers, etc.). Such decisions must be related to objectives of the service.

4. *Operations*: Decisions are directed toward monitoring the level of quality and efficiency in rendering the service.

5. *Output*: Decisions are related to assessing output in terms of specified objectives.[10]

The key idea to be noted is that the process of input-throughput-output must also be viewed in terms of outcomes. The system, for success and survival, must achieve goals; this calls for specificity of overall objectives and lesser objectives and their achievement by various departments/units/sections/subsections in a planned, integrative system. The system is thus highly dependent upon effective decision-making. Figure 6-2 portrays an adaptation of the model relating appropriateness of informational inputs to key decisional areas.

## SUMMARY

This chapter introduced the concept of the common decision-making process, noting that it is a pervasive organizational process with a cynical nature that depends upon information to be effective.

The normative view implies that there is a need to be proactive in decision making, to assertively seek out the necessary information rather than leave decisions to chance.

10.   Ibid, p. 367–369.

# FIGURE 6-2 Effective Decision Making Depends On Information At Key Points

Decision making involves the assessment of the input information in light of the information required for decision related to Objectives, Control, Input, Operations, Output, and Feedback. Hence, we ask key questions at each point: Why is the action required? What action is to be taken? What resources will be required to support the action? What will the action accomplish? When are the results of the action expected? What objectives and conditions must be met?

| INFORMATION INPUTS → CHECK APPROPRIATENESS | IN LIGHT OF → INFORMATION REQUIRED | FOR DECISIONS ON | IN ORDER TO |
|---|---|---|---|
| *EFFECTIVE DATA* can be assessed by its:<br><br>1. *Do I want these data?* (If not, skip remainder) | On quantity, quality and cost of manpower, facilities, and other factors needed for the service and related community efforts. | OBJECTIVES → | Determine type of target group and level of service |
| 2. *Is it relevant to my position?* (Do I need it to make better decisions?) | On availability of funds, staff, and facilities and levels of performance in terms of quality and productivity, costs, efficiency, and subsequent changes in objectives. | CONTROL → | Determine the levels of efficiency, quality and effectiveness in meeting the specified objectives |
| RELEVANCE<br>TIMELINESS<br>ACCURACY<br>PRESENTATION<br><br>3. *Does it come in time?* | | | |
| 4. *Does it come at the right frequency?* (More or less often than it should?) | On subject needs and availability of resources (staff, funds, facilities) that meet quality standards and match needs of subject group. | INPUT → | Determine the number and type of people accepted and specific uses of available resources |
| ASK:<br><br>5. *Is it accurate (enough)?* Not too inaccurate or unnecessarily accurate. | In form of time, cost, and operations data and data on subject progress. | OPERATIONS → | Monitor the quantity, quality and efficiency of services rendered |
| 6. *Is its presentation in the best form for me?* | Expressed in quantative or qualitative terms depending upon which of 4 levels of efficiency measures are used (see below). | OUTPUT → | Assess the output of the service in terms of the specified objectives |

# CHAPTER 7

---

# planning, program planning, and organization

## INTRODUCTION

In the introduction to Part 2, the planning process was described as an analysis of pertinent information from the past and present, and prediction of the most likely future developments so that a course of action may be formulated to enable an organization to attain its stated objectives.

A major emphasis in this book is on the interactive relationship of the four key management processes with the foundation process of decision making. The planning process requires the determination of an organization's objectives and the assessment of means and resources needed to achieve the objectives.

The social agency director, under pressure from a volatile external environment characterized by rapid political, economic, and social changes, often responds solely to external stimuli. This places the director in a systems transaction—a state of affairs characterized by being almost wholly dependent and reactive. The mark of the competent, effective administrator is his or her ability to anticipate, project, plan, and thus have some positive control over the delivery and maintenance of services. The former state of affairs is reactive, whereas the latter stresses proactivity— that is, the ability to practice self-direction, to be task and problem centered, and to move from need assessment to planning to implementation to evaluation.

This chapter is broken into two major sections. The first is planning, its definition and relationship to decision making; types of planning and time relationships, the planning cycle and the relationship of planning to other processes of the management cycle. Second, program planning and organization, that is, linking planning to the organization of resources by the use of objectives, and a discussion of alternative resources.

## DEFINITION OF PLANNING

Writers describe planning in fairly consonant terms. Cleland and King describe planning as "an organic function which precedes the complementary functions of organizing, motivating, and controlling. It is concerned with the development of a plan; it involves mental activity, and specifies what should be done, how it should be done, when action is to be effected, who is responsible, and why such action is necessary. Planning is the selection of suitable alternatives from a myriad of choices."[1] Ewell considers planning as "deciding what to do and how to do it before action is required."[2] Kast and Rosenzweig state simply that "a plan is a predetermined course of action."[3]

In short, such writers note some basic characteristics of planning: a sense of the future, a sense of action, and a sense of decision making—the need to select and evaluate alternatives. Through these characteristics we can see the relationship between decision making and planning: all planning depends upon the determination of ends and means—which, in a very real sense, is the core of decision making. The planning functions are indeed a broad foundation upon which the administrative role is based. It is decision making because it involves obtaining information, assessing alternatives and their costs and benefits, selecting the best alternatives, and implementing them.

1. David S. Cleland and William R. King, *Systems Analysis and Project Management* (New York: McGraw-Hill Book Company, 1968), p. 93.

2. Charles M. Ewell, Jr., "Setting Objectives: First Step in Planning," *Hospital Progress,* 53, no. 9 (September, 1972), 68.

3. Fremont E. Kast and James E. Rosenzweig, *Organization and Management* (New York: McGraw-Hill Book Company, 1970), p. 436.

In light of these thoughts, planning will be defined simply as a course of action decided upon before any details are worked out. This definition emphasizes the concept of *process*—that is, objectively determining in advance what to do, how to do it, when to do it, and who is to do it. It implies not only decision-making activity, but also the need to organize resources, monitor (control) activities, and motivate people to carry out activities.

### types of planning

There are several types of planning. McFarland offers a useful classification by relating, as seen in Figure 7-1, the kind of planning needed at various levels of the organization.[4]

Another way to look at planning is to introduce the critical dimension of time, that is, long-run and short-run planning. Long-run planning depends greatly upon the action of external environmental influences. The administrator of a care-giving organization is faced with the need to make assumptions concerning the future of the organization and to plan accordingly for these circumstances. Although the planning must extend more than one or two years into the future, it has more than just a time dimension. It is a broad, continuous planning process that cyclically sets and resets the purpose and direction of the organization. It utilizes forecasting and projection aids in its aim to realize the organization's objectives. Short-run, or tactical, planning stems from the long-run planning process. Short-run plans ordinarily refer to operational program planning of less than one year's duration. This type of planning is more specific, detail- and activity-oriented, and addresses the means of implementation. As one works up the organizational ladder from nonmanagerial staff to top management, one moves from having the responsibility for short-run tactical planning to overall long-run planning.

**FIGURE 7-1**   *Planning Activity by Levels*

| LEVELS OF ORGANIZATION | TYPES OF PLANNING |
| --- | --- |
| Top Management | Goals, policies, long-range plans, company-wide sphere. |
| Middle Management | Quotas, programs, supplementary goals, policies. |
| Supervising Management | Projects, schedules, short-range goals, supplementary policies, operational planning. |
| Managerial Workers | Limited to work routines and minor procedures. |

4.   Dalton E. McFarland, *Management: Principles and Practices,* 3d ed. (New York: Macmillan, Inc., 1970), p. 149.

Long-run and short-run planning are closely related. Each short-run plan, for effectiveness, is integrated into, and supportive of, the long-run plan. In short, planning should be viewed as a total, interdependent process in which long-run planning establishes the necessary framework upon which more detailed operational planning takes place. The strategic plan addresses such questions as: "What long-run strategies are required to move our service organization to fulfill these goals?" Whereas the short-run plan addresses such questions as: "In light of our overall plan: 1. What actions are to be taken? 2. What resources are required and are they available? and 3. Who will do what activities and when?"

In brief, the care-giving organization, for service delivery and innovation, as well as stability and survival, must engage in effective planning activity. Subactivity occurs at all levels, with varying time frames. It gives a sense of direction and stability. As a purposeful approach, it promotes a holistic sense of the organization and combines the stability and survival necessary to maintain the sense of organizational purpose, along with innovation, by contributing to the long-term purpose of helping people.

A different view of planning activity in light of time frames is the concept of normative planning. Bergwall, Reaves, and Woodside distinguish normative planning, which establishes goals, from technical planning, which deals with objectives.[5]

> The relationship between goals and objectives is that objectives, essentially, are steps toward goals, and they are guided by policies that link goals and objectives. This is accomplished by setting forth the acceptable means that are to be used in working towards goals.

They further point out that normative planning is a

> hierarchy of goals, policies, and objectives. . . . [G]oals might be those end results toward which efforts are directed . . . ; policies might be those courses of action undertaken to emphasize such ends . . . ; and objectives might be the establishment of certain programs . . . ; therefore . . . the progression is from the abstract as we go from goals to objectives.[6]

Normative planning, then, once again introduces the sense of desirability of the ideal. Its focus is on final outcomes and their consequences for people in the future and it works backward from them to set up plans for the present that will enable long-run ideals to be achieved.

Complementary to the previous discussion, one last way of looking at planning is through the concepts of strategic planning and management planning. Strategic planning is "the process of deciding on the objectives

5. David F. Bergwall, Philip M. Reaves, and Nina B. Woodside, *Health Planning* (Washington, D.C.: Information Resources Press, 1974), p. 77.

6. Bergwall, Reaves, and Woodside, pp. 77-78.

of organizations, on changes in these objectives, on the resources to achieve these objectives, and on the policies that are to govern the acquisition, use, and disposition of these resources."[7] In the context of human services, strategic planning is concerned with:

1.  plan formulation—the process of developing and finalizing annual and long-range plans;
2.  the formulation of the policies for plan implementation—decisions as to which services will be provided by the official agencies, which through contract mechanisms, and which will be provided through the private sector;
3.  the formulation of criteria for setting priorities and patterns of resource allocation—the process by which decisions are made to deliver specific amounts of services to target population groups and geographic areas; and
4.  monitoring and evaluation—decisions here would deal with information requirements, storage and retrieval issues, as well as criteria to be used.

Management planning is the process by which the planners and managers insure that the resources, once obtained, are used to reach the organization's objectives efficiently and effectively. In the context of human services, it is concerned with:

1.  the development of operating rules for public agencies—the regulations dealing with service eligibility, the receipt and use of public funds;
2.  the development of guidelines to assist public and private agencies in the formulation of projects and evaluation of the impact of these programs; and
3.  the design and implementation of service delivery systems—the actual programs.

In short, then, strategic planning, like normative and long-run planning, is concerned with setting objectives, establishing priorities, and resource acquisition and deployment. Management planning, like technical and short-run planning, emphasizes the management of these resources.

Although these types of planning differ in time, specificity, and locational dimensions, they employ similar techniques. They all should be viewed as interdependent processes and, for effectiveness, depend upon a series of interrelated stages. In short, they all conform to the systems concept of being cyclical in nature—moving from stages of analysis and assessment to design to feedback to selection to feedback to implementation and returning to assessment. Beginning with desired outputs (which involves output/objective determination) the administrator then identifies

7.   Robert N. Anthony, "Planning and Control Systems" (unpublished paper, Graduate School of Business Administration, Harvard University, 1965). p. 69.

and moves to obtain those specific input resources needed to accomplish the desired outcomes, plans the means (throughput process) to most effectively reach these outcomes, and finally assesses both the process and results of the activities. This cyclical planning process is discussed in the next section.

### the cyclical steps in the planning process

Writers are in general agreement about the cyclical steps of the planning process. Kast and Rosenzweig include the following steps:

1. Appraising the future political, economic, competitive, or other environment;
2. Visualizing the desired role of the organization in this environment;
3. Perceiving needs and requirements of the clientele;
4. Determining changes in the needs and requirements of other interested groups;
5. Providing a system of communication and information flow—whereby organizational members can participate in the planning process;
6. Developing broad goals and plans which will direct the efforts of the total organization;
7. Translating this broad planning into functional efforts on a more detailed basis —research, design and development, production, distribution, and service;
8. Developing more detailed planning and control of resource utilization within each of these functional areas—always related to the overall planning effort.[8]

In a similar vein, management authority Peter Drucker recommends five steps: establishing objectives, determining priority of objectives, identifying resources, executing action programs, and maintaining control.[9]

George Terry, in a classic work, has outlined a series of steps in the process, similar to those described by the previously mentioned writers, that are especially adaptable to the planning needs of the administrator of a care-giving organization.[10] He discusses eight steps:

1. Clarify the problem;
2. Obtain complete information about the activities involved;
3. Analyze and classify the information;
4. Establish planning premise and constraints;
5. Determine alternate plans;

8. Kast and Rosenzweig, *Organization and Management*, p. 452.

9. Peter Drucker, *The Effective Executive* (London: Heinemam, 1967), p. 125.

10. George Terry, *Principles of Management* (Homewood: Richard D. Irwin, Inc., 1968), pp. 253–260.

6. Choose proposed plan;
7. Arrange detailed sequence and timing of proposed plan; and
8. Provide progress checkup to proposed plan.

Note that all three processes delineated above are dynamic rather than static activities—that is, that the steps need not be sequential, and that each step may be affected by the future events that result in adaptation of planning activities.

In Chapter 1, steps leading to a normative stance within an organization were discussed. Some have special relevance to the planning process. These include the steps which state: decisions need to be based on rational inquiry; administrative decisions should lead to consequence; and staff should foster support and growth among themselves. The first implies that a great effort should be made to obtain information and assess it for relevance to the planning process in order to make a sound plan. The second suggests that just consequences will result only when people affected by a plan have the opportunity to influence it. Early involvement, wherever and whenever possible, of the organization's constituents or consumers in plan formulation is desirable. The third step implies that staff personnel want to influence any planning activity that affects their work activities, and that they bring skills, ability, and imagination to the process.

When these normative steps are not present, organizational plans and their implementation meet with resistance. The following example serves to illustrate this point.

A large Midwestern health care organization set up a major planning and implementation program to decentralize its clinics and ambulatory care programs, which included the closing of an existing building. The process involved top administrative and medical staff, board members, and some political support. One such decentralized facility was opened and two years later was greatly underutilized and experiencing staff morale problems.

The facility was planned and implemented upon what seemed to be a sound, logical basis of projected demographic flow and geographic accessibility. What was missing was any consideration of the need for consumer involvement. The site, though accessible, proved to be unacceptable to consumers due to habit, fear (unfounded or not) of location, and lack of initial participation. Staff carrying out the programs were confronted with a major change without the opportunity to affect it. As a result, the organization had to undertake a major recruitment drive and attempt to rebuild staff morale.

In the normative sense, then, care should be taken to assure the presence of rational inquiry, just decisions, and proper use of staff. Rational inquiry calls for attention to be given to the premises on which the administrator bases the planning activities. These premises, relating to the external and internal environment of the organization are, in reality, predictions of the future. Koontz and O'Donnell classify the external premises into three groups:[11] the general environment, which includes political, economic, social, and technological conditions; the product market, which includes factors affecting demand for an organization's services; and the factor market, which includes such items as labor, capital, location, and so forth. For the care-giving organization, assumptions would be made, for example, concerning future federal, state, Title XX or federation funding; supply of adequate professional staff; potential centralization or decentralization of programs due to changes in demand, utilization patterns, and demographic changes; and the like. Internal environmental premises deal with such matters as internal demands (shifts in demands between units), capital investments, programs already committed, and the like.

A means to assure that administrative decisions lead to just consequences is to involve consumers in the process of the planning that affects their lives. In the normative sense, this means a pragmatic, as well as philisophical, belief in the positive contributions that consumers/constituents/board members have to offer. They have the opportunity to bring knowledge, skill, and perceptions to the planning process in a number of ways: pointing out gaps in the process; giving feedback on quality and quantity considerations; providing links to other consumers and other power bases; and bringing legitimacy to the process.

A detailed discussion of how staff can foster support and growth among themselves is presented in Chapter 13.[12]

Having discussed the normative stance, we can proceed to formulate a normative planning process. Based upon Terry's discussion of the planning steps and the key questions to be faced,[13] the authors have adapted and modified the process for use in human services organizations as follows:

1. CLARIFY THE PROBLEM.  State it concisely—a problem well defined is one half-solved. Ask these questions:

   a. What is the real aim or purpose of the plan to be formulated?
   b. Does this aim or purpose require a brand new plan, or will a modified existing plan suffice?
   c. What will the accomplishment of this aim mean to the organization?
   d. Is the contemplated aim in conflict with any existing goals of the organization so that adjustments or eliminations will be in order?
   e. What consumers/constituents/staff should be involved and are affected?

---

11.  Harold Koontz and Cyril O'Donnell, *Principles of Management: An Analysis of Managerial Functions* (New York: McGraw-Hill Book Company, 1968), p. 124.

12.  For a fuller discussion of consumer functions, see Henrik Blum, *Planning for Health* (New York: Human Sciences Press, 1974).

13.  See Terry, *Principles of Management*, pp. 4–12.

2. Obtain Complete Information About the Activities Involved. Experience, past solutions to problems, practices of other enterprises, observation, looking over records, and data secured from research and experiments constitute popular sources of usable information. The following questions may be asked:

a. Have all pertinent data been collected?
b. Have any reasonable sources of data been overlooked?
c. Have consumers/constituents/board members/operating personnel been solicited for suggestions?

3. Analyze and Classify the Information. Each component of information is examined both separately and in relation to the whole of the information. As a guide in this step, ask:

a. Are apparent relationships among data real and confirmed by key operating personnel as well as by consumer/constituent experiences?
b. Are all usable data being included?
c. With further study, can steps in the present work flow probably be eliminated?

4. Establish Planning Premises and Constraints. These premises and constraints will point out the background that presumably already exists or will exist to validate the plan. Ask the following questions:

a. What assumptions regarding the future are being made in order to develop the plan?
b. Are the premises inclusive and do they cover all important contingencies?
c. Has all reasonably available information concerning the planning premises been obtained and evaluated?
d. What premises and constraints must be carefully watched in order to detect changes that might seriously affect any plan based upon these assumptions?

5. Determine Alternate Plans. Usually several alternate plans exist, and the various possibilities are evolved during this step. These questions may be considered:

a. Are these possible plans in keeping with the organization's basic objectives and method of operation?
b. How much adjustment will be needed for each plan in the event it is adopted?
c. Are cost, speed, and quality requirements satisfied?

6. Choose Proposed Plan. Adequate consideration of expediency, adaptability, and cost must be made. In this step, the choice includes that

of doing nothing. Considerations contributing to the proper solution include:

 a. Is the proposed plan simple or complex?
 b. Will it be readily accepted by the operating personnel?
 c. Does it possess the flexibility to adjust to varying conditions?
 d. What new equipment, space, personnel, training, and supervising will be, needed?

7. ARRANGE DETAILED SEQUENCING AND TIMING OF PROPOSED PLAN. The details of where, when, and by whom the planned action should be done put in proper order for the intended purpose. Questions which might be asked are:

 a. Has a carefully worked out time schedule been established?
 b. Is the proposed installation, both in content and timing, in keeping with maximum acceptance by those affected by the plan?
 c. Have detailed instructions to cover the plan been written?

8. PROVIDE PROGRESS CHECKUP OF PROPOSED PLAN. Provision for adequate follow-up to determine compliance and results should be included in the planning work. For this step, ask:

 a. Have records and reports to keep consumers/constituents/board members/ operating personnel advised of progress been included?
 b. Will sufficient data over a reasonable period be collected to measure the results?
 c. In what range or within what limits will results be considered satisfactory?
 d. What remedial action is proposed if results indicate weaknesses?[14]

### example: an alcoholism services center's planning process for a new program

A very brief example may serve to portray the planning process. Such a process might take the following shape:

 1. *Clarify the problem.* An alcoholism center has determined that there is a major need for the provision of alcoholism services, preventive and therapeutic, to teens in the city in which it is located.
    a. Real aim: To develop services to meet very real needs of teenagers that are not now being met.
    b. New/modified plan: This program does not exist and will require a separate plan.
    c. Accomplishment: Will yield a definite positive meaning for the center by enabling it to furnish a comprehensive service, as well as increase its credibility.

14. See Terry, *Principles of Management,* pp. 253–60.

    d. Such a plan fits within the purview of, and does not conflict with, the organization's existing goals, but will require increased staff, monies, time, etc.

    e. The center's planning committee, key staff/director/program director, school officials, and teens themselves are to be involved in the process.

2. & 3. *Gather and classify information.*

    a. Data from schools, the public, hospitals, and other service agencies within the area must be obtained in order to document the need.

    b. Process should be organized to obtain suggestions from consumers, constituents, board members, operating personnel, and others.

    c. Data on similar programs in other communities should be obtained.

    d. Such data should be examined by key personnel as to, for instance, identified need, potential population at risk, success of other programs, and so forth.

4. *Define premises.* The center has recieved permission to embark on the planning process by the regional alcoholism planning organization and can assume a range of funding and support if the plan seems warranted.

5., 6., 7., & 8. *Determine and select a proposed plan from a series of alternative plans.* The center would begin a process of weighing alternative objectives, subobjectives, action programs, time frames, assignments, work plans, and performance standards in order to select the most feasible plan. (This process is detailed more completely in the next section on Program Planning and Organization.)

Some of the previous material needs further elaboration, specifically the preparatory exercise of certifying the premises or assumptions of the organization, and clarifying the problem. These two activities are closely related in that a care-giving organization has to make predictions about what will happen in the future and formulate its objectives in light of these predictions. Such premises or predictions are crucial if effective plans to meet an organization's objectives are to be made. Hence, any activity that serves to reduce the uncertainty of the future is warranted. A basic method for predicting uncertainties is *forecasting,* which serves to project future conditions and performances facing many care-giving organizations. A number of forecasting techniques are available to the administrator. Some of the most important ones are discussed in Chapter 14, "The Wise Administrator."

## PROGRAM PLANNING
## AND ORGANIZATION

### *introduction*

The previous section introduced the planning process in the human services organization. This section continues this discussion by first linking the planning process to the process of organizing resources by the use of objectives; and then discussing alternative organizational structures.

### program planning objectives and structure

The cyclical steps of planning—from problem clarification to plan selection to implementation to evaluation—all depend greatly on activity directed toward setting the targets that the human service organization is committed to achieve. These objectives exist in a time frame and many require reformulation as conditions change. A more detailed discussion of the setting of objectives will be found in the Chapter 12 section, "Management by Objectives." However, a few points should be introduced here to lead into the discussion of the link between planning and the organization of resources.

Theorists discuss the concepts of "nesting" and hierarchy of objectives. By this they mean that objectives never exist in isolation—they "nest" within each other in a hierarchical relationship. Beginning with the goals of the organization, objectives are set to enable the organization to meet the goals, then subobjectives—departmental or supportive—are set to guarantee the meeting of the organizational objectives, and so on down the hierarchical ladder. They key point is that the completion of lower-level activities and the attainment of their objectives serve to fulfill higher-level objectives and act as means to assess the order and direction of other activities.

The concept of planning is dependent on the setting up of a system of objectives. For the administrator of a care-giving organization, this is manifested in the area of program planning and its relationship to program structure. Program planning in a social agency refers to that mental activity on the part of organizational leadership that specifies what should be done, how it should be done, when certain necessary action is to be undertaken, and who will be responsible. All this is predicated upon the fact that such action is deemed necessary and that something will be done. In short, a program plan is a combination of objectives, policies and procedures, budgets, and other elements and activities deemed necessary to carry out predetermined objectives. Program planning calls for a hierarchical arrangement of goals and objectives that portrays the relationships of programs, services, and activities to goals and objectives. A particular program, then, is the set of activities that contributes to one of the social agency's objectives.

Program planning precedes the complementary function of organizing agency resources and sets in motion the depiction of program structure. Working from a hierarchical foundation, program objectives must be delineated, followed by a specification of program categories, services, and related activities.

Figure 7-2 depicts a program structure that has as its broad goal: to provide a service to help young people in a neighborhood area increase their reading ability. At the next level three major objectives are delineated. Within the provision of reading services, as one example, a series of subobjectives and program activities are linked vertically. These hierarchical linkages portray a workable program structure and program.

Figure 7-3 involves a more specific objective and structure that is more adaptable to evaluation. A time frame could be delineated for noting when certain subactivities, activities, and subobjectives are to be

**FIGURE 7-2**   *A Program Structure*

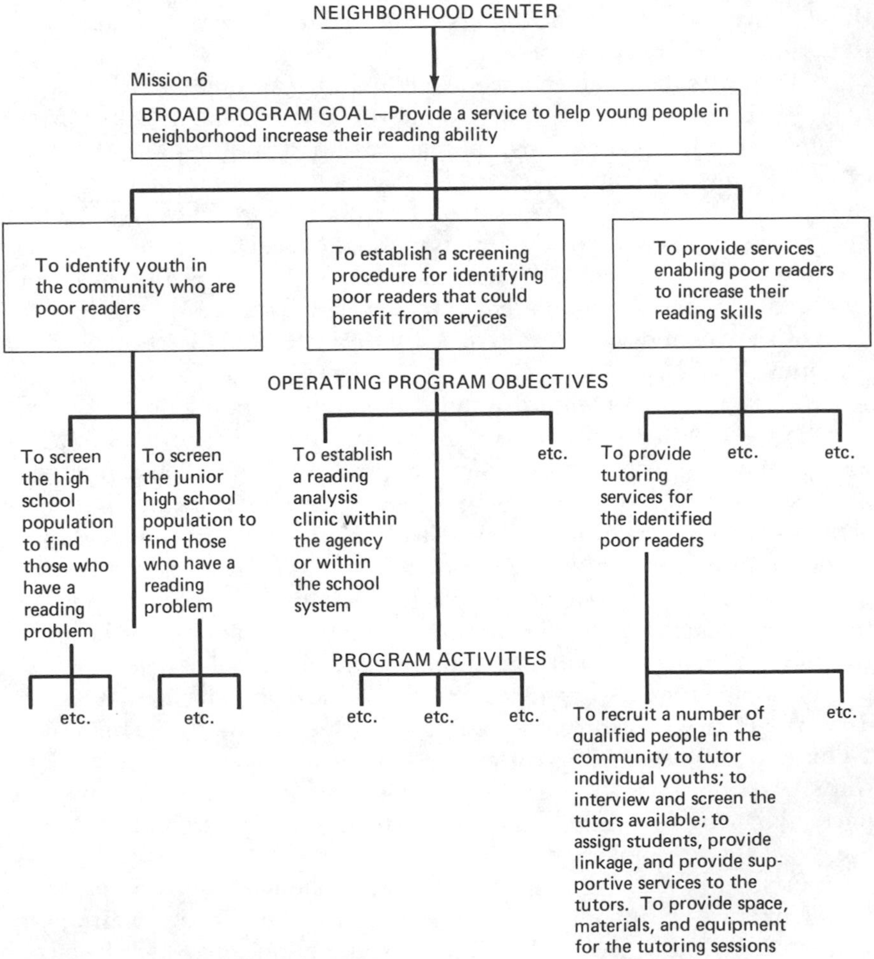

NEIGHBORHOOD CENTER

Mission 6

BROAD PROGRAM GOAL—Provide a service to help young people in neighborhood increase their reading ability

To identify youth in the community who are poor readers

To establish a screening procedure for identifying poor readers that could benefit from services

To provide services enabling poor readers to increase their reading skills

OPERATING PROGRAM OBJECTIVES

To screen the high school population to find those who have a reading problem

To screen the junior high school population to find those who have a reading problem

To establish a reading analysis clinic within the agency or within the school system

etc.

To provide tutoring services for the identified poor readers

etc.          etc.

PROGRAM ACTIVITIES

etc.          etc.          etc.          etc.          etc.

To recruit a number of qualified people in the community to tutor individual youths; to interview and screen the tutors available; to assign students, provide linkage, and provide supportive services to the tutors. To provide space, materials, and equipment for the tutoring sessions carried out. Thus, at certain time intervals, an administrator could monitor the work process.

In both examples, the relationship of objectives to subobjectives to activities is reflected in a hierarchical arrangement. The key point is to achieve a final program structure that will ease the analysis and assessment of programs, services, activities, and their many interrelationships.[15]

Figure 7-4 is an example of a summarized program worksheet for a neighborhood organization program. It includes some other features that must be considered, such as resource allocations, measurements, and additional collaborating units. It further introduces a sense of organizational determination of priorities among the operating unit's objectives.

This section introduced the concept of linking program planning to program structure by the use of objectives. The next section discusses organizational principles and alternative structures.

**FIGURE 7-3**    *A More Specific Program Structure*

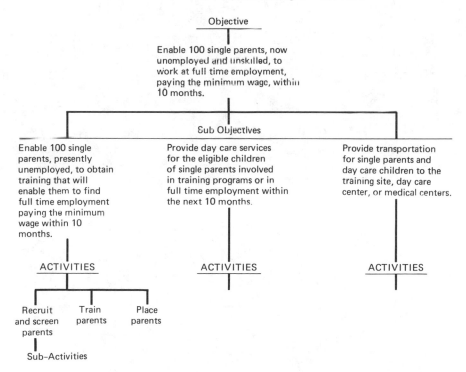

15.   A common problem in planning a program is that not enough analysis has been involved to assure that programs, services, and activities are as mutually exclusive as possible. The results are conflicting priorities, "too many bosses," and misdirection and duplication of effort.

# FIGURE 7-4 Neighborhood Organization Program

UNIT OBJECTIVES WORKSHEET (with Resource Allocation)

| (1) CODE | (2) OPERATING UNIT OBJECTIVES | (3) OTHER COLLABORATING UNITS/ ORGANIZATIONS | (4) INDEX OF NEED | (5) ACHIEVEMENT MEASURES OR INDICES | (6) ESTIMATED RESOURCE ALLOCATION % |
|---|---|---|---|---|---|
| B1 | To develop and implement a Community Information System (CIS) which could be used by neighborhood groups to monitor local govt. applications for assistance under the Hsg. & Comm. Dev. Act of 1974. | Neighborhood Groups | 1 | Number of requests for information. | 1% |
| B2 | To conduct a conference on the Housing and Community Development Act of 1974 and to publish a summary of the proceedings of the conference. | Case Western Reserve University Law School | 3 | Number of participants attending the conference and amount of circulation of the published proceedings. | 1% |
| B3 | To plan & establish neighborhood councils in 20 of the 60 municipalities using quadrant target priorities dev. from application of the "Desegregation Index" to 1980 Census Data. | Community leaders, major institutions, & key organizations committed to open housing. | 1 | Number of the 60 municipalities represented. | 8% |
| B4 | To organize a county-wide housing council of neighborhood representatives. | Community leaders, major institutions, & key organizations committed to open housing. | 1 | Number of the 20 municipalities mobilized. | 1% |

YEAR:

OPERATIONAL GOAL
Organization of neighborhood programs.

NAME OF UNIT:
Neighborhood Organization Programs

1. Urgent Need
2. Important Need
3. Moderate Need
4. Minimum Need

## ORGANIZATION OF RESOURCES

Administrative organizing is viewed as the process of the determination and allocation of roles, resources, and activities so as to achieve the organization's goals. This involves the creation of a formal series of role structures based upon authority-responsibility relationships. The previous section addressed this administrative function in the discussion on program and program structure. This section will elaborate upon that discussion by commenting upon the principles of organization, outlining the basic steps in developing an organizational/program structure; and comparing alternative organizational structures.

### *principles of organization*

Classical organizational theorists, as noted in Chapter 3, discuss several basic principles relevant to the building of an organizational structure for a human service agency.

SPAN OF CONTROL. The administrator must select an organizational structure that does not overload a manager with more people than can be effectively controlled. However, there seems to be no consensus on what constitutes the ideal number. Much of the success of a particular organization will depend upon not only the control area, but also upon formal and informal lines of communication, the respective abilities of the supervisor and those supervised, and the nature of the work—complex vs. routine.

Depending upon one's viewpoint, two types of structures—tall and short—evolve from this principle. Tall structures usually have increased levels of authority, with fewer people being supervised, and are accompanied by problems in vertical communication. Short structures have few levels of authority, an increased number of subordinates per supervisor, and are accompanied by problems of horizontal communication.

AUTHORITY LEVEL. The administrator must insure that responsibility for decisions is held and made at each manager's level of authority competence and not referred up or down the authority structure.

UNITY OF COMMAND. The administrator should create an organizational structure in which each member of an organization is responsible to, relates to, and receives orders from only one individual. This is sometimes difficult to achieve in care-giving organizations due to the lack of clarity of objectives, staffing difficulties, the size and domain of organizations (public and private bureaucracies), and the complexity of organizations dealing with multiple service needs.

SCALAR PRINCIPLE.   The administrator must select an organizational structure that has clear authority lines from top authority to middle management to supervisors to every subordinate. This relates to the principle of unity of command. People need to know the line of authority and, in increasingly complex and multidemand organizations, to whom to relate for what activities.

PARITY OF AUTHORITY AND RESPONSIBILITY.   There needs to be equality between the authority that a manager exercises and his or her delegated responsibilities. One cannot act upon a decision without having the authority for discharging it.

FLEXIBILITY.   Especially necessary for care-giving organizations existing in today's fast-changing environment, is an organizational structure flexible enough to respond to external and internal changes. The tendency is to design an organizational structure and to stick to it despite many changes in such areas as population at risk, emerging client/ constituent demands, and funding patterns. The need to build in adjustment mechanisms capable of initiating change when needed is paramount.[16]

### steps in the organizing process

Earlier in this chapter the concepts of program and program structure were discussed. The discussion centered upon the need to relate objectives and plan services and activities as a unified whole. This organizing process must also relate to the human factors (motivation, skill, experience), the environmental factors (external and internal factors that impinge upon the organization), and the basic principles outlined above. Development of the organizing process, then, leads to some fairly basic, principlelike steps that seem common to organizing resources in a care-giving organization. Such steps flow sequentially in the following order:

1. Establishment of the agency's goals and objectives. If this is a continuing program, the agency's goals and objectives should be reviewed.
2. Establishment of supportive objectives, policies, and plans.
3. Determination and classification of the activities deemed necessary to fulfilling these goals, objectives, policies, and plans.
4. Organizing these activities into workable groupings in light of the resources (human, capital, financial) available.
5. Assigning the authority to the manager of each grouping to carry out the activities.

16.   For classic discussions of these and other organizational principles, see: Henri Fayol, *General and Industrial Management,* trans. Constance Storrs (London: Sir Isaac Pittman and Sons, Ltd., 1949), and Luther Gulick, *The Elements of Administration* (New York: Harper & Row, Publishers, Inc., 1947).

6. Linking these groupings together through both authority-responsibility relationships and information systems. This requires delineation of both the horizontal and vertical relationships necessary to carry out the organization's objectives, policies, plans, and activities.

## alternative organizational structuring of resources

In the normative sense, no one organizational structure seems best for all human service organizations. The authors contend that the human service administrator must look at the organization in a systematic, dynamic way and not get locked into selecting the same organizational structure under all circumstances. Organizational structures of care-giving organizations vary according to type of organization, size, auspices, and even managerial style. The following represent fairly common variations of organizational design and are depicted in Figure 7-5.

*Line Organization* centers around the primary source of authority responsible for the major functions of the organization. A *Line and Staff Organization* is one with a supportive responsibility staff that advises line personnel. The *Line Organization*, in which a superior exercises direct control over a subordinate, makes for a clear and simple division of authority. The addition of the *Staff Organization* enables specialists to render expert advice to line personnel. However, this may be a source of conflict if there is a lack of understanding of basic authority channels and a lack of respect for differentiated roles, or extremely authoritative programs.

*Functional Organization* emphasizes the functional authority over certain practices, processes, or activities that are delegated to particular departments or individuals. This means a particular delegation may be carried over into other departments because of a lack of particular expertise in such departments. An example would be control over information systems by an expert in a functional department carried over into out-patient, in-patient, and day-care departments of a community mental health center. This provides an organizational vehicle for utilizing expertise, as well as relieving line personnel of routine activities. However, if the organization does not have a built-in coordination process and clear perception of authority-responsibility relationships, conflict among personnel is a distinct possibility.

Another type of organizational design is the *Matrix Organization*, which stresses temporary groupings, with resources organized around a particular task or project, rather than on departmental or functional lines. Personnel from key departments are brought together, full time, in order to carry out major assignments.

**FIGURE 7-5** *Three Organizational Types*

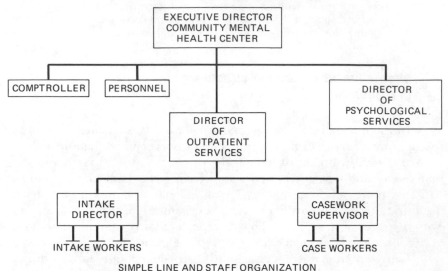

SIMPLE LINE AND STAFF ORGANIZATION

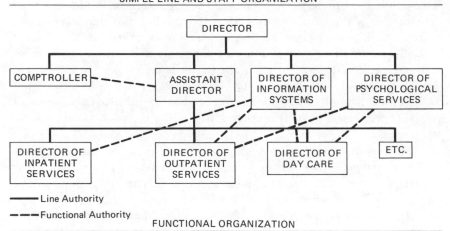

FUNCTIONAL ORGANIZATION

MATRIX ORGANIZATION
TYPES OF ORGANIZATION

A typical example is bringing together key agency staff to develop a funding proposal for a new service, as depicted in Figure 7-5. Here, the proposal convenor is assigned the proposal and is given the authority and responsibility to draw key people from relevant departments in order to develop the proposal. These personnel, upon completion of the proposal, return to their respective departments. Once again, in order to minimize conflicts, clear relationships of authority, delegation, and responsibility are needed.

## SUMMARY

This chapter discussed program structure and its relationship to objectives. Principles of organizational structure, steps in the organizing process, and alternative structures were explored. The conclusion can be drawn that the best structure is one that is adaptive to: the nature of the work and type of technology used by the care-giving organization; characteristics of the organization's personnel; the organization's size and complexity; and the impact and needs of the organization's publics, the most important being the needs of the care-giving organization's patients, clients, or constituents.

# CHAPTER 8

---

# control:
# monitoring
# and evaluation

## INTRODUCTION

Control was described earlier as the creation of a process for monitoring, measuring, and correcting to assure the organization's ability to attain its stated objectives, and includes the creation of evaluating tools. This process is receiving increasing attention as care-giving organizations are scrutinized by public and private funding bodies, commissions, boards of directors, and the public at large. Internal to the organization is the need for personal accountability.

"Do we know whether we are reaching our objectives?" "Are we operating efficiently and effectively?" "Have we structured our programs to maximize our potential service delivery?" "Are we expending our financial resources so as to assure minimum loss and more 'clout' for our dollars?" Such questions and concerns from both internal and external environments emphasize a need for more concentration on control processes.

This section will discuss the relationship of control to the other processes of the management cycle, evaluation as a positive control and feedback system, and the concept of budgeting as a planning-control system.

## RELATIONSHIPS

The control process is an integral part of the decision-making—planning cycle. Decisions are made to establish goals and objectives, plan alternative programs, and allocate human and capital resources. Control fits into this cycle by the use of comparisons. Monitoring is an on-going control function that compares actual performance with planned performance and makes any necessary adjustments on the basis of the information that has been gathered. Later, one evaluates the end results by comparing the achievements-results of the program with the program as originally planned. Thus, both monitoring and program evaluation affect initial program changes and changes in objectives, as well as future aims of the care-giving organization.

Another way of looking at control is to frame the above discussion in "systems" terms. Outpatient/outcome control is the use of evaluation to measure the outcomes of programmatic activities/services in light of whether they met or did not meet measurable preconceived output standards. Throughput/activity control is the difficult attempt to monitor the activities of the organization (such as modality of counselling, structuring of workload, organizational structure, use of time and monies) to determine whether the activities are soundly contributing to the fulfillment of the organization's objectives. Some writers also emphasize the use of input control. On the basis of previous research, other organizational experiences, professional norms, and the like serve to control the type and number of certain resources (e.g., professional training and experience of desired staff members) that are recruited as inputs to an organization.

## EVALUATION AND MONITORING
## AS A POSITIVE CONTROL
## AND FEEDBACK SYSTEM

As noted above, the external environments of public and private human service organizations today, reflect a series of factors including: limited resources, increasing demands for services, evolving perceptions of social problems and needs, integration of services, and changing social conditions. One of the results of such volatile external environments has been the emergence of the need for accountability. Social agencies, in order to survive in what seems to be a most competitive world, are now generating evaluation efforts. This is due to the demands of funding bodies for comprehensive feedback from recipients on the benefits resulting from their expenditure of monies, as well as the need of service organizations to know how well they are doing. Evaluation, as a positive control and feedback system, presents an opportunity for agencies to receive valuable and comprehensive information that can lead to improved service delivery and program development and design.

This section will present key concepts in evaluation and, within the systems framework of this book, will emphasize the place for evaluation in the implementation, planning, and program management processes.

## EVALUATION DEFINED

Writers generally define evaluation as an effort to determine what changes have occurred as the result of a planned service program by comparing actual results with desired results (i.e., goals and objectives) and by identifying the degree to which the program is responsible for the difference. Suchman, for instance, described evaluation as ". . .the determination (whether based on opinions, records, subjective or objective data) of the results (whether desirable or undesirable; transient or permanent; immediate or delayed) attained by some activity (whether a program, a part of a program, a drug or a theory, an ongoing or one-shot approach) designed to accomplish some valued goal or objective (whether ultimate, intermediate, or immediate, effort or performance, long- or short-range.)"[1] In short, evaluation aims at measuring the program's effects in relation to the goals it has set out to accomplish in order to contribute to future decision making about the present program and improvement of future programs.

Each of the aforementioned definitions refers to "what we are doing" and "what we did." In other words, evaluation takes place within two time frames: the present, when evaluations are made of current activities in order to monitor how well a particular program or activity is working; and the past, in that after the program is completed, an evaluation as to whether we accomplished what we said we would do is made.

The former refers to a process type of evaluation sometimes called

1.   Edwin A. Suchman, *Evaluative Record: Principles and Practice in Public Service and Action Programs* (New York: Russell Sage Foundation, 1967), p. 78.

"on-going evaluation" or "status monitoring" or "program monitoring." It is a central function, the results of which help the administrator to correct a program or an activity that does not seem to be working. Fitting the concept within the later discussion on management by objectives (M.B.O.), this evaluation collects information on the progress of a program on an on-going basis and then compares it with preset objectives. The systematic collection of information in this kind of evaluation helps decisions on allocation of resources, as well as providing an early identification of actual or potential problems.

The latter, sometimes called "program evaluation" or "in-depth assessment," is results-oriented and is concerned with comparing actual and planned results. It centers, then, upon causal relationships between inputs, throughputs, outputs, and outcomes.

Figure 8-1 portrays these types of evaluation in graphic form to illustrate their time frames. In the on-going evaluation, the agency director attempts to identify key incidents in a program. On the basis of the key incidents, a collection of information would be initiated, the goal of which is to inform the director how well these incidents are being achieved. In the program evaluation, data would have been identified, collected, and displayed in such a way that the director could identify the success or failure of the program and the factors leading to its success or failure.

Examples of critical incidents to be monitored in the on-going evaluation:

1. Monitoring of the agency's outreach program;
2. Monitoring the intake process;
3. Monitoring the counselling and referral process; and
4. Monitoring the disposition of the case.

**FIGURE 8-1**   *The Two Time Frames of Evaluation*

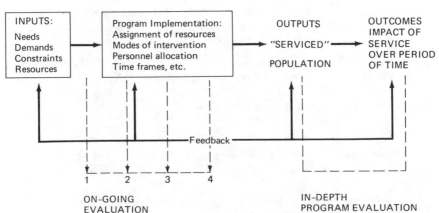

## steps in the evaluation process

Five basic steps are frequently ascribed to the program evaluation process. They are:

1. Assess needs;
2. Formulate program goals and objectives;
3. Define program methodologies;
4. Conduct an evaluation process; and
5. Conduct a program evaluation.

Weiss, however, formulates four steps:

1. Find out the program's goals;
2. Translate the goals into measurable indicators of goal achievement;
3. Collect data on the indicators from who participated in the program (and for an equivalent control group who did not);
4. Compare the program on participants (and controls) with the goal criteria.[2]

Both series move through a process of delineating objectives to means of implementation to data collecting to comparison with objectives. It is the premise of this book, with its systems bias, that in-depth assessment and on-going evaluation are closely related and serve to buttress each other in their joint purpose of aiding decision making. Hence, the steps in the evaluation process of a social agency will involve an expansion of the steps noted above in order to cover both types. These steps conform to the systems approach and can be viewed in a cyclical manner as moving from identification of objectives, to development of performance indicators, to evaluation design, to data collection, to data analysis, to reporting of results, to recommendations and implementation, to return to original view of objectives. Note the strong similarity to the cyclical nature of decision making and planning and their common reliance on gathering relevant information in order to be successful.

This section will outline the steps in the evaluation process. It will point out, where necessary, the need for differentiation in approach depending on whether on-going or program evaluation is used.

### Step 1—*Identification of Objectives*

The entire process of evaluation depends heavily upon the ability of an organization to specify its objectives. The role of the director is paramount in assuring that these objectives are realistic and, thus, will

2. Carol Weiss, *Evaluation Research and Methods* (Englewood Cliffs, N.J.: Prentice-Hall, Inc., 1972), pp. 24–25.

contribute to an effective evaluation. Chapter 11 will discuss the three criteria of realistic objectives: measurability; the setting of a level of acceptable performance; and the setting of the conditions or boundaries within which the objective is to be met. The more the stated objectives conform to these criteria, the more certainty there is in having an effective evaluation analysis.

As stated above, objectives should provide information relevant to a program's direction. However, they may not provide performance targets. That is, objectives may be focused upon individual points (characteristics of the objectives, i.e., accessibility, acceptability, etc.), but may not be focused upon a performance target. The performance target assures a way to compare planned and actual accomplishments. For example:

*Objective*: To assure that patients have ready access to the ambulatory care center in the northeast area of the city.

*Focal Point* (characteristic): ready access.

*Performance Indicator* (measure of performance): patients within one-half hour walking time of the ambulatory care center.

*Target* (success criteria): no less than eighty percent of the patients living within one-half hour walking time of the ambulatory care center.

After program implementation, the actual number of patients living within the walking time area would be compared against the target figures of the evaluation stage.

It cannot be emphasized enough that the activity of the director in setting targets is crucial. The director needs to identify key information in order to arrive at workable objectives and targets. Such information comes from a host of sources: previous program experience; previous experiences of similar programs in the locality or elsewhere; dictates of the enabling legislative or funding body; standards of accrediting organizations; or previous personal experiences.

**Step 2**—*Development of Performance Indicators*

The second step in the evaluation process is to develop measures of the expected program accomplishment as described in the objectives. There are a number of performance indicators vis-a-vis objective characteristics that are common to most human service organizations. These indicators usually deal with factors of efficiency, effectiveness, personal acceptability, and people to be served. In order to make an effective evaluation, the director should be considering multiple performance indicators in the planning stage. The following is a sample of objective characteristics that are made measurable by appropriate performance indicators:

| OBJECTIVE CHARACTERISTICS | EXAMPLES OF PERFORMANCE INDICATORS |
|---|---|
| Service Objectives | Percentage of service recipients in employment program working on planned jobs. |
| Population Served | Percentage of service recipients by race, income, and location receiving health services. |
| Accessibility | Percentage of patients living within one-half hour commuting time of ambulatory care center. |
| Acceptability | Patient's ratings of service providers. |
| Efficiency | Cost per unit of service. |
| Time | Average time per unit of service. |

Such performance indicators must be agreed upon by relevant staff as reliable indicators of the program's effect upon the people to be served if adequate data is to be obtained.

## Step 3—*Evaluation Design*

Once the evaluator knows "what" is to be studied, the questions to be faced next are, "How to study it?" and "Where is the information?" Step 3 relates to the "how" question. It is aimed at organizing the means necessary to gather and analyze the data called for in Step 2. On-going evaluation requires developing a feedback system that will deliver the reliable collection and retrieval of data relating to performance indicators. This implies setting up time schedules for data collection, their manner of presentation, and a periodic review of such data. This is consonant with the feedback processes built in to the milestones of the M.B.O. process (see Chapter 11).

Program evaluation, unlike on-going monitoring, aims at explaining program performance. There are a number of useful evaluation designs available to the human services organization. Their use depends upon feasibility, time, sophistication of the evaluator, and costs. The more sophisticated the design and the more time involved, obviously, the higher the cost. The following are brief examples of different evaluation designs available to the program evaluator:[3]

3. For excellent full discussion of evaluation design, see: Phyllis L. Solomon, "Approaches to Program Evaluation: Experimental, Quasi-, Pre-, and Non-Experimental Designs," *Allocation Guidelines Project* (unpublished mimeo, Cleveland, Ohio, August, 1976); Carol H. Weiss, *Evaluation Research and Methods,* Chapter 4, pp. 60–91; and Edwin A. Suchman, *Evaluative Record,* pp. 91–114.

THE EXPERIMENTAL DESIGN.    This is the most costly, time-consuming, and complex of evaluation designs. It involves the use of control and experimental groups within which program individuals or areas are randomly assigned. Then the impact of the program upon the experimental groups is compared to the control groups, which have not received any program services. This design approaches a true measurement of program effectiveness but has some problems. It is quite expensive; its requirements are quite stringent (e.g., no self-selection on the part of consumers, clearly defined program outcomes, clear separation between control and experimental groups, and the like). Another important consideration is an ethical one: Can some people (the control group) ethically be denied the program's services?

QUASI-CONTROL DESIGN.    In this design, an attempt is made to match, as closely as possible and prior to program implementation, the group to be served by the program with a control group that will not be served. Again, the aim is to assess the program's effectiveness. The difficulty is in finding close matches among the characteristics of the two groups.

TIME-SERIES DESIGN.    This design is quite practical but does not fulfill the stringent requirements of the experimental design. It involves measurements to be made at calculated intervals before a program begins, during its existence, and after a program ends. In other words, progress during a program is observed and compared to previous conditions. The group being studied acts as its own control group.

PRE-POST PROGRAM STUDY.    This is a simpler version of the time-series design, in which data collected only prior to and after program implementation is compared.

An extension of the program evaluation design is the cost-benefit analysis. Given development of performance indicators and the use of an evaluation design usually utilizing comparison groups, the analyst attempts to identify the program's direct and indirect costs and its tangible and intangible effects. Such analysis has come increasingly into vogue in the human services arena.

### Step   4—*Data Collection*

The entire process of on-going and program evaluation depends upon the ability to collect accurate and timely data. Weiss points out that the only limits to effective data collection are the ingenuity and imagination of the evaluator and suggests a number of possible sources. These include:

> 1) interviews; 2) questionnaires; 3) observation; 4) ratings (by peers, staff, experts); 5) psychometric tests of attitudes, values, personality, preferences, norms, beliefs; 6) institutional records; 7) government statistics; 8) tests of information, interpretation, skills, application of knowledge; 9) projective tests; 10) situational tests presenting the respondent with simulated life situations; 11) diary records; 12) physical evidence; 13) clinical examinations; 14) financial records; and 15) documents (minutes of board meetings, newspaper accounts of policy actions, transcripts of trials).[4]

For effective evaluation, the use of a number of such sources of performance indicators may be necessary. On-going evaluation requires a system for collecting data. Such a system involves: an analysis of information needs regarding performance indicators (e.g., baseline data on program consumers, staff, and monies utilized; data on program objectives and outputs, etc.); identification of sources of information (see above); development of a system of collection, handling, and retrieval of the information; and a feedback system concerning the workability of the information system. For program evaluation, information is collected in a more concentrated way, depending on the type of research design being utilized. This calls for precise compilation of performance indicator information and, at times, can also use the information gathered through the on-going evaluation system. Depending upon the type of design, four common data collection techniques are available to the human services administrator:

1. consumer/constituent surveys;
2. community/general citizen surveys;
3. analysis of existing data (records, statistics, etc.); and
4. professional (expert) ratings.

The first three techniques ordinarily collect data from random representative samplings.

## Step  5—*Data Analysis*

Judgment must be made about the meaning of the collected data regarding performance indicators. This analysis is based on a comparison of actual and planned performance. Hence, the importance of Steps 1 and 2, "Specification of Objectives" and "Performance Indicators." If the objectives are unclear, the evaluation will be meaningless.

---

4.   Carol H. Weiss, *Evaluation Research and Methods,* p. 53.

In brief, there are two methods of analysis, quantitative and qualitative. The quantitative method involves the use of numbers and/or statistics to describe trends or relationships. The qualitative method involves nonstatistical analysis in the absence of numerical data or resource availability. It is an impressionistic analysis based upon the evaluator's professional expertise. The methods can be complementary, providing a fuller, richer analysis of performance indicator data. Both rely upon human judgment. Care should be taken to recognize the effect of external factors when drawing conclusions from the data to see whether or not the program was successful.

**Step 6**—*Reporting of Results*

The next step is to prepare a useful evaluation report based on the data analysis. This implies taking the time to develop a format to display the analysis so that it is comprehensible, timely, and useful to program decision makers. The use of professional jargon and unclear language can damage the evaluation as much as a faulty research design or unclear objectives. If the results are reported to a decision maker too late to facilitate a more effective decision, then the evaluation is useless as an action tool. Further, if the report is completely undecipherable to the key decision makers, it will not be used. In brief, the report should be carefully documented, organized, and presented in a format that aims at the intended audience (the decision maker). For on-going evaluation, this calls for a series of regular reports, so an agreed-upon format can be formulated early. For program evaluation, although the report is usually issued at the end of the program, it is useful for the evaluator and the decision maker to arrive at a mutually-determined report format early in the evaluation process.

**Step 7**—*Recommendations and Implementation*

This step is not necessarily included in the evaluation process. Generally and increasingly, decision makers are calling for evaluators to develop recommendations on the basis of the evaluation for future directions of human service organizations. Recommendations must be linked to suggestions for implementation. Recommendations, without a commentary on the "how" of implementation and the possible resistance to them, is only half of the evaluator's job. A certain amount of personal risk-taking is involved but, in the normative sense, making recommendations seems to be a requirement for planning the "action" in action-research. Evaluation without some sort of action serves no purpose.

In on-going evaluation, such recommendations would be directed to potentially increasing the efficiency and continuing effectiveness of the program. In program evaluation, this step would be addressed to continuance or discontinuance, or to means designed to improve the program's effective performance.

So far this section has addressed the concept of evaluation and monitoring as positive control and feedback mechanisms that can aid in planning and decision-making processes. It outlined the typical seven-step evaluation process for both on-going and program evaluation and placed the process in a cyclical, systems framework.

Two other considerations call for discussion: the use of on-going evaluation as an aid to staff evaluation and training and the politics of evaluation.

Chapter 5, "Motivation," and subsequently Chapter 11, including "Management by Objectives (M.B.O.)" and Chapter 12, "The Creative Organization," all stress the importance of the human element to whether a human-service organization is efficient and effective. A motivated, well-trained, competent staff immeasurably increases the potential for successfully meeting an organization's goals and objectives. On-going evaluation can aid in this process. Suchman points out that evaluation can "build morale of staff by involving them in evaluation of their efforts. . .by providing goals and standards against which to measure progress and achievement."[5] By objectively relating staff activity to performance goals, an administrator can more effectively determine potential areas for staff training and development, as well as better staff utilization. These staffing considerations will be more fully discussed in Chapter 12.

Another consideration deserving comment is the politics of evaluation. We have discussed the volatile environment of the human services organization. Various external publics (e.g., funding bodies, planning bodies, governmental agencies, and the like) and internal publics (line-workers, supervisors, staff, administrators, and the like) face both the on-going evaluation process and the program evaluation process and react with mixed perceptions. Critical questions, never posed, arise: "Am I doing my job right. . .?" "Are they doing their jobs right. . .?" "Will we lose our funding. . .our staff. . .?" "Shall we fund them. . .?" "Can we gain further funding. . .?" "Are we efficient. . .?" "Are we aiming too high. . .too low. . .?" "Does this give us an excuse to cut the program. . .?" and so forth. Depending upon one's perspective, these questions determine the resistances, success, use, and nonuse of evaluation. Evaluation can take place, then, in an extremely political arena. The evaluator who does not recognize this factor runs the risk of having his or her results abused, misinterpreted, or ignored. It behooves the evaluator to acknowledge that evaluation can be initiated for nonrational as well as rational purposes.[6]

    5.   Edwin A. Suchman, *Evaluative Record,* p. 141.
    6.   For a discussion on covert purposes of research, see Carol Weiss, *Evaluation Research and Methods,* pp. 11–12.

Weiss presents some sound advice for the evaluator in initiating an evaluation: "Find out who initiated the idea of having an evaluation of the program and for what purposes. Were there other groups in the organization who questioned or objected to the evaluation? What were their motives? Is there real commitment among practitioners, administrators and/or funders to using the results of the evaluation to improve future decision-making?"[7] The answers to such questions should enable the evaluator to make his or her own personal decision as to the potential merits of pursuing the evaluation.

In short, whether to conduct an evaluation and the potential use of its findings will hinge upon what Suchman calls: "Forces Related to Program and Organizational Forces" and "Forces Related to Public Reaction."[8] The former refers to potential internal environmental interests and resistances, the latter to potential external environmental interests and resistances.

However, with all its problems and pitfalls, proper evaluation, in the normative sense, can be an effective aid in the planning, controlling, organizing, motivating, and decision-making processes of the human services administrator.

7. Carol H. Weiss, p 13.
8. See Edwin A. Suchman, *Evaluative Record*, pp. 164–66.

# CHAPTER 9

---

# the concept of budgeting as a planning control system

**INTRODUCTION**

The concept of control is more popularly recognized in the use of the social agency budget. It is the authors' contention that the budget is more than "just" a control device, and that it interrelates closely with planning and the organization of resources.

This chapter will explore the use of budgets in human service organizations, noting the various types, and describing the budget process.

Most writers conform to Kast and Rosenzweig's description of a budget as "a plan set forth in financial terms."[1] This description attempts to focus on the budget as a key part of an organization's planning and control system and to focus on it positively as a control as opposed to a monitor. There is an added emphasis on the planning element in the

---

1.   Fremont E. Kast and James E. Rosenzweig, *Organization and Management* (New York: McGraw-Hill Book Company, 1970), p. 486.

budgeting process, rather than its curbing and checking aspects (see Figure 9-1).

In human service organizations we have seen, and are seeing, a continuing evolution of the budget from only strict monitoring control to management control to a planning phase. Alan Schick in a classic article, discusses how the major orientations have changed over the years.[2] The first orientation, from 1920 to 1935, was one that emphasized the control of improprieties. The second orientation, from 1936 to 1965, was one of management, and emphasized the assessment of work efficiency and performance measurement. The third orientation, from 1966 to the present, is one of planning, that is, the attempt to use the budget to emphasize programmatic outcomes and policy formulation for the future. One way to view these orientations is to relate the types of current budgeting practices (line-by-line, functional, and programmatic) to them in light of the management cycle.

**FIGURE 9-1** *Budget as Planning and Control*

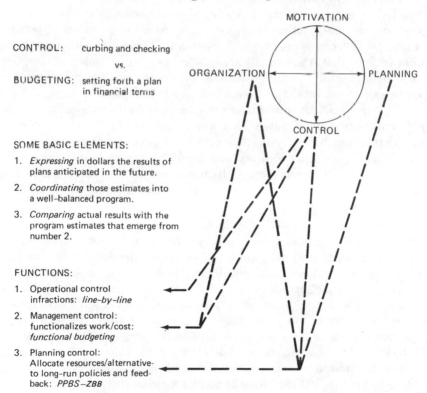

CONTROL: curbing and checking

vs.

BUDGETING: setting forth a plan in financial terms

MOTIVATION

ORGANIZATION ← → PLANNING

CONTROL

SOME BASIC ELEMENTS:

1. *Expressing* in dollars the results of plans anticipated in the future.

2. *Coordinating* those estimates into a well-balanced program.

3. *Comparing* actual results with the program estimates that emerge from number 2.

FUNCTIONS:

1. Operational control infractions: *line-by-line*

2. Management control: functionalizes work/cost: *functional budgeting*

3. Planning control: Allocate resources/alternative- to long-run policies and feedback: *PPBS–ZBB*

2. Alan Schick, "The Road to PPB: The Stress of Budget Reform," *Public Administration Review,* XXVI, no. 4 (December 1966), 243–58.

However, there are two basic elements common to all budgets. One is that in every budget there is a delineation in financial terms of the anticipated results of plans for the future. Second is that there is an attempt to coordinate these estimated plans within a balanced program. Each of the current budget practices fulfills these to a greater or lesser degree depending upon its emphasis.

Given these common elements, the following section will discuss each budget type in relation to its orientation within the cycle of the key management process of planning, organizing, controlling, and motivating.

## TYPES OF BUDGETS

### line-by-line

A line-by-line budget, often called the object accounting budget and practiced by human service organizations for many years, relates only to the management function of control. It focuses on operational control as depicted in Figure 9-1 and has proved worthwhile in catching budget improprieties and noting changes in line items (e.g., salaries, rentals, income, etc.) from previous years. Such a budget reflects an accounting point of view that traditionally accumulated expenses (salaries, supplies, transportation, etc.) and then summarized these into an overall budget. Organizations would simply review how much was spent on such objects of expenditure and how much income was received by line sources of income (e.g. contributions, memberships, fees, and the like). The projected budget then was based upon these previous figures, and projections were made that would take into account these figures plus an increase for inflation and other cost factors. In the normative sense, a line-by-line budget is an excellent mechanism for operational control.

Table 9-1 depicts a community mental health center's line-by-line budget request to a United Way. Notice that it lists income and expenditures for a three-year period: the previous year, the current year's operating budget, and the estimated budget for the next year. It reflects an agency that experienced rapid growth due to increased objectives, numbers of people served, geographic area, as well as several increases in sources and amounts of income. This budget lends itself to horizontal analysis by which line items may be compared over the years (e.g., program service fees increasing from $36,100 to $99,500 to a projected $140,000). At the same time, it lends itself to a vertical analysis as a comparative tool (e.g. salaries, benefits, and payroll taxes, $862,000 plus $43,300 plus $18,000 for a total of $923,300 represents approximately 92 percent of the total projected budget). Such a figure could be compared

## TABLE 9-1  Line-by-Line Budget

| Support/Revenue for Current Operations | 2<br>Actual<br>Last<br>Period<br>(Last Year) | Projected For<br>Period Ahead | |
|---|---|---|---|
| | | 3<br>Current Year<br>Budget | 4<br>Next Year<br>Estimated |
| Contributions – General | | | |
| Special Events | | | 10,000 |
| Requests, Non-Endowment | | | |
| Associated Organizations | | | |
| Allocated From Other United Ways | 73,000 | 120,600 | 157,000 |
| Unassociated, Non-Fed. Fund Raising Orgs. | | | |
| Fees and Grants from Gov. Agencies | 114,000 | 226,600 | 621,000 |
| Membership Dues – Individuals | 11,500 | 6,000 | 20,000 |
| Assessments and Dues – Local Member Units | | | |
| Program Service Fees | 36,100 | 99,500 | 140,000 |
| Sales of Supplies and Services to Local Members | | | |
| Sales to Public | | | |
| Investment Income | 14,900 | 16,025 | 20,000 |
| Miscellaneous Revenue | | | |
| (B)  TOTAL SUPPORT/REVENUE | 249,500 | 468,725 | 968,000 |
| DEFICIT – (A) minus (B) | 41,960 | 41,075 | 37,350 |

| Expenditures For<br>Current Service Operations | 2<br>Actual<br>Last<br>Period | Projected For<br>Period Ahead | |
|---|---|---|---|
| | | 3<br>Budget | 4<br>Estimated |
| Salaries | 234,000 | 413,000 | 862,000 |
| Employee Health & Retirement Benefits | 8,700 | 35,000 | 43,300 |
| Payroll Taxes | 8,600 | 12,000 | 18,000 |
| Prof. Fees & Contract Service Payment | 3,100 | 600 | 750 |
| Supplies | 5,400 | 6,900 | 9,700 |
| Telephone & Telegraph | 3,600 | 5,200 | 13,400 |
| Postage & Shipping | 760 | 1,000 | 1,200 |
| Occupancy (Buildings & Grounds) | 1,700 | 10,200 | 10,300 |
| Outside Printing, Art Work, etc. | -- | 1,000 | 1,500 |
| Local Transportation | 12,600 | 8,200 | 19,300 |
| Conferences, Conventions, Meetings, Maj. Trips | 2,000 | 9,300 | 11,400 |
| Subscriptions & Reference Publications | -- | -- | -- |
| Specific Assistance to Individuals | 1,000 | 4,100 | 2,600 |
| Organization Dues | 1,600 | 400 | 5,000 |
| Awards & Grants | -- | -- | -- |
| Equipment & Other Fixed Assets | 7,900 | 1,500 | 3,500 |
| Miscellaneous | 1,500 | 1,400 | 2,400 |
| Dues/Support Pay. to Nat'l "Parent" Org. | | | |
| (A)  GRAND TOTAL EXPENDITURES | 292,480 | 500,800 | 1,005,350 |

with that of other community mental health centers to see whether they are comparable in a positive manner.

However, there is a strong tendency for administrators, budget committees, officers, boards of directors, and funding bodies to emphasize the incremental nature of the budget. That is, there is a tendency to compare the dollars of an expense category from one year compared to another, rather than relating the dollar numbers to the programs that the organization is planning. By only looking at monies spent in current years, monies being spent now, and adding a percentage increase due to cost-of-living changes, the sense of the "future" in budgeting is negated.

### functional budget – program budget

The functional budget was an evolutionary attempt to increase the efficiency and comprehension of a budget. Relating to Figure 9-1, this type of budget emphasizes a movement toward a concept of managerial control that embraces the two functions of control and organization of resources in the management cycle.

Here the organization aims at managerial control to assure that resources are obtained to accomplish the organization's objectives. This type of budget distributes revenue and overhead expenses, such as general supportive management functions, as well as particularly identifiable programs or services provided by the human services organization. The process distributes line item costs and revenues for each program as well as the management function and thus gives a more accurate picture of the organization's program. By distributing overhead costs, it serves to deal with functional activities and utilizes work-cost measurements to organize the work process. Such tools as time management and time studies can increase the efficacy of such a budget.

This type of budget is known also as a program budget in that it can ultimately lead to a program budget. The state of the art for most human service organizations is really a hybrid of both forms, a functional program budget. The functional budget does not include the planning element whereas a functional program budget attempts to introduce a form of planning into the process.

An example of this process is depicted in Table 9-2, a modified functional program budget of an area mental health budget requesting monies from a funding body. The total line items for the organization are to be found in Column 1, "Total." These items have been distributed among supporting services (management) and programs. In this case, there are seven programs (services) being provided by the organization (outpatient, inpatient, day care, 24-hour emergency care, consultation and education, research and evaluation, and after care). This budget is a worthwhile tool because it enables both an organization and its funding sources to compare costs of various services as well as overhead.

The budget also presents opportunities for horizontal and vertical analysis. Management costs are seen to be 8.7 percent of the total budget ($88,206 of a total budget of $1,013,862) and this could be compared to other agencies' management costs. Similarly, costs of programs can be compared internally (e.g., outpatient to inpatient) and externally with particular programs of other agencies.

However, as Goodman notes there is a "catch" in this type of budget. There may be no built-in orientation toward the ultimate objectives of organizational policy and, there is a danger that an agency's objectives will be defined in terms of activities rather than the social problem that needs to be addressed.[3]

The functional budget can, in an indirect sense, lead to identifying organizational purposes, but still focuses only upon an itemization of the monies required to continue an old program or commence a new one. Program budgeting attempts to emphasize the long-run policies of the care-giving organization with the aim of relating program and expenditure choices. In other words, it attempts to allocate resources to alternative choices by careful analysis of these alternatives and by linking program costs to potential outputs. In Figure 9-1 this is reflected by the emphasis on planning in addition to control and organization of resources in the management cycle. Whereas functional budgeting is concerned with the work process, program budgeting is concerned with the purpose of work.

The program budgeting process sequentially attempts to:

1. narratively describe the agency's programs in light of objectives, programs, subprograms, and targets;
2. identify budgetary allocations by functional programs;
3. delineate and quantify program results;
4. utilize cost-benefit analysis;
5. explore alternative methods and priorities within the overall program; and
6. develop a long-run (over three years) planning process with the assurance of considerable feedback.

Steps 1 and 2 in the aforementioned process do not present overly strenuous problems for most human service organizations, large or small. However, the succeeding steps call for a great deal of time and expertise that may not be present in an organization, regardless of size.

At present, program budgeting is in its infancy at most human service organizations due to difficulties in measuring and defining outputs, lack of expertise, monies, and implementation time, receptivity, and

3. Nathaniel Goodman, "The Catch in Functional Budgeting: To What End?" *Social Work*, 14, no. 3 (July 1969), 40–48.

**TABLE 9-2**  *Proposed Budget by*

UNITED WAY OF _____

Executive's Signature _____

| | | | *Supporting Services* | |
| | (1) Total Col. 4 + 5 | (2) Mgmt. & General | (3) Fund Raising | (4) Total Col. 2 + 3 |
| *Item* | | | | |
|---|---|---|---|---|
| No. EXPENSES | | | | |
| Salaries | | | | |
| Health and retirement benefits | | | | |
| Payroll taxes, etc. | | | | |
| (A) TOTAL SALARIES AND RELATED EXPENSES | 923,612 | 80,354.27 | | 80,354.27 |
| Professional fees, contract services | 750 | 65.25 | | 65.25 |
| Supplies | 11,500 | 1,000.50 | | 1,000.50 |
| Telephone | 13,400 | 1,165.80 | | 1,165.80 |
| Postage and shipping | 1,200 | 104.40 | | 104.40 |
| Occupancy | 10,300 | 896.10 | | 896.10 |
| Rental/maintenance of equipment | 4,000 | 348.00 | | 348.00 |
| Printing and publications | 1,500 | 130.50 | | 130.50 |
| Travel | 26,200 | 2,279.40 | | 2,279.40 |
| Conferences, conventions,meetings | 11,400 | 991.80 | | 991.80 |
| Specific assistance to individuals | 2,600 | 226.20 | | 226.20 |
| Membership dues (incl. national support) | 5,000 | 435.00 | | 435.00 |
| Awards and grants | | | | |
| Miscellaneous | 2,400 | 208.80 | | 208.80 |
| (B) TOTAL EXPENSE BEFORE DEPRECIATION | | | | |
| Depreciation of buildings, equipment | | | | |
| (C) TOTAL EXPENSE | 1,013,862 | 88,206.00 | | 88,206.00 |
| (D) BUDGETED SUPPORT/REVENUE, CURRENT YEAR | | | | |
| Contributions | 45,624 | 1,359.00 | | 1,359.00 |
| Net proceeds of special events, Town and State | 71,168 | 14,891.00 | | 14,891.00 |
| Fees and grants, government (FED) | 620,713 | 54,002.04 | | 54,002.04 |
| Membership dues | | | | |
| Program revenue, including sales | 136,287 | 11,857.02 | | 11,857.02 |
| Investment Income | 20,000 | 1,740.00 | | 1,740.00 |
| Miscellaneous | 3,600 | 313.20 | | 313.20 |
| (E) TOTAL SUPPORT/REVENUE | 967,392 | 84,162.00 | | 84,162.00 |
| (F) (DEFICIT) BEFORE DEPRECIATION (B minus D) | 46,470 | | | |
| (G) (DEFICIT) AFTER DEPRECIATION (C minus D) | | | | |

AGENCY _____

Date Submitted _____

| | | | Program Services | | | | |
|---|---|---|---|---|---|---|---|
| (5)<br>Total<br>Program | (6)<br>Outpat. | (7)<br>Inpat. | (8)<br>Day<br>Care | (9)<br>24 Hr.<br>E. R. | (10)<br>C & E | (11)<br>Res. &<br>Eval. | (12)<br>After<br>Care |
| 843,258 | 235,268.00 | 107,937.00 | 95,288.00 | 63,244.00 | 183,830.00 | 30,357.00 | 2,733.00 |
| 685 | 191.04 | 87.65 | 95.36 | 51.36 | 149.28 | 24.65 | 85.00 |
| 10,500 | 2,929.36 | 1,343.94 | 1,186.44 | 787.46 | 2,288.89 | 377.98 | 1,585.00 |
| 12,235 | 3,413.34 | 1,565.98 | 1,382.46 | 917.57 | 2,667.06 | 440.43 | 1,847.00 |
| 1,096 | 305.67 | 140.24 | 123.80 | 82.17 | 238.84 | 39.44 | 165.00 |
| 9,404 | 2,623.69 | 1,203.70 | 1,062.64 | 705.29 | 2,050.05 | 338.54 | 1,419.00 |
| 3,652 | 1,018.91 | 467.46 | 412.68 | 273.90 | 796.14 | 131.47 | 551.00 |
| 1,370 | 382.09 | 175.30 | 154.75 | 102.71 | 298.55 | 49.30 | 206.00 |
| 23,921 | 6,673.85 | 3,062.53 | 2,702.96 | 1,795.00 | 5,214.69 | 861.14 | 3,611.00 |
| 87,780 | 2,903.89 | 1,332.25 | 1,176.13 | 780.60 | 2,268.95 | 374.70 | 1,571.00 |
| 2,374 | 662.29 | 303.85 | 268.24 | 178.04 | 517.49 | 85.46 | 358.00 |
| 4,565 | 1,273.64 | 584.32 | 515.85 | 342.38 | 995.17 | 164.34 | 689.00 |
| 2,192 | 611.84 | 280.47 | 247.61 | 273.90 | 796.14 | 78.88 | 330.00 |
| 925,656 | 282,857.00 | 129,775.00 | 114,584.00 | 76,039.67 | 221,021.00 | 36,499.04 | 1,530.00 |
| 44,264 | 3,479.00 | 1,825.00 | 1,621.00 | 1,060.00 | 3,109.00 | 554.00 | 211.00 |
| 156,277.00 | 43,600.00 | 20,003.00 | 17,658.00 | 11,720.00 | 34,067.00 | 5,625.00 | 2,359.00 |
| | 158,112.00 | 72,539.01 | 64,038.34 | 42,503.33 | 123,543.00 | 20,401.60 | 8,557.00 |
| 124,430 | 34,716.14 | 15,927.12 | 14,060.59 | 9,332.25 | 27,125.00 | 4,479.48 | 1,878.00 |
| 18,260 | 5,094.54 | 2,337.28 | 2,063.38 | 1,369.50 | 3,980.68 | 657.36 | 2,757.00 |
| 3,287 | 917.02 | 420.71 | 371.40 | 246.51 | 716.52 | 118.32 | 496.00 |
| 883,230 | 84,162 | | | | | | |

the fact that the political process in budgeting thus far has bypassed the purely rational process.

The state of the art of such program budget methodologies is, as stated above, at the beginning phase. There is, however, an increasing impetus toward seeking sounder means for planning, budgeting, and controlling organizations on the basis of rational decision making. In the normative sense this is a positive step—if organizations do not become bogged down with the budgeting process to the detriment of the outcome. It is crucial for an organization to strive for self-evaluation in order to determine what it is trying to accomplish, what its objectives will be over the next few years, and to analyze its present programs as related to the overall objectives of the agency to meet community needs.

The care-giving organization must balance the sense of the ideal with the requirements of reality. To be adaptable, regardless of size and complexity, it makes sense for all organizations to attempt to answer the following questions as a basis for a planned program budget.

1. How do the various activities compare and what is their value in terms of their specific contribution to the stated agency objectives?
2. Is it possible to develop programs that would cost less but perhaps accomplish the same objectives?
3. Are there some activities or programs which cannot be definitively evaluated in one year or two years, but instead require long-term appraisal?
4. How do the organization's plans fit in with what other human service organizations are doing in a similar field or toward a similar objective?
5. In the light of an exploration of programs, should certain changes be effected in the stated objectives or mission to make them more consistent with changing community needs?

Such questions serve to focus an organization on the future.

A word should be said about two fairly recent forms of program budgeting: the Program, Planning, Budgeting System (PPBS) and Zero-Base Budgeting (ZBB). Both are emphatic attempts to introduce the use of planning and decision-making rationality to the management process. Both involve a heavy emphasis on analysis of various alternatives in program services, activities, and measurement of outcomes.

A very brief comparison of PPBS and ZBB is depicted in Figure 9-2. A prime difference between the two is that ZBB purports to omit any reference to the previous level of appropriations.

A number of public and private human service organizations have tried one or the other budgeting process with varied results. The key seems to be an selective, adaptable use of the techniques. Both require a great deal of time, paper work, money, and expertise in order to develop

**FIGURE 9-2** *PPBS and ZBB Compared*

## PPBS

*Purpose*

To plan more effective utilization of resources and to enable consistent translation of plans into program decisions and, ultimately, budgets.

*Basic Components*

1. *Statement of Objectives*—General to specific delineation of program objectives, alternatives, and performance measures.

2. *Program Structure*—Systematic grouping that permits cost-effective comparisons of categories, subcategories, and elements (activities).

3. *Program Memoranda and Special Analytical Studies*—The analytical materials that document the organization's choices and strategies.

4. *Program and Financial Plan*—The compilation of information relating to expected output, costs, and financing of the program for the first five years.

5. *Allocation*—Decision made to allocate resources with built-in, continuous feedback.

## ZBB

*Purpose*

To start from base zero and reanalyze an organization's activities and priorities with a view to creating new and more effective sets of alternatives for the upcoming budget year.

*Basic Components*

1. *Decision Packages*—Comprehensive documents that identify and describe specific activities in the organization, thus permitting management to evaluate each activity and rank it in comparison to other activities. This includes such information as goal statements, costs, manpower, measurements, and analysis of alternative means of action in light of benefits or consequences.

2. *Evaluation and Ranking of all Decision Packages*—Use of a cost-benefit approach to evaluate and rank the aforementioned decision packages.

3. *Allocation*—Decision made to allocate resources in light of the above activity.

and evaluate program memoranda and/or decision packages. These requirements have hindered any widespread use of PPBS and ZBB in human service organizations at this time.

## THE BUDGET PROCESS

There are marked similarities in the budget processes of most public and private organizations. Ideally, budgeting is an integral part of the program planning process. A sequence of the process might be portrayed in the following manner:

1. The Public Administration, possibly with an Advising Committee or the Board of Directors in the private organization, authorizes a committee, often the Program Planning Committee, to develop the planning process.

2. This committee in turn sets a time frame and works towards developing its planning base (goals, objectives, data collection, analysis of the organization's internal and external environments, predictions of the future, and prioritizing of its objectives and alternatives, as noted in Chapter 7).

3. This committee develops an integrated plan of goals, objectives, and action programs, and means of assessing their effectiveness.

4. A delineation of the budgeting process is initiated at this point. That is, feasible monetary figures are then assigned to the program. If the budget process is an integral part of the program planning committee, then that committee will undertake this work. In some organizations a finance committee undertakes this process, and the finance committee will then recommend a budgeting process to be integrated with the planning process recommended by the Program Planning Committee. Depending on the type of organization, such a process may include forecasts of income items (fees, endowment income, gifts, unsolicited gifts, a range of other public and private funding sources, and so forth), as well as forecasts of costs based on the work plan for the year.

5. A fully integrated program plan and budget is prepared, refined, and presented to the key decision-making body for approval (Administrator, Board of Directors).

6. This integrated package is then submitted to the key funding body (County Commissioners, State Budget Committee, a United Way or other federated funding body) depending on type of organization.

7. Depending upon the funding body's analysis, the integrated package may be fully implemented, or need some amendments or revisions. In the latter case a review process then would be initiated.

8. Cycle of implementation of the program then begins.

## SUMMARY

This chapter introduced the concept of the budget as a joint administrative process that helps bridge the gap between an organization's need to have fiscal control and accountability and its need to allocate financial and organizational resources to a plan. Too much reliance on one process over the other makes the budget unidimensional and can result in either a budget that does not have fiscal integrity or a budget that turns inward, presenting no opportunities for change. Types of budgeting and the typical budgeting process were also discussed.

# CHAPTER 10

---

# fund raising

**INTRODUCTION**

Several earlier chapters in Part Two have discussed the need for proactivity in relation to the internal and external environments of the human service organization. Every function of the organization depends upon the availability of financial resources in order to be effective. Similarly, in Chapter 4, dealing specifically with critical environments, stress was placed on the need for the administrator to proactively analyze the external environment and its many elements. Otherwise, the organization becomes reactive, often acting on the basis of faulty or incomplete information and operating with a crisis-management mentality. It is the importance of fund raising that moved the authors to include this underpinning of the Management Cycle in Part Two.

Probably the need to deal proactively with the environment as a state of dependency is never more manifest than in the area of organizational financial dependency. No organization, public or private, could afford not to be continually sensing and forecasting actual and potential sources of financial support. The government, at all levels, has assumed a large part of charitable functions, the result of which has been to increase the complexity of the "how" of organizational financing. This is due to several factors:

1. the systems approach of the 1960s in which "both public and private organizations attempted to syphon off funds provided for federal and state programs;[1]
2. shifts in governmental appropriations, especially for social services in the areas of Title XX ($2.5 billion annually in the program that incorporates all previous public welfare provisions of the Social Security Act into a single social service entity);
3. the influence of public and private contracting, alluded to above; and
4. revised tax and accountability measures.[2]

An additional reason for the growing complexity is increased competition for monetary support as a result of rapid inflation and in anticipation of the potential effect of California's Proposition 13 on the funding of care-giving organizations.

Hence, any organization, public or private, must continually renew its efforts to more effectively raise funds. Administrators will find a systems approach to the organization's environment beneficial. Organizations need to define and implement their own fund-raising systems by selecting relevant parts (funding sources, contributors, information, staff, etc.) and developing relevant connections between parts, methods of data collection, and activities. In implementing the systems approach to an agency's fund-raising endeavors, the administrator must "describe the basic fund-raising systems flows that trace inputs (staff, resources) into and outputs (money raised) from each system elements; compile processing requirements (what is needed) at each step; devise an improved fund-raising system and assess whether it is effective, inexpensive and practical; organize the tasks to be accomplished (who will do what and when); and implement the campaign system and build in feedback to control the system."[3] This system approach is depicted in Figure 10-1.

An example of this approach is the systematic tracing of a membership campaign. A particular approach to membership campaigns involves a concerted effort by lay professional leadership. Starting with a desired goal, the leadership must analyze what a successful campaign would be.

1.  Michael J. Murphy, "Financing Social Welfare," *Encyclopedia of Social Work,* 1, 17th issue, (Washington, D.C.: National Association of Social Workers, 1977), p. 478.

2.  See Murphy, "Financing Social Welfare," pp. 478–83.

3.  Michael J. Murphy, "Fundraising Curriculum Components," *Professional Components in Education for Fundraising,* ed. Frank M. Loewenberg (New York: Council on Social Work Education, 1975), p. 43.

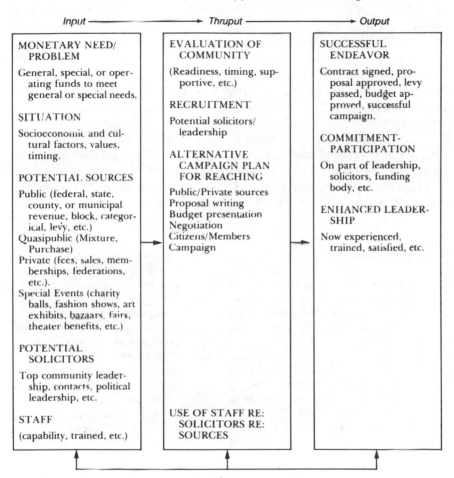

**FIGURE 10-1** *Systems Approach to Fund Raising*

Input                 →     Thruput            →     Output

| | | |
|---|---|---|
| **MONETARY NEED/ PROBLEM**<br><br>General, special, or operating funds to meet general or special needs.<br><br>**SITUATION**<br><br>Socioeconomic and cultural factors, values, timing.<br><br>**POTENTIAL SOURCES**<br><br>Public (federal, state, county, or municipal revenue, block, categorical, levy, etc.)<br>Quasipublic (Mixture, Purchase)<br>Private (fees, sales, memberships, federations, etc.).<br>Special Events (charity balls, fashion shows, art exhibits, bazaars, fairs, theater benefits, etc.)<br><br>**POTENTIAL SOLICITORS**<br><br>Top community leadership, contacts, political leadership, etc.<br><br>**STAFF**<br><br>(capability, trained, etc.) | **EVALUATION OF COMMUNITY**<br><br>(Readiness, timing, supportive, etc.)<br><br>**RECRUITMENT**<br><br>Potential solicitors/ leadership<br><br>**ALTERNATIVE CAMPAIGN PLAN FOR REACHING**<br><br>Public/Private sources<br>Proposal writing<br>Budget presentation<br>Negotiation<br>Citizens/Members<br>Campaign<br><br><br><br><br><br><br><br>**USE OF STAFF RE: SOLICITORS RE: SOURCES** | **SUCCESSFUL ENDEAVOR**<br><br>Contract signed, proposal approved, levy passed, budget approved, successful campaign.<br><br>**COMMITMENT-PARTICIPATION**<br><br>On part of leadership, solicitors, funding body, etc.<br><br>**ENHANCED LEADER-SHIP**<br><br>Now experienced, trained, satisfied, etc. |

The overall goal is a successful financial result, the more latent desired result is enhanced leadership and a committed body of constituents. Given agreement on a goal, a general statement of the monetary need would have to be developed. Information about several elements would have to be gathered: any situational factors touching on the campaign; what and where are the potential sources (old, new) of memberships; what type of leadership/solicitors are needed, and are they available; is there capable backup staff resources? Once this information was obtained, actual evaluation of these factors would take place. An active strategy would be laid out for recruitment of desired leadership and solicitors and development and implementation of a campaign plan and organization ("when" and "how" questions are faced—solicitation by geographic residence, size of gift, mail, direct contact, combination, matching of staff with solicitors, etc.). Finally a built-in evaluation system for on-going monitoring and reporting would be implemented (report meetings, etc.) and plans made for a final evaluation at the end of the time period.

This procedure—moving from desired result to analysis of environmental factors to implementation of a strategy and plan—is similar for all types of endeavors, be it a levy, purchase of service contract, a budget meeting with public officials or private funding bodies, or proposal writing.

The concept of organizational fund raising, then, involves a great deal of both "rational" and "nonrational" activity. By rational we mean the clearly defined plan for fund raising, the proposal writing, the budget committee approach, the council hearing, and so on, each usually involving the following elements:

| RATIONAL | NONRATIONAL |
|---|---|
| 1. Statement of need/needs assessment. (Specification and documentation of need(s) to be met.) | 1. Identification of potential resource(s) that is (are) the best source(s) of support. |
| 2. Objectives of the program. (Specific, realistic, measurable, and feasible outcomes over a time frame.) | 2. Analysis of the benefits/constraints of this resource(s). |
| 3. Methodology of the Program. (Selection of particular activities after analyzing alternatives.) | 3. Identification of the resource's peculiarities (e.g., methods/time/display format, etc.). |
| 4. Evaluation. (Design for on-going monitoring and final evaluation.) | 4. Identification of the key "actors" in this resource (How do we influence them to favor our cause?) |
| 5. Budget. (Financial cost of personnel, activities, etc. in funding body's terms.) | 5. Analysis of the advantages/disadvantages of multi vs. single resource(s). |
| 6. Future support, if needed. (Plans for potential support at end of time period.) | |

A planned approach is quite necessary to a fund-raising endeavor. However, this rational approach is usually only one-half of the effort. Often times the old axiom is true—"It's not what's being said—but who is saying it." The nonrational approach is related to this axiom by calling for a planned approach to the nonrational elements, such as timing, right solicitor for right contact, the matching of lay decision maker with key "influencer;" the key board member contact; and the like. A planned attempt is made to predispose the funding body to look favorably upon the organization's request for financial support.

Public and private agencies traditionally have derived income from nine sources: 1. fees for services, 2. membership dues, 3. investment earnings, 4. use of capital resources, 5. sale of goods and publications, 6. bequests, 7. tax funds, 8. grants or contracts for services, and 9. donor contributions.[4] Some of these areas lend themselves to individual discussion.

SERVICE FEES. Organizations must continually review their fee schedules and balance sliding fee scales with cost-of-living increases to cover service costs without making needed services prohibitively expensive.

MEMBERSHIP DUES. All too often, when organizations join federated bodies, such as the United Way, Jewish Federation, Urban League, or Catholic Charities, they no longer attempt to maintain their membership rolls. This has proven to be a great loss. Membership activity is not only a source of financial support. It is also a means of identifying constituents and potential leadership that became closely associated with the organization. A belated, but necessary, interest in redeveloping enthusiastic and informed volunteers seems to be evolving throughout the country.

BEQUESTS AND DEFERRED INCOME PLANS. An ever-increasing area of funding support is that of bequests (designation of a gift in a donor's will, either as an outright gift, a residuary portion of the estate, or a contingency bequest) and deferred income plans (pooled income plans, charitable gifts annuities, deferred gift annuities, charitable remainder annuity trusts, and the like). Agencies like the Salvation Army, Jewish Community Federation, and Y.W.C.A. have been in the forefront of these particular fund-raising sources, and are now being joined by other private and public agencies.

TAX MONIES/PURCHASE OF SERVICE. With the advent of Title XX and the "New Federalism" that initiated General and Special Revenue Funding, Community Block Grants, and Purchase-of-Service Contracting, fund-raising complexity increased. Now, public and private agencies must participate in planning and accountability processes. Most planning processes involve a linear progression that moves from problem analysis/needs assessment, to goals and objectives, to resource inventory, to program development, to program implementation. Similarly, the accountability process usually relates to moving from goal formulation, to translation of goals into measureable indicators of goal achievement, to collection of data on indicators for program's participants, to comparison of program with goal criteria.

Both these processes are deemed "rational" but the "nonrational" processes of bargaining, negotiation, contacts, and overall "potential" action are equally necessary. The dilemma for administrators is to ascertain whether it is worthwhile to spend large segments of time on the rational and nonrational processes in order to both render services and maintain the organization.

4. Murphy, "Financing Social Welfare," p. 479.

DONOR CONTRIBUTIONS.   A final source of potential funding is the federated funding body. This involves submission of budgeting and allocation requirements. Unfortunately, in many communities, the yearly cost of living is increasing more rapidly than the annual increase in donations to such bodies. One result has been a tightening or strengthening of the budget process, depending upon one's perspective. The agency that only reacts faces a difficult task to even maintain itself. The proactive agency analyzes the key elements of the funding body (its decision makers, its budgetary activities, its budget committee membership, and the like) and initiates positive steps to interest the funding body in its present and potential activities.

Another area of donor funding activity is the foundation from which human service organizations have been able to obtain pilot, developmental, one-time-only, research, and some operating funds. In general, these foundations can be grouped by donor type or restrictions:

> *Community Foundations* (from and usually limited to a particular geographic area or municipality; wide interests in funding);
> *Corporate/Company Foundations* (ordinarily incorporated separately from the corporation; funding to a geographic area);
> *Family Foundations* (narrow funding forms, usually reflecting the family's particular personal interests);
> *General Purpose Foundation* (few legal restrictions on funding; usually reflects interests in many fields);
> *Special Purpose Foundations* (monies given for definite purposes).

Foundations today are confronted with a number of forces that impinge upon how and what they finance. A major force has been changes in the tax laws to require more reporting, more accountability, and regulation of expenditures—such as requiring foundations to expend more of their yearly income than in the past. The vagaries of the stock market have also influenced some foundations' portfolios. Between poor stock selection and a generally depressed economy, the investment principal of some foundations has depreciated, thus reducing the monies available to fund human service organizations. Several foundations have funded ill-advised and unsuccessful programs in the past, which has resulted in both a more cautious view of what is a viable potential candidate for funding and increased accountability measures.

Foundations, however, remain the best sources of venture capital available to human services organizations. New, innovative, and, sometimes, high-risk activities can and are being funded by foundations. Ordinarily, operating funds are given for a three-year maximum period, with a provision that requires the recipient organization to have a plan for future maintenance if needed.

## SUMMARY

This brief discussion has focused upon the need for the administrator of a care-giving organization to actively analyze the external community for potential sources of financial support. The ever-changing character of this environment makes it necessary for the administrator to attempt to forecast trends in support and to develop relationships in the short run and maintain them in the long run with actual and potential funding sources. Such relationships should be analyzed as to their efficacy: Does this source interfere with the prime objectives of the organization? . . . Is this source the "best" source of support? . . . Are there "strings" attached to this support? . . . Should one or many diversified sources be pursued?

Some final cautions should be given about funding. Organizational fund raising for human services does present opportunities for individuals to have a sense of involvement, self-determination, and participation in an effort to support services for human needs. Caution must always be taken, however, to assure that "people should never be used as a means, but rather are always to be viewed as ends. While raising money is a valid target, this should never be achieved at the expense of people."[5] Another caution is related to need for organizational maintenance. There is the temptation, always present when organizational funding is necessary for survival, to "cater to neuroses" of the funding body—that is, to seek funding regardless of its effect on organizational goals and services. When survival becomes the primary goal and services become secondary, organizations lose their reason for being.

5.  Frank M. Loewenberg, "Some Observations on Fundraising in the Context of Social Work Values and Practices," *Professional Components in Education for Fundraising* (New York: Council on Social Work Education, 1975), p. 13.

# part 3

---

# CREATIVE
# ADMINISTRATION

# CHAPTER 11

---

# convivial
# approaches

One of the major distinguishing marks of the human's long trek on the evolutionary path is the ability to develop and use tools. The concept "convivial" has been selected to represent our belief that the tools to be used by administrators need to be basic and adaptable enough to be used by any administrator. He or she needs to be able to grasp the major ideas and put them into practice within a relatively short period of time, and without painful cerebral struggles.

Complicated budgeting processes, which would call for an accountant's skills or computer programming techniques, may be useful to most administrators, but are not easily mastered. Convivial tools are simple tools that can be used by most people. To the extent that they lend themselves to easy use, they are convivial; to the extent that they are shrouded in jargon and "fancy gaming," they are not for the average person. As far as our investigations have been able to ascertain, all of the convivial tools in the following chapters can be easily and effectively used.

This does not mean that other, more complex (but not necessarily more effective) tools are not seen by us to be valuable. We will recommend them and explain their use, but we will not attempt to relate them as carefully to the reader's needs.

We should remind the reader that the purpose of a tool is to enable a person to do a job more simply or effectively. The job of the administrator is to facilitate the work of the agency. To the extent that the administrator is accessible and helpful to staff, he or she, too, can be considered a convivial tool.

In the administration of human service organizations, one would expect to find positive attempts being made to reduce the conflict between the needs of the organization and the needs of the individual working within the organization. All too often, however, under pressure, one finds a management style that is autocratic, has one-way directive communication, and is lacking in consideration for subordinates' needs. This results in inefficiency, in decisions made upon faulty and inappropriate information, in lack of morale, and in high employee turnover.

However, several convivial approaches to management have found their way into the human services arena. These approaches attempt to combine the tools of the scientific management, human relations, and human resources schools in order to obtain efficiency and effectiveness. By placing these approaches within a systems framework, their adaptation seems especially useful in building and maintaining a human services organization. It is not surprising that such approaches have evolved. After all, the administrator of a social agency, in order to survive, must adapt to the organization's environment and the demands and resources of both society and technology on the current situation. This chapter discusses those approaches that seem particularly adaptive to the needs of the human services organization.

## THREE CONVIVIAL APPROACHES: MANAGEMENT BY OBJECTIVES

Management by Objectives (M.B.O.), which is derived from a systems approach, encompasses several key factors: the systematic focus on the organization's and the individual's goals and objectives; the building of a worker/program structure; and the importance of goal achievement to worker morale, satisfaction, and recognition.

A workable definition of M.B.O. is furnished by Odiorne. He describes M.B.O. as "a process whereby the superior and subordinate managers of an organization jointly identify its common goals, define each individual's major areas of responsibility in terms of the results expected of him/her, and use those measures as guides for operating the unit and assessing the contribution of each of its members."[1]

The key concept in the M.B.O. process is the *mutual* setting of objectives and the systematic application of these objectives within the organizational structure. However, the initial step of mutually setting goals may be fruitless unless one can relate the process to organizational/ departmental/group/individual objectives that have been determined. There is a strong temptation to jump in without giving enough thought to the final results. The initial requirement is to work on specifying objectives in a clear-cut and mutually understood manner. This involves a three-step process on the part of the manager and the subordinate, one of moving from general problem/need determination, to determination of general objectives, to setting of specific objectives.

### the three-step process

Most organizational problem areas can be ascribed to two general ideas, system dissonance and/or system development. System dissonance refers to a problem in the care-giving organization itself, in which there is present a dysfunctional, disturbing, inadequate, inefficient, or unsatisfactory system phenomenon that renders it less functional, less efficient, and less effective than it could be. Examples of dissonant system elements include: decreasing morale, back-up in an intake department, absenteeism, lack of financial resources, and so on. The phenomenon may be developmental, that is, it may involve the development of a new program, new manual, and so forth. As we proceed through the three-step process, we will illustrate with examples from both areas and apply them to a Maternal and Infant Care Program (M & I) and a Regional Crippled Children's Program.

**Step 1**—*General Problem Formulation (Determination of Need)*

In the chapter on systematic approaches to the cycle of planning, organization, control, and feedback, the importance of problem formulation was discussed. A brief, additional comment may be made. Often what are defined as needs are first seen as problems. Problems and needs can sometimes be stated in almost identical terms, but occasionally a problem may have to be "translated" to be understood as a need.

For example, here is a statement of a problem:

M & I outreach workers are frustrated because they are not able to give mothers who need medical care adequate help or information.

1. George Odiorne, *Management by Objectives* (New York: Pitman Publishing Company, 1965), p. 6.

It may be translated into a statement of need, thusly:

M & I outreach workers *need* to become familiar with basic M & I criteria and procedures.

Note that this is an example of system dissonance.

## Step 2—*General Objectives*

The statement of the organization's or department's general objectives emanates from a need or problem and, as a rule, is not difficult to present. A general objective is more easily defined than the need statement, but utilizes words that are imprecise and generally not measurable. Thus, such phrases as: "to know," "to fully understand," "to know relevant ways," "to know how," and so on, are appropriate terms for general objectives, but do not refer to specific behaviors—that is, they represent nonmeasurable values. Here is an example of a general objective emanating from the previous need example:

To help M & I outreach workers know the basic M & I criteria and procedures in order to enable mothers to obtain the services to which they are entitled.

This statement emanates from the need, but "to know" is not a measurable objective, and thus it is a general rather than a specific objective.

## Step 3—*Specific Objectives*

In order to eventually evaluate the M.B.O. process, the manager and the subordinate must mutually determine where the action is going and be able to tell when the action has been effective. This involves setting specific objectives, a difficult but necessary task if evaluation is to be accomplished. Specifying objectives entails meeting three conditions: a) making the objective measurable; b) determining the level of satisfactory performance; and c) determining limitations.

a. *Making the Objectives Measurable*.
   This involves stating the objective in a manner that will enable the manager and subordinate to measure the results. Helpful for this purpose are action verbs: "to design," "to terminate," "to solve," "to identify," "to list," "to state," and so on. Each refers to measurable, specific behaviors. Recall the previous general objective:

   To help M & I outreach workers know the basic M & I criteria and procedures in order to enable mothers to obtain the services to which they are entitled.

   As was noted above, the statement emanated from the need, but "to know" is not a measurable objective and, hence, it is more appropriately a general objective. However, we can convert it to a specific objective by making it measurable, thusly:

> M & I outreach workers will be able to state eight criteria that mothers must meet to be eligible for M & I services.

b. *Determining the Level of Acceptable Performance.*
This involves stating how well an objective must be met. For instance:

> M & I outreach workers will be able to state eight of ten criteria for M & I service eligibility.

We have set a level of eight to ten. Anything less than eight will be considered unacceptable.

c. *Determining the Limitations.*
This requires a decision by the manager and subordinate regarding the limitations or boundaries within which the objective must be met. For example:

> At the end of a one-hour orientation session, an M & I outreach worker will be able to state eight of ten criteria for M & I service eligibility as listed in State M & I instructions without referring to M & I guidelines.

This objective is measurable, states a predetermined level of acceptable performance, and states the limitations within which the specific task must be performed.

This particular example of an M & I staff person reflects a system dissonance issue. The process of moving from need to general objective to specific objective can be applied to a system development issue as well. For instance:

| | |
|---|---|
| *Need/Problems:* | The Regional Crippled Children's Program needs to decentralize its service programs. |
| *General Objective:* | To help the Regional Crippled Children's Program to plan a decentralized program of services. |
| *Specific Objectives:* | At the end of three months, three specific plans for decentralization of the Regional Crippled Children's Program will be presented for review; none of the three plans will exceed a $10,000 implementation cost. |

Note that the specific objective is measurable and states a predetermined level of acceptable performance, as well as the limitations under which the objective must be performed.

All three steps—need, general objectives, specific objectives—are necessary to achieve future evaluation. Note, however, the introduction of a time element in the previous example of a system development issue. It served to specify the objective to a greater extent. Further, it also lets one know how "well" the M.B.O. process seems to be moving. For instance, if at the end of two months only one plan was partially designed, then possible completion of the full objective (i.e., three plans) seems in jeopardy. The concept of time is but one element that adds to the measurability of the objectives. The following represent some pragmatic ways to achieve measurability and introduce aspects of time, quantity, quality, and cost.

1. *Time:*  
This element may be included by using certain abbreviations such as, $B$ = Beginning July 1, 1981; $DUR$ = During fiscal year 1981; $SPEC$ = Specific time—On February 1; $EO$ = End form, by the end of July 1981.

2. *Quantity:*  
A. State using a base with which a comparison can be made— compared with last year at this time, etc.  
B. Further, utilize number terminology whenever possible. For example: Objective—"Prepared a criteria manual for M & I outreach workers." Convert to: "85% of M & I outreach workers will be able to supply 80% of manual eligibility by EO February 1981."  
C. Avoid terms that indicate direction, but lack quantification (i.e., terms such as: "increase," "decrease," "maximize," "minimize," "optimize," etc.) Add the amount: e.g., "increase service delivery by 25%," "reduce initial procedure time by 10%," etc.

3. *Quality:*  
Translate qualitative into quantitative objectives, e.g., "Conduct monthly parent education classes for new families in family management techniques," convert to, "50% of parents in program will be able to use family management techniques by EO March, 1981."

In other words, where possible, convert qualitative objectives (activities) by asking the purpose of the activities which, in turn, helps to derive the quantitative objectives.

*Cost:*  
Simple enumeration of costing (see the previous example of system development)—introducing a cost boundary ($10,000 for each plan).

The process and pragmatic questions regarding the setting of specific objectives is portrayed in Figure 11-1. This illustration can be used as a worksheet for determining the logic of the process.

Note the linear progression on the Specific Objective form. This was designed precisely to draw attention to the linear procedures followed in seeking to reach an objective. There may very well be a series of short-run objectives that have to be met prior to or in order to ensure attainment of the long-run objective (i.e., completion of three plans in three months). Examples of short run-objectives would be: completion of a general format for the plans in three weeks; completion of Plan 1 in five weeks; Plan 2 in six weeks; Plan 3 in seven weeks; cost-benefit analysis of all three plans in eight weeks; and so on. In other words, specific objectives represent short-run or interim ones that lead toward the ultimate outcome objectives.

**FIGURE 11-1** *Specific Objective Process*

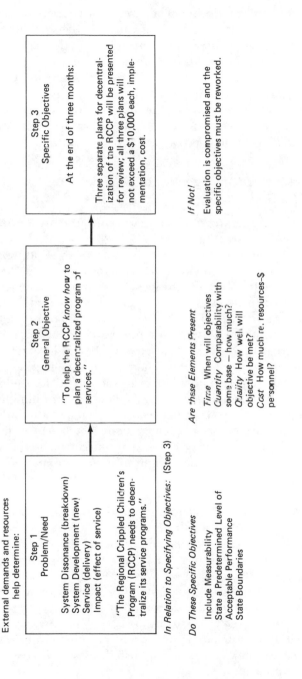

External demands and resources help determine:

Step 1
Problem/Need

System Dissonance (breakdown)
System Development (new)
Service (delivery)
Impact (effect of service)

"The Regional Crippled Children's Program (RCCP) needs to decentralize its service programs."

Step 2
General Objective

"To help the RCCP *know how* to plan a decentralized program of services."

Step 3
Specific Objectives

At the end of three months:

Three separate plans for decentralization of the RCCP will be presented for review; all three plans will not exceed a $10,000 each, implementation, cost.

*If Not!*

Evaluation is compromised and the specific objectives must be reworked.

*In Relation to Specifying Objectives:* (Step 3)

*Do These Specific Objectives*

Include Measurability
State a Predetermined Level of Acceptable Performance
State Boundaries

*Are These Elements Present*

*Time* When will objectives
*Quantity* Comparability with some base — how much?
*Quality* How well will objective be met?
*Cost* How much re. resources—$ personnel?

175

Note here that the initial mutual proposals and then subsequent joint agreement will relate to the long-run objectives of the M.B.O. process. Short-run objectives may also be formulated in this particular action phase of the M.B.O. process. Mutual movement promotes the development of feedback on interim results, that is, any progress indicators that can be clarified and stated. Thus, both manager and subordinate have mutual feedback on progress toward the ultimate goal. Overall indicators of the success of the action are necessary, but indicators of the attainment of the short-run or interim objectives are necessary as well.

### the cycle of management by objectives (M.B.O.)

Given the setting of objectives as core, the process of implementing M.B.O. is ready to commence.

It is the authors' contention that social service administrators should avail themselves of an open systems approach and the techniques of management by objectives to improve service delivery, as well as staff morale and effectiveness. Open systems theory, or rather the utilization of the systems approach, is a *rational* means of exploring the raison d'etre of an organization—that is, finding the "why" of the organization (its goals and objectives) and working back to see what makes it tick, whether or not it reaches its goals—and why. There is a fear, sometimes valid, that such an approach may become too mechanistic and fail for the same reason that the "Scientific Management" school failed—an unwillingness to recognize that there may be conflict between the needs of the individual and the needs of the organization. Management by Objectives, however, implies that an organization can be effective if one considers the *emotional* aspects present in an organization in light of overall organizational needs. This process may founder for the same reasons that systems theory may. The two wedded together, however, bring a *holistic* element to the administrative process by accounting for the rational-human aspects in light of end results—a systematic approach. It suggests that objective rational analysis, coupled with acceptance of the need for people to have a hand in making decisions that affect them, is a way of bettering the administrative process.

OPEN SYSTEMS. As mentioned previously, open systems refers to a set of parts coordinated to accomplish selected goals, whereas Management by Objectives refers to the process whereby a superior (administrator) and subodinates jointly participate in setting the subordinate's objectives and major areas of responsibility, as well as using such measures for operational guides.

Recall that the concept of an open-systems approach to a human service organization implies that the major point of reference is the *whole* rather than the individual parts. There are key parts to any care-giving organization, such as: the reality of need on the part of client/patient/constituent; the sense of need and commitment on the part of staff/board/etc.; the meshing, translation, and utilization of information/resources/materials/energy; the sense of timing/goal of achievement/outcomes. Each of these parts may be viewed as a point of reference in human service organizations, but the systems approach views them as parts of a whole and in relation to each other. It implies that, prior to the implementation of an organization decision at any level, someone should examine its *ultimate impact upon the objective(s)* of the organizational system.

To define a care-giving system means to select relevant parts (patients, contributors, constituents, clients, data, staff, etc.), relevant connections between parts, methods of data collection, and activities in light of overall and unit objectives. In operationalizing systems theory for the care-giving endeavor we must:

1. describe the basic systems flows which trace inputs (staff, resources) into, and outputs (service delivery) from, each system element;
2. compile processing requirements (what is needed) at each step;
3. devise an improved system and assess whether it is effective, not costly, and practical;
4. organize the tasks to be accomplished (who will do what, how, and when);
5. and then implement the system and build in feedback to control the system.

In human service organizations, therefore, the diverse but interdependent and interacting activities consist of: needs, situational and environmental resources, potential clients/patients/constituents, supporters, and staff, which must be so organized that they all work toward the common purpose of optimizing the organization's effectiveness in achieving its goals (people served effectively and efficiently, consistent supporters, etc.), and thereby the organization's maintenance.

One must try to identify the input-throughput-output process of a care-giving system, but the effort is worthless unless one relates the process to the objectives and goals of the system. We must consider the acquisition of inputs in light of their ability to help the organization achieve its goals and objectives; we must consider throughputs in light of whether our processes/activities are the most effective and efficient way of reaching our goals and objectives (that is, are there alternative activities that can be measured against each other for better results?); we must consider our outputs in light of the objectives and goals of the organization (did we miss our objectives; can we evaluate how well/badly we have done; etc.?). Therefore, we use a process that involves a systematic method of setting the organizational objectives, making plans to achieve these objectives, allocating resources, implementing the plans, and controlling and evaluating the system performance. Each step of the process must be considered in light of the organization's goals and objectives.

The key is to view the process of input-throughput-output also in terms of outcomes. The system, for successful service delivery and survival, must achieve goals. This calls for specificity of overall objectives and subobjectives and their achievement by various departments/units/sections/subsections in a planned and integrated system.

Too many social service administrators look primarily at inputs rather than outputs—they tend to become ossified at the point of recruitment of inputs and never measure outcomes in light of objectives. The beauty of the systems approach is that it focuses not only upon final outcomes, but also upon processes, and therefore serves to highlight the systems' intermediate outputs as well.

This is where M.B.O. comes into the picture. The success of the human services organization depends to a large extent upon the throughput-output process—that is, on how well one's staff can meet their objectives/subobjectives.

The distribution of work activities designed to meet objectives and goals, and the resultant distribution of responsibilities to various organizational units can be, if handled well, a positive, motivating, effective factor in a human service organization's success. Distribution of such activities, *without regard for the situation* (socioeconomic trends, external resources and demands) and organizational capacities (manpower and otherwise), can be debilitating. Further, distribution of such activities *without regard for the human factors* present in every organization can be equally debilitating and can result in strong resistance. Given a rational approach to offset the former, management by objectives is a technique to offset the latter.

M.B.O., relating to McGregor's "Y" theory, is based upon the premise that people who work together for any purpose can decide what they want to accomplish, set a date for that accomplishment, then schedule all the activities/efforts that will be needed. In short, it is mutual decision making at every step in the process and is built upon collaboration and agreement. It avers that people wish a strong input into the rendering and carrying out of decisions that affect their lives. The administrator who does not recognize this fact, and exercises only autocratic leadership, can expect failure, absenteeism, high rates of turnover, and low staff morale. Surely, human service organizations, built upon the premise of the dignity and worth of the individual, should recognize this fact more than most organizations.

Relating M.B.O. to the human service organization, in light of systems theory, calls for three basic elements.

1.  A specific definition of goals/objectives or subobjectives.

2. A delineation of specific tasks necessary to reach these goals.
3. A collaboration and worked-out agreement between the administrator and his subordinate(s).

Specific goals plus specific implementing tasks plus agreement make up a statement of an objective for an organization, department, or other unit. It is a cyclical process (similar to the cyclical systems process) that includes:

1. assessment of needs/desires on a broad basis;
2. agreement on objectives for the department/unit/section/group and commitment to achieving these objectives;
3. working on a prescribed schedule with set dates for each step (milestones) in achieving these objectives; and
4. measured results.

Figure 11-2 portrays this cyclical process. Note the similarity between the M.B.O. cycle and the systems (decision) cycle described in Chapter 7. Implementing the M.B.O. process involves identifying goals, developing a working structure, mutual determination of objectives by the manager and the subordinate, a joint program of activities and performance, and planned feedback and review.

Note the encircled steps in the cycle (Steps 3 and 4). It is these particular steps that differentiate the M.B.O. process from other managerial techniques. The autocratic process, for instance, implies a one-way communication of a directive to a subordinate. The administrator determines the objective(s), the subordinate's standards of performance, time frames, and needed resources. Concomitant results of such a process are low morale, absenteeism, excuses, and turnover. The M.B.O. process attempts to change this activity by tapping into the skills that subordinates can bring to an organization. The comprise between the views, perceptions, and on-the-line experience of the subordinate should result in a more realistic definition of what might be accomplished.

Interestingly, while the M.B.O. system in Steps 3 and 4 is unique in that it enables people to have a say in decisions that affect them, these same steps can become a source of failure and resistance. Subordinates and administrators can become mechanical, threatened, and stifled. The implication is that human involvement is crucial. Yet, every time a change is brought to an organization, one must be cognizant that resistance is normal. Typically, organizations must loosen up, develop a positive climate for change, account for the human side of the change, and develop supports to sustain the change in a positive manner. Otherwise, the beneficial effects of installing an M.B.O. program in a human services organization will be compromised.

FIGURE 11-2 *The Management by Objective Cycle*

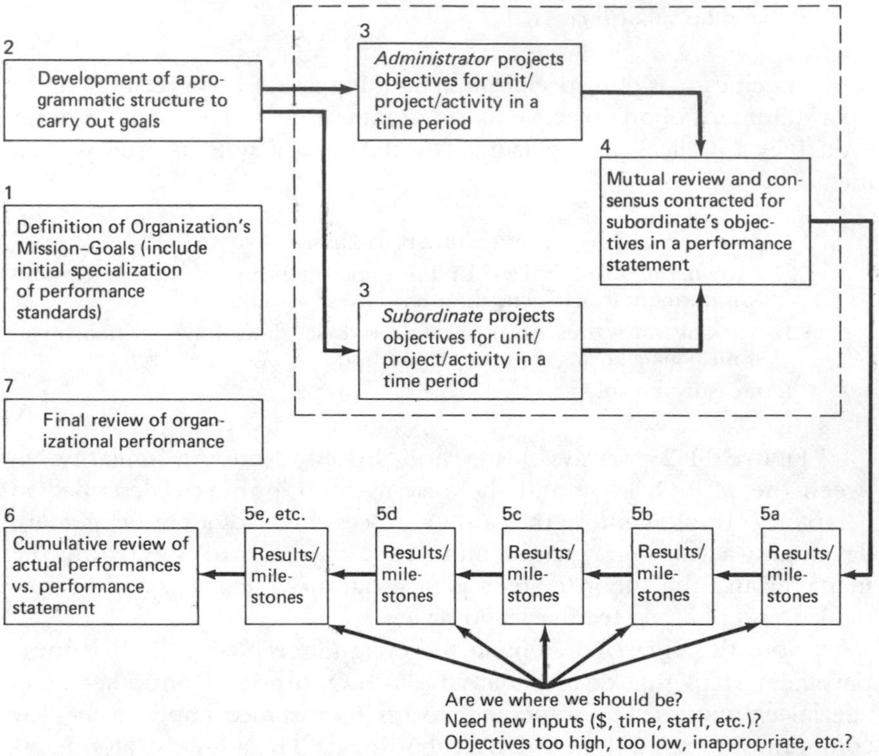

2
Development of a pro-
grammatic structure to
carry out goals

3
*Administrator* projects
objectives for unit/
project/activity in a
time period

4
Mutual review and con-
sensus contracted for
subordinate's objec-
tives in a performance
statement

1
Definition of Organization's
Mission–Goals (include
initial specialization
of performance
standards)

3
*Subordinate* projects
objectives for unit/
project/activity in a
time period

7
Final review of organ-
izational performance

6
Cumulative review of
actual performances
vs. performance
statement

5e, etc.
Results/
mile-
stones

5d
Results/
mile-
stones

5c
Results/
mile-
stones

5b
Results/
mile-
stones

5a
Results/
mile-
stones

Are we where we should be?
Need new inputs ($, time, staff, etc.)?
Objectives too high, too low, inappropriate, etc.?

The process of M.B.O. calls for a series of questions about the nature of the system, such as: What outputs are desired? What structural process should we develop? What inputs does the manager need? What inputs does the subordinate need? How do "we" develop adequate feedback? Do we have to change our desired goals in light of resources, external, internal constraints, etc.? How do we review outcomes in light of feasible goals? and so on.

In short, there are positive features for an administrator to use an open systems approach plus M.B.O. as a joint means of improving a human service organization's services. They, together, can be a powerful tool to rationalize the organization and gain staff commitment and involvement. They call for increased training (e.g., how to specify objectives); increased willingness to take a risk (i.e., for the administrator to trust the staff, for the subordinate to act, as well as to trust, the administrator); increased give-and-take; and increased planning and evaluation activity.

## an example

A brief example to highlight the M.B.O. process seems fruitful at this time. Recall the earlier example of the specific objective:

At the end of three months, three separate plans for decentralization of the RCCP will be presented for board review. None of the three plans will exceed a $10,000 implementation cost.

This example could be construed as the result of Steps 3 and 4 of the M.B.O. process.

The M.B.O. process in this example would be used in the following manner:

*Step 1:* Define mission: Need to decentralize.

*Step 2:* Assignment to a unit in the organization: Considerations such as selection of a task force, special unit, or person.

*Steps 3 and 4:* Projection of objectives by the administrator and the subordinate, and a mutually agreed upon performance statement. In these two steps: 1. consideration would be given to the feasibility of this specific objective. 2. A series of questions would be explored: Is three months adequate? Is the cost-out adequate? Is this the proper unit? Should more people be assigned? Is experience present? What supportive role does the administrator take? What interim results do we need?

*Step 5:* Feedback on results versus agreed-upon milestones; consideration of, for example, such reporting dates as a single two-week interim plan versus a one-month interim for all three plans; completion dates for such a plan(s); a two-month compilation of costs and benefits for each other; a final write-up in ten weeks; etc.

*Step 6:* Cumulative review: Analysis of the actual performance as compared to the specific objective stated above, that is; were three plans ready for review within the boundaries of numbers, time, and cost?

*Step 7:* Review of organizational performance: Where this particular three-month activity fits in overall organizational performance.

This section has thus far presented the possibility of utilizing a systematic approach to objective definition, as well as the integration of objectives into a management-by-objectives process. Such mutual approaches have great potential for improving both the administration of human service organizations and the effectiveness of service delivery.

In the normative sense, we must reemphasize potential problem areas within the M.B.O. process:

A poorly designed M.B.O. program can set back organizational effectiveness, efficiency, and morale;

A rigid, mechanistic format will discourage activity by subordinates;

Too little support from top management or failure of top management to accept the concept of negotiation will decrease its effectiveness;

Imposition of objectives from top management, under the guise of "joint" decision making, will reduce subordinate activity;

Too short an implementation period does not allow for a full testing of the process.

Despite these potential problem areas, M.B.O. does offer an opportunity to positively manage human and nonhuman resources in an effective manner.

## ORGANIZATIONAL DEVELOPMENT TECHNIQUES

Another major area of convivial approaches to the management of human services is the use of organizational development (O.D.) techniques. Evolving in the business arena over the past three decades, O.D. is now finding its way into the human services. That it has taken so long is in itself surprising because O.D. does draw very much upon behavioral science and structural intervention, as do the human services.

French and Bell offer a comprehensive definition of organizational development, defining it as: "a long-range effort to improve an organization's problem-solving and renewal processes, particularly through a more effective and collaborative management of organizational cultures."[2] They believe that a systematic action-research analysis of the formal and informal processes of an organization, based upon teams of basic units of organizational change, and with the assistance of consultants, has great merit in improving and renewing an organization.

O.D. fits into the premise of this book in its reliance upon a full systems view of the organization. Further, there is an opportunity for O.D. to complement the M.B.O. process as both techniques are based upon the assumption that people affected by change or decisions desire involvement in the planning and implementation of such changes or decisions. Finally, most human service organizations pragmatically apply theories

---

2.   Wendall L. French and Cecil H. Bell, Jr., *Organization Development* (Englewood Cliffs, N.J.: Prentice-Hall, Inc., 1973), p. 15.

(organizational, psychological, learning, developmental, group, change, communication, leadership, etc.) from the social behavior sciences. These theories serve as the basis for O.D. activity as well.

In short, an organizational development effort is a planned, organization-wide, managed-from-the-top intervention in an organization's process with the aim of increasing its effectiveness and health.

French and Bell pointed out that the basic model underlying most O.D. activities is the action-research model.[3] This is a feedback model that usually requires the following steps:[4]

1. Identification of a problem area about which an individual/group is concerned (e.g., a breakdown in communication, morale, and work capacity on the part of intake and income maintenance in a public welfare department);
2. Selection of a specific problem and a prediction with a goal and activity statement (e.g., to reduce overload and back-up of worker's cases by initiating intake hours at 10:00 A.M. except for emergencies and allowing the time from 8:30 to 10:00 A.M. to be utilized for uninterrupted paper work on backlog cases);
3. Record actions taken along with data regarding the degree of goal attainment (e.g., Did it work? Was overload and back-up reduced? Did worker morale and communication correspondingly improve?);
4. Drawing inferences, in relation to the goal, from the actions taken (Should this change be permanently implemented? Any problems? Any needed improvements?); and finally,
5. The continuing retesting of the process on the basis of emerging information.

Action research, then, along with behavioral science and systems theories, are at the heart of the O.D. techniques. Such techniques and interventions can be classified into four types: Team Development; Intergroup Relationships; Goal-Setting and Planning; and Education.

Briefly, team development consists of interventive activities aimed toward increased team effectiveness (e.g., team-building activities, process consultation, and role analysis). Team training will be discussed in more depth in the section on destratification approaches. *Intergroup relations* are interventive activities aimed at increasing intergroup effectiveness (e.g., between various departments or units utilizing intergroup team building). *Goal-setting and planning* are characterized by interventive activities aimed at improving total overall organizational change (e.g., confrontation meetings, survey feedback activities). *Education* intervention techniques

3.  French and Bell, *Organization Development*, see pp. 84–96.
4.  For a full discussion, see: Stephen M. Correy, *Action Research to Improve School Practices* (New York: Bureau of Publications, Teachers College, Columbia University, 1953), pp. 35–42.

are aimed at improving individual effectiveness (e.g., coaching, T-groups, career planning, etc.).[5]

There is a large, ever-increasing inventory of useful O.D. interventive techniques with great potential for application in human service organizations. Because it is still evolving, O.D. does present problems for the human services administrator similar to the potential problems in employing M.B.O. Organizational development is not a panacea, and if used to manipulate staff will result in failure and lack of credibility. Another problem is the occasional reluctance of the O.D. consultant or in-house practitioner to confront power issues. Finally O.D. knowledge still is not being integrated into a major theory base, with the result that human services have to attempt some selectivity in application.

## PERT (PROGRAM EVALUATION AND REVIEW TECHNIQUE) AND CPM (CRITICAL PATH METHOD)

In Chapters 7 and 8 the relationship between planning and control was discussed. There is a need to define and integrate any series of events and activities that has to be accomplished over a period of time. Out of systems theory and operations research two particular tools have potential application for the human services administrator. They are network schedules called, for convenience, PERT (Program Evaluation and Review Technique) and CPM (Critical Path Method). The former is a planning and control tool primarily oriented toward time control, and the latter is a closely-related tool that adds the dimension of identifying key activities that may potentially delay an entire project if not completed prior to other activities. The former is similar in principle to management by objectives, the latter is similar in principle to management by exception. The former relates to probable time values, the latter relates to determined time values.

Such network plans seek, through a flow chart, to depict how certain parts of a project depend on each other, and how certain tasks must be completed before other tasks can be initiated. CPM adds the dimension of identifying the longest path through the network of events and activities needing to be accomplished in order to complete a project. It therefore equals the minimum time required to accomplish the project.

5.    For fuller elaboration on these techniques, see: French and Bell, *Organization Development,* pp. 97–146; W. W. Burke and H. A. Hornstein, *The Social Technology of Organization Development* (Washington D.C.: NTL Learning Resources Corporation, 1971); and W. Warner Burke, *Current Issues and Strategies in Organizational Development* (New York: Human Sciences Press, 1977).

The working procedure of a PERT/CPM network involves four steps:

1. Analyze the project in light of specific events and activities. An event is a specific accomplishment (represented by circles in Figure 11-3) that marks the start or completion of certain tasks, activities, objectives attained, and so on. In systems/MBO terms they are referred to as milestones. Events do not require expenditures of time or resources. Events are placed in circles (see Figure 11-3) and are further identified as either predecessor or successor events. Predecessor events come immediately before another event(s) and successor events immediately follow another event. Activities are the consumption of time and/or resources required to accomplish events. Activities are represented by the lines and arrows connecting the circles (events).

2. Produce a network of these events and activities by determining the sequence of the activities. This involves determining which activities must be completed before other activities can be initiated.

3. Identify the estimated time required for the various activities. In PERT these are based upon three types of time estimates: an optimistic, a pessimistic, and a most-likely estimate. In CPM, the time estimate is determined. This one estimate is arrived at by pooling the expertise of all persons involved in the project.

4. Identify the critical path through the network. As indicated above, this refers to the longest time required to complete a project. In short, it requires the determination of which part(s) of a project will require the most time to arrive at the final event from the initial event. Extra time for any particular event along the critical path will cause the final event(s) to fall behind by the same amount of time.

Figure 11-3 depicts a simplified example of how PERT/CPM can be used in a typical private human services organization's proposal to a public agency for a purchase-of-service program. The circles A to M represent identified events, the arrow-lines represent time-determined events required to complete activities. The heavy line represents the critical path.

This network plan shows, through a flow chart, how the various events of a project depend upon each other and how certain activities must be finished before others can be initiated. Figure 11-3 does not specifically list the activities. A typical series of activities would be the single week's activities between Events B and C; for example: staff analyzing the previously collected data regarding human needs; developing a data display; preparing a statement of the problem initially determining the gap between services needed and services presently available, and so on. These activities were projected (determined) to take two weeks.

In short, PERT/CPM is a valuable technique that is an excellent planning tool for projecting key events and activities in light of objectives to be attained. They are useful ways to look at the time dimensions of a project. Some view the three time estimates in PERT as potentially

*A Learning Environment*

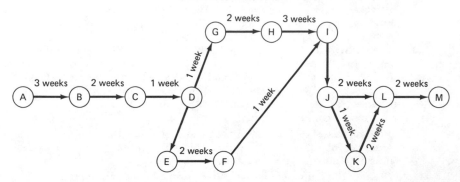

introducing a personal-bias disadvantage, and claim that there is a tendency to portray only optimistic times. CPM adds the critical dimension of determining the minimum time required to complete a project. Thus, it presents an opportunity to reanalyze key events in light of changing demands and resources, in order to potentially shorten the project's time period. Neither tool will make decisions for the administrator, but they can assist in making more rational decisions on what to stress and not stress in a program. If objectives are not determined, PERT/CPM cannot be used as they both assume an objective-based program. In other words, they act as supplements to the implementation, sequencing, and progress check-up phases of the planning process.

### events in figure 11-3:

A. Board authorization to staff for needs assessment study.
B. Data collection completed by staff.
C. Staff problem definition determined.
D. Board approval of problem definition.
E. Initial contact with public agency regarding potential funding feasibility in problem area.
F. Reactions received from public agency.
G. Priorities of objectives established.
H. Program alternatives selected.
I. Program plan developed.
J. Board approval of program plan.
K. Preliminary plan informally presented to public agency for informal review.

L. Completion of revised purchase-of-service proposal on basis of public agency's concerns.

M. Submission of formal plan for funding.
Total time for proposal submission: 19 weeks.
Critical Path: A, B, C, D, G, H, I, J, K, L, M.

## SUMMARY

This chapter discussed the usage of M.B.O., O.D., and PERT/CPM as potential tools for the human services organization. They bring the concepts of objective-setting, planned intervention, timing, and staff enhancement to an organization. Each is based upon sound assumptions. They are "convivial" tools in that they are basic and adaptable, but will require continuous effort in order to be successful.

The major normative point is that an M.B.O. system that is superficially imposed from the top does not allow a true sense of participation by subordinates. Individuals, if one follows the exposition of Maslow and Herzberg, find motivation and satisfaction by participating in self-esteem building and self-actualizing activities. These activities imply that people do wish to take control of the decisions that affect their lives. Adherence to this concept calls for the human services manager to be open to mutual deliberation. If that sense of openness and security is not present, then the M.B.O. process is compromised at its most basic foundation.

This also holds true in the use of O.D. and PERT/CPM as potential tools for the human services organization. If applied in a mechanistic and manipulative manner, one can expect strong and warranted resistance on the part of staff. Methods of staff enrichment will be discussed in Chapter 12.

# CHAPTER 12

---

# the creative
# organization

Creativity is the art and science of thinking and behaving with a measure of subjectivity and objectivity, modulating a give and take between feeling and knowing, the known and unknown, the familiar and the strange. Its purpose is to provide coping processes which lead to effective solutions. Creativity depends on an openness to new ideas and an ability to suspend judgments about options which may appear contrary to one's own methods or which may appear too "way out."

An organization is creative when its staff is able to establish or adapt to new situations in ways which have "good" consequences for the members served, as well as for the organization. All people can be creative when environmental forces support creativity, and staff can learn to be proactive rather than reactive. George Prince in his approach to creative action "synectics" has evolved a number of techniques to help people become more proactive, including ways to make the "familiar strange and the strange familiar."[1]

1.  George M. Prince, *The Practice of Creativity* (New York: Collier Books, 1970), p. 80.

We have been trained to look for solutions to problems rather than to think creatively. Although a particular solution to a problem may suffice, in that it works, it may be a poor solution. Creative thought processes might permit a more satisfactory solution, that is, one in which the consequences would be better. "Creative problem solutions are those which lead, which inspire, which provoke, those which help us to imagine more advanced problems, and which provide us with the models for solving other similar problems, and which generally turn others on to their correctness, obviousness or to their simplicity."[2]

In this chapter we will explore the agency ecology and administrative processes needed to help an agency achieve its creative potential. The key, naturally, is the people in the organization, and the unleashing of their energy in creative modes. But among the people in the agency, the administrator's process of self-renewal and transformation from manager to designer is the creative model that will set the mode for the agency metamorphosis.

All people are creative and adaptive. Some are more so than others, but clearly creative reactions and proactions are learned behaviors. There are, of course, creative geniuses, the group which has "God-given talents," but even the great creative individual's talent needs to be cultivated and nurtured in a receptive environment. The "synectics" group has used the ability to think synergistically and to train their teams to work together creatively as a way to establish a creative management consultant firm.[3]

## A HOLISTIC VIEW
## OF AGENCY CREATIVITY

We believe that the creative organization requires a balance of five crucial elements: 1. the context and climate which permits creative work; 2. a creative administrative unit; 3. creative staff; 4. clients who are helped to develop their creative growth potential; and 5. important work. These can be brought together in an engagement process for work and change.

### the context

Prior to looking at the human creative experience, we must again note the importance of the environment's effect on the individual. People are motivated to work when they are treated with respect, feel they have

2. Don Koberg and J. Bagnall, *The Universal Traveler* (Los Altos, Calif.: Kaufman, 1972), p. 9.

3. William Gordon, *Synectics* (New York: Collier Books, 1961).

the opportunity to function with some autonomy, and believe what they do will make a difference.

A climate must exist within the agency that permits staff to move about in 1. a psychological space, which gives them the freedom to be and do, and 2. a time space, which allows time to reflect on the needed actions. When this type of climate does exist, emergency situations in which hurried "executive decisions" need to be made can be accepted by staff, because they know this to be a rare occurrence. The executive has built up credibility, and people's energies are not wasted on anger over being misused.

In discussing his approach to the teaching of adults, "andragogy," Malcolm Knowles suggests that to help people learn, they must be treated with respect and dignity. Under the concept of climate, he also suggests an inviting workplace, with some degree of comfort for both teacher and student.[4] We would add that the climate must also permit sufficient privacy and time for staff thought and an atmosphere of client confidentiality. Knowles' andragogy process consists of seven steps:

1.  Setting a climate for learning.
2.  Establishing a structure for mutual planning.
3.  Assessing interests, needs, and values.
4.  Formulating objectives.
5.  Assessing learning activities.
6.  Implementing learning activities.
7.  Evaluating results.[5]

A great deal of research supports the important effects of space, comfort, and color on the emotions and productivity of people. One of the first agencies to make use of color in its total impact on clients was Bruno Bettelheim's Orthogenic Clinic in Chicago.

Bertha Reynolds notes, "it is not possible to do good social work without equipment. Buildings are necessary in order to meet people, facilities for administration, equipment for recreation, education, medical care, or whatever the programming of the agency demands."[6]

The hierarchical and communication structures within the agency should also promote a climate of openness and egalitarianism. People should not only have access to the decision-making processes, but opportunities for open consideration of things they feel are abused.

John Ingalls, a supporter of the andragogy approach to organizational function, suggests that climate setting involves the integration of

    4.   Malcolm Knowles, *The Modern Practice of Adult Education* (New York: Association Press, 1970).

    5.   Knowles, pp. 15–20.

    6.   Bertha Reynolds, *Social Work and Social Living* (Washington D.C.: NASW, 1971), p. 2.

**FIGURE 12-1** *A Learning Environment*[7]

Human and
interpersonal
relations

Physical surroundings

Organizational policy
and structure

three major elements: the physical, human, and organizational.

Ingalls attempts to incorporate the basically education-oriented andragogy model into an organizational-planning and change approach that parallels some of the normative approaches to administration.[8]

### the creative administrative unit

Our use of the word "unit" is meant to signify that we are not merely talking about one person, but of the human resource "gestalt" involved in fulfilling the administrative tasks. Regardless of who is the administrator, however, it is important to note that he or she is a human being who has hopes, fears, and plans, and who retains memories of many experiences —a person who has learned patterns of actions which almost demand specific responses to specific situations. The important point is that if a person has learned one way of acting, he or she can learn other ways.

This learning process can be motivated by a desire to become a "different" kind of administrator, or the behavior can be shaped to some degree by other staff. Indeed, a situation can be developed in which staff are not permitted to act poorly. The processes which we discuss in this section are for use by all staff, but when introduced and supported by the administrative units, they are more likely to be successfully used in the agency. The administrative staff are in a position to recruit consultants, establish workshops, and provide other learning opportunities for the staff. The importance of the executive presence in new learning situations with staff is highlighted by the research of R. Wayne Bass, which indicates that staff want the administrator involved in training sessions.[9] Staff see these sessions as an opportunity to bring about change.

7. John D. Ingalls, *A Trainers Guide to Andragogy* (Washington D.C.: United States Department of Health, Education and Welfare, 1972), pp. 15 – 19.

8. Ingalls, *A Trainers Guide to Andragogy,* pp. 102 – 3.

9. F. Wayne Bass, "The Effects of Leader Absences on a Confrontation Team-Building Design," *Journal of Applied Behavioral Science,* 14, no. 4 (1978), pp. 467 – 77.

### creative staff

Throughout the book we have discussed what we have chosen to call convivial tools" (see Chapter 11), techniques which help people think about problems so that they can act in logical ways toward desired outcomes. Most had built-in mechanisms aimed at alerting administrators as to whether or not the process was achieving the outcomes. Although we may have provided some new and important ways to look at and solve problems, tools themselves can become institutionalized and limit creativity. Their special language—"input," "pathanalysis," "PERT,"—creates a boundary that can separate people from each other. They provide methods of thinking and doing that become tracks or patterns for us, and these patterns can become limiting and, in fact, thwart new creative attempts. The new approaches, created to deal with problems in new ways, often go on to become obstacles to new thinking. Their advocates, once they master the techniques, try to institutionalize them—with themselves as the experts. Some managers, for example, have used the M.B.O. goal-setting processes only to create tons of paper work.[10]

### pattern busting as creativity

When one is part of the problem, or too close to it, it is often difficult to find the way out. Many approaches to creative thinking suggest that one needs to "step back" or "out" in order to get a different perspective on the situation.[11] Meetings which have suffered from a lack of ideas due to apathy or fear can often be improved by simply altering the way ideas are introduced into the meetings. Permitting brainstorming at meetings, rather than requiring formal, itemized proposals often opens meetings up to new ideas. Full agendas often suggest there really isn't any room to hear a new view.

This might be illustrated by the following Sufi tale, which can also serve as a tool for examining patterned behavior.

> A cat teacher was discussing her class with some other cat teacher. "I don't know what's wrong with those two rabbits in my class," she complained. "They just don't have any motivation. Yesterday, I gave a wonderful session on how to catch mice, and none of them payed any attention."[12]

People develop patterns of behavior based on the frames of reference they believe to be true. Their perceptions of the world are influenced

10.   *Small Business Report,* June 1978, p. 26.

11.   See for example: James L. Adams, *Conceptual Blockbusting* (San Francisco: W. H. Freeman, 1974) and Edward de Bono, *Lateral Thinking* (New York: Harper Corporation Books, 1973).

12.   Indries Shah, *The Magic Monastery* (New York: E. P. Dutton & Co., 1972), p. 21.

192

by these patterns, which in turn often determine the types of responses they make to the world.

The "cat" story has meaning on several levels and is used purposefully by the Sufi storyteller to raise the consciousness of the recipient. "There is the joke, the moral, and the little extra which brings the consciousness. . .a little further on the way to realization."[13] It serves to soften the fixed patterns of understanding and response.

In helping professions, we too have developed patterns of practice, learning, and administration which are entrenched and which are usually only altered by an extreme demand for change or by a slowly emerging awareness that there are other ways. Although "there may be many ways to skin a cat," most of us usually feel that we need only one, and we generally use it all our lives. Likewise, although there may be many ways to "understand" our administrative roles, the pattern of thinking we use to solve problems may limit our use of a helping tool. Creative thinking processes are aimed at restructuring administrative patterns, particularly those which have not led to synergistic consequences.

## SYNERGY

"Synergy" is the term Ruth Benedict uses to represent the "gamut that runs from one pole, where any act or skill that advantages the individual at the same time advantages the group, to the other pole, where every act that advantages the individual is at the expense of others."[14]

Synergistic transactions have an excellent chance of success in most supervisory situations in social work. Generally, the major emphasis rests on what needs to be done to be helpful to the client. The transactions between the supervisor and the supervised need not take on the nature of a contest since neither party has anything to gain by overcoming the other. In fact, each, as well as the client and the agency, has something to gain if the transaction leads not only to better service for the client, but also to increased knowledge and understanding for the worker, and satisfaction for the supervisor.

Why then is there an adversary situation? A partial answer may be found in some of the communication patterns that both parties to the transaction have developed. It may be related to games they play, to a fear of being seen as dependent, or to uncertainty as to their authority. A basic reason might be each person's sense of ego and fear of losing self-esteem. This can be minimized if people treat each other with respect.

13.   Indries Shah, *The Sufis* (New York: Anchor Books, 1964), p. 63.
14.   Ruth Benedict, "Patterns of the Good Culture," *Psychology Today*, IV, no. 1 (June 1970), 54.

What is important for our work, however, is not the possible motivating cause, but rather an examination of the methods through which new synergistic ways of working together might be developed and integrated into the on-going supervisory relationship. Naturally the "culture" of the agency, as Benedict has suggested, will determine the extent to which synergistic interactions within subunits or "subcultures" can expand, survive, or influence other parts of the system.

> In all corporate societies the social order makes certain provisions for synergy. All homologous segmented societies depend upon and build up in their members an experience of social solidarity with each. . .segment of society, however small. . . .
> If other factors in the social order make synergy low, their own group also is less dependable; but it is still there.[15]

Industry and education have also been receptive to many of the ideas of synergy, particularly its potential for creative problem-solving methods. Two books dealing with "synectics" illustrate the use of synergistic concepts to develop new models of thinking as well as new products for industry.[16] Prince, looking at attempts to "teach" creative thinking approaches, points out some of the difficulties caused by noncreative thinking. He suggests that we often attack new ideas because they threaten us, or because we fear the people who have initiated them. We stress the bad points of an idea, often attempting to make it look worse then it might be. Naturally, when we attack someone's idea, he or she in turn will attack ours. That is the nature of competition and retribution. Prince suggests instead a "spectrum" approach to new ideas.

The "spectrum" approach requires that no idea that is suggested be attacked. Traditionally, it is assumed that "if you attack my idea, I will attack yours," no matter how good or beneficial the ideas may be. With this method, we instead, search for the good part of the idea within the broad spectrum of concepts lurking in the suggestion. It is often natural in our culture to attack the bad aspects of an idea because these, indeed, are the parts that would be most threatening, were it to be accepted.

The "spectrum" of an idea can be diagrammed in several ways, depending on the relative amounts of "good" and "bad" it contains. Only the good parts of the idea are discussed and built upon. If no one can find

a. good ... bad      b. good ... bad

15.   Ruth Benedict, "Patterns of the Good Culture," p. 55.

16.   George M. Prince, *The Practice of Creativity* (New York: Collier Books, 1970), p. 70; William J. Gordon, *Synectics* (New York: Collier Books, 1961).

a good part, the idea is ignored and fades away. After one idea is worked on, a second, third, and fourth might be subjected to the same approach so that all staff ideas are considered

The result can be a synergistic solution. The ideas are now group-worked ideas with known potentials that can be evaluated when the specific idea choice needs to be made. The procedure restructures the thinking processes in ways that alter traditional patterns. The use of analogy, metaphor, and teaching stories also permits this kind of restructuring. Our "cat" story represents a traditional "teaching" method used by the Sufis. The story has meaning on various levels, and permits the learner to tune into what he or she is ready for. Discussion with others permits expanded awareness. Indries Shah, discussing Sufi tales about a folk hero, Nasrudin, states, "Superficially most of the Nasrudin story may be used as jokes. . .but it is inherent in the Nasrudin story that it may be understood at any one of many depths."[17]

The "cat" story might be about relevance of teaching content, or techniques, motivations, status, power, the choice of a wrong teacher (Why not a wise owl?), feedback, fear, or it might reflect the Sufi's own acknowledged disregard for formal hierarchical structures such as the student/teacher relationship.

Although it might be important for synergistic administrative transactions to be introduced and supported from the top, it is not impossible to have them start within any working relationship, small society, or a community.

It is the synergistic approach, whether in the supervisory relationship, staff meetings, or committee work, that provides one method for innovation within the agency. It is the ability to take in new ideas and build on them that provides variation in approach and eventually in the nature of the staff's self-image and output.

Were all workers to remain fixed in their ideas or be required to adopt the ideas of the supervisor or the agency director, not only would there be a lack of growth in their own ability to function as autonomous workers, but the agency's level of growth would likewise suffer. Clearly, setting the culture of the agency at a high synergy level not only benefits staff growth, but also serves to insure agency survival. In the long run—in competition with agencies that are more flexible, creative, and able to use innovative, high-synergy approaches—agency survival may require, in fact demand, a synergistic approach to administration.

What is suggested, therefore, is that the adoption on an agency-wide basis of a commitment to synergistic growth environment would:

1. Benefit the supervised, by permitting and structuring autonomous, creative growth.

17. Shah, *The Sufis*, p. 63.

2. Minimize the bosslike qualities of the supervisor, which often force "good" social workers to become "bad" supervisors, and permit the supervisor's own growth on the job.
3. Mobilize a "force" of workers for the agency who are creative, excited, and constantly moving toward higher levels of performance.
4. Benefit the clients by providing innovative attempts to help, and a sense of being worked with in a synergistic manner.

## THE STAFF GROUP

In our section on motivation, we discussed the needs of individuals and interpretations of hierarchical need levels that often lead to paradoxical behavior.

Similar to that of individuals, the paradoxical surface behavior of groups has led to examination of their basic motivations. Gregory Bateson, Jay Haley, and other communication specialists have pointed out how organizations purport to do things for clients, but the underlying message is often clear to all—do what's easier for the agency.[18]

### group dynamics

In order to do his or her best work with work groups, the administrator must have some understanding of group dynamics, much of which, of course, comes from experience. Picture, if you will, a staff meeting where an attempt is made to decide what type of procedures might be developed to make referrals from the Intake Department more helpful.

| | |
|---|---|
| Director: | There have been a number of complaints that the intake process does not operate in a way that is helpful to clients and staff. A number of staff people feel they don't get enough information, whereas clients feel they have to go over the same ground twice. At our last meeting we said we would look at the process. |
| Worker A: | Part of the problem is that we don't have consistency in the Intake Department. |
| Worker B: | They don't want to cooperate. |
| Worker C: | They should be given clear directions as to what to look for. |
| Worker B: | That's been tried; it doesn't work. |
| Worker C: | Try again. |
| Director: | Are there other ideas? |

18. Gregory Bateson and Jay Haley, "The Cybernetics of Self: A Theory of Alcoholism," *Psychology*, vol. 34 (November 1971).

Worker A:         Why not find out how they do it at Family Service?

Worker C:         Who cares?

Worker B:         (whispering to Worker A) Did you hear about what hap-
                  pened to Joe on the way to work?

Worker D:         I think a subcommittee should take this up; I want to talk
                  about the new regulations.

Director:         I don't feel we're getting anywhere. . .

And so it goes. . .on and on. Many of us have been at meetings that go round and round and never seem to get anywhere. Our experience doesn't help direct the action, but we can use Bion's analysis as one quick way of assessing the group's dynamics. He suggests that groups develop emotionally based orientations that prevent them from working toward the avowed goals of the group. These nonwork styles, which he calls "basic assumptions," are unknown to the group and take the form of "dependency," "fight-flight," and "pairing." Groups will develop their own methods of non-work, but each is related to one of the three basic assumptions.[19]

The nonwork group will act "as if" it believed it existed in order to fight or to be dependent, however, "the basic assumptions of the basic assumption groups are usually outside of awareness."[20] The task for the administrator is to demand that the group work toward its contractual goals and transform the energy going into basic assumptions into work. In a sense, nonwork is transformed into its opposite—work—or at least made subservient to work.

He maintains that, in a broad sense, a group can be seen as doing either of two things: work or nonwork. If they are working on the task for which they have gathered, there is no problem. If they are not working, we need to assess what is happening and why. Remember that nonwork consists of three types of behavior. The first is "fight-flight." The response to any idea is that it is "not good, won't work, absurd, not worth the effort, or dumb." The other side of the coin is, "too hard—we can't do it; we don't have the power-skill-time." Each represents an attempt to run away from the problem. In a sense, this is one of our most primitive emotional responses, and would normally be a successful maneuver if we hadn't developed our thinking brains.

Another way of not working is to be dependent. "You tell us what to do." "Let's get an expert from Chicago." Anything—as long as we don't have to work. "Let's get a beer." Dependency permits us to not work but still obtain some benefits, particularly if others are doing the job.

The third technique of not working is what Bion calls "pairing."

19.  Wilfred Bion, *Experiences in Groups* (New York: Basic Books, 1959).

20.  Margaret J. Rioch, "The Work of Wilfred Bion on Groups," *Psychiatry*, 33, no. 1 (Jan. 1970), 59.

People talk among themselves, tell jokes, flirt, form cliques and so on. It shows that the group is warm and friendly, but little work gets done. Because of the outward friendliness, it is difficult to move the group into a work situation. There is a great deal of satisfaction in these warm surroundings.

It should be noted that some of these forces of nonwork are natural and occur in most groups. In some groups, however, it becomes a "way of life"—and a learned way of not working. It becomes their style—a culture—or what Bion refers to as the "basic assumption of the group." Once this becomes part of the life of the group it is difficult to alter the group's basic assumption. For this reason, supervisors must place a demand for work upon those in worker roles from the start of the relationship.

In any reciprocal relationship, such as that between worker and supervisor, the mode of the group will influence the supervisor and vice versa. If the group does not want to work, it will try to get the supervisor not to demand work of them. If the supervisor doesn't want to work or wants the group to be dependent, he or she will "set them up" for that experience. "Know yourself" is a worthy piece of advice in analyzing any experience with people.

Bion's theoretical projections grow out of his own experiences and limited data. The summations are psychodynamically oriented, and not particularly contextual. It is offered as one of many ways to perceive group action. Sherif's use of environmental manipulation in a boy's camp illustrates another view, namely, how environment, peers, interaction, and program shape the nature of work that takes place in a group.[21] The motivations are clear—the need to cooperate in order to get the work done.

In most organizations the structure (pattern of interaction) is influenced by the fact that usually one member of the group, the administrator, is immediately seen as a person with a different, if not higher, status than some of the others.[22] That person's interactions are seen as more important, though not necessarily better, than those of others. The status of administrator may imply boss, teacher, evaluator, or parent, and the pattern often tends to reflect the hierarchical structures first symbolized by the family. This status-oriented structure may likewise lead to repetition of many of the family's problems of authority, rivalry, and competition. This historical pattern is structured into all groups and must be dealt with because it will cause the most well-intentioned administrator to fulfill the parental role. The pattern can be transformed into alternative

21. Muzafer Sherif, *Intergroup Conflict and Cooperation: The Robbers Cave Experiment* (Norman, Oklahoma: University of Oklahoma, 1961).

22. Florence Kaslow, *Issues in Human Services* (San Francisco: Jossey Bass, 1972), p. 131.

structures, such as a brotherhood or a community. These alternative structures offer other action options. "A certain type of structure permits certain kinds of mental operations to occur, so that certain behavior, feelings, perceptions, language and thinking are the necessary consequences of that particular kind of structure."[23]

Systems analysis suggests that the structure of agencies will influence the parts creating the structure, just as the parts will influence the appearance and functioning of the whole structure. We are dealing with a system of interrelated parts, and with reciprocal feedback and dynamics. The structure becomes a system at the point where the interacting parts are working toward a similar goal. To a great extent, the work of most organizations is carried out by small subsystems or groups.

A valuable concept for our understanding of the surface structure is that by modifying one part of the system, we can often bring about changes in the total system. Generally, it does not matter which part we select as the entry point, change will take place in all as they move to a new equilibrium.

Thus, in an administrative or work group, the entrance of new members or the leaving of powerful members will alter the nature of the exchanges and modify the bonds of feeling and/or power relationships. Improving the feelings members have about each other or themselves will alter their ability to interact. Modifying the administrator's status by having him or her take a reduced power role will open the way for other members of the group to function—or at least help them reassess their own relationship to power. Homans has ably demonstrated the relationship of emotions and status as they determine a group's ability to function.[24]

Leadership roles are important in all organizations, and these roles are generally related to carrying out the two functions of a work group: the accomplishment of the task and the maintenance of the group so that the task can be accomplished. All groups carry on both functions simultaneously in order to attain their goals. The fact is often overlooked that, in truth, groups often cannot accomplish their goals if members' personal concerns—that is, process—are neglected.

When people join together in groups, they explore their similarities and discover common concerns. They can support and help each other. They feel stronger and less alone. The more they interact with one another as equals, the more likely they are to like each other, and to become like each other in their behavior. Because people joining groups

23. Melvin L. Weiner, *The Cognitive Unconscious* (New York: International Psychiatry Press, 1975), p. 118.

24. George Homans, *The Human Group* (New York: Harcourt Brace Jovanovich, 1950).

have varied goals, one of the first tasks is to develop a common goal. A common goal is something the members will achieve as a group at some future time and which they must first decide they can all work toward. In a staff group, the common goal is more visible in that it should be related in some way to improved agency functioning, or meeting the organizational goals.

However, it is important to remember that in addition to achieving the agency goals for which the group was organized, the group must also meet the needs of its individual members. Where a choice exists, the group member will remain involved as long as the rewards of being a member are greater than the costs. As the rewards become fewer, the members will tend to feel ambivalent toward the group. If the rewards should disappear, so, in all likelihood, will the members.

Rewards seem to be related to two major areas:

1. SATISFACTION: The feeling that the group is accomplishing its tasks. It is getting the job done that it started out to do (TASK).
2. SECURITY: The feeling of acceptance as a member of part of the group. Comfortable group climate (MAINTENANCE).

Where members treat each other with respect and dignity, value each other's needs and contributions, and where the goals are clear and agreed upon by the membership, the chances of a success are enhanced. Naturally, success in some groups also is dependent on various environmental factors supporting the group's ability to achieve its goals.

Thelen notes four problems which all groups face: 1. the publicly stated problem the group was brought together to solve; 2. the hidden problems of dealing with shared anxieties which usually are not explicitly formulated; 3. individual efforts to achieve publicly stated ends; and 4. individuals' efforts to deal with their own hidden problems of membership anxiety, self-integration, and adaptation.[25]

The administrator who recognizes the systematic relationship among these factors cannot consider process and goal in any way as a real dichotomy, and must accept their functional relationship. The administrator who understands this relationship can structure the work situation in a way that rewards creative processes even if they are not always successful.

### structure follows function

Structure is the manner in which the group organizes itself to get its work done. Structure starts to develop in small groups as they interact, and roles evolve over time (patterns of association, such as, like-dislike,

---

25.  Herbert Thelen, "Emotionality and Work in Groups," in *The State of the Social Sciences*, ed. L. D. White (Chicago: University of Chicago Press, 1956). p. 10.

status-interests). Some people volunteer to carry out tasks, and they start to be seen as leaders.

What is the function of structure? Efficient job performance seems to be the major benefit. But it also:

1. Serves to control both tasks and behavior at meetings.
2. Provides a division of labor (who-does-what begins to become institutionalized).
3. Helps internalize obligations: to lead, to communicate.
4. Supports psychological processes, such as tension reduction and a common need to predict group behavior.
5. Supports the individual need to be able to count on the stability of attendance and times of meetings, so they feel their work is not wasted.

The structure of a group affects its work (ability to solve the task of the group) and the mental health of the members. It helps to solve the social problems of the group. Some research has shown that a person's position in the group is related to his or her feeling that the group is worthwhile, as well as that of self-worth.

Research on behavior settings indicates that a group's activities can often be influenced and even reduced by other factors, such as meeting time, the space it acts within, and the mode of dress. Thus, we expect a group meeting in a gym to do physical things, a group meeting in a small room to talk, a well-dressed group not to fight, a group meeting at 12 noon to eat, a group meeting at 5:00 P.M. to drink. The administrator, then, can help structure the group's ability to work by the nature of the setting provided, including comfort, food, a rest area, and so on.

Roles are seen as basic units for understanding some of the behavior of members of groups of all types. A great many personal and societal problems are interpreted in terms of role analysis. In addition to the roles that appear on tables of organizations, roles evolve in groups over time as members begin to develop patterns of actions. Some people volunteer to do certain tasks, some become "jokers," and so forth. Roles tend to fall into three major areas: task-oriented roles, group maintenance roles, and individual-oriented roles.

Tables of organizations usually indicate what the formal structure of a group looks like. Often, however, there is an informal structure made up of subgroups, or cliques, which may differ from the formal power structure, but which may be equally or even more influential in decision making. When the roles taken by members of the informal subgroups subvert the goals of the formal structure, the whole group can become disoriented and disintegrate, or it can alter its actions to be more in keeping with the needs of all its members.

Some important research on the "bureaucratic personality" has shed light on the survival mechanisms used by staff as they come to terms with some of the demands of the organization which may conflict with their own values and/or aspirations.[26]

In staff groups, the administrator often assumes, or is delegated, the role of leader, expert, judge, parent, boss, evaluator, friend, etc. Can one person carry all of these roles equally well? Should he or she do so? A major asset of a supervisory group is that there are many people who can assume supervisory roles if urged to, permitted to, and rewarded. There is a need to understand the roles of various actors in the environmental arena.

### communication and the group

The structure of the group not only helps define tasks, but permits certain channels of communication to operate. Communication is the art of getting information from the mind of one person to that of another. The purpose of communication is to get the needed information processed through the organization so that the job can be done.

THE CERTAINTY OF A TWO-HEADED COIN. If the purpose of communications is to transmit an idea to another person from the mind of the first, then one must be concerned with the notion of expectations or probability. The essence of successful communication is to anticipate in some way what the correct message will be for the person to whom it is directed. What is the probability that the thing that I am trying to say will be received by the person to whom I am directing the message, will be interpreted in the way that I feel it should, and will elicit the anticipated response?

Communication channels consist of a message sender, a message, and a receiver. Although the message may have been thought by the sender to be extremely clear, there is the possibility that either: 1. something might have happened between the sending and the receiving of the message to cloud it (or create static); or 2. the receiver, for numerous reasons, may interpret the message in a way different from that anticipated by the sender, even if nothing has happened to the message itself in the transmission.

We are most likely to be able to send a "clear" message if we understand the receiver and how he or she is liable to perceive the message. For example, most people know how best to phrase a question or request to close friends, their wives or husbands, but less so to their children. When we try to communicate with people with whom we have not had much contact, the problems of communicating a clear message are

26.   See Norma M. Williams, Gideon Sjoberg and Andree F. Sjoberg, "The Bureaucratic Personality: An Alternate View," *Journal of Applied Behavioral Science*, 16, no. 3 (1980), 389.

more difficult. The reason, naturally, has to do with the amount of time that we have spent together, and our understanding of what is usually the most successful way of confronting the issue with this particular person. At another level, we might even know what probably would be an appropriate message to certain wives, that is, flowers. This is so because we have some expectation of what wives traditionally like to receive from their husbands. This example may serve to accentuate another important point—that not sending flowers when your wife thinks you should have may also be seen as a message, "you don't care." *It is impossible not to communicate!*[27]

In essence then, successful rewards in communication are often related to the ability to search out precedents that help us ascertain with greater success the type of message transmittal most likely to bring the desired results from the receiver. We must now alter our model to include both a precedent search and a feedback loop to help us determine whether or not we should be satisfied with our communicative act (see Figure 12-2).

COMMUNICATION CREDIBILITY. People's past experiences in inter-action (communication) with others help them to develop a psychological "set," a predisposition based on expectations to treat in certain ways certain inputs from the environment. When we offer our hand to help someone we expect that person to show some degree of gratitude; to be thankful; to appreciate what we have done and we have gained "satis-faction." What a violation of expectations occurs when we are told that our help is not wanted, or our motives as supervisor or administrator are questioned. We may feel that we are trying to help a person become a better worker, whereas the person feels we are only interested in "looking good." Somehow it doesn't fit with our expectations of what people should do in these situations. We are disoriented; we retreat. We try to find some explanations that would somehow account for the phenomenon and still maintain for us our dignity and feeling of being in control of the situation. Festinger has discussed aspects of this phenomenon and called it "Cog-nitive Dissonance." He explains that "if a person knows various things are not psychologically consistent with one another, he/she will in a variety of ways try to make them more consistent. . . .A major way to reduce dissonance is to change one's opinions and evaluations in order to bring them closer in line with one's actual behavior."[28]

We can no longer trust the things we know to be true. We must bring them into line with our concept of reality. But look at the communication

27. Note the "double bind": "If you can't communicate, keep quiet!" For further comments on not not being able to communicate see Paul Watzlawick, Janet Ceavin and Don Jackson, *Pragmatics of Human Communication* (New York: W. W. Norton & Co., 1967), pp. 48–50.

28. L. Festinger, "Cognitive Dissonance," *Scientific American*, 207, no. 4 (Oct. 1962), 93–95.

**FIGURE 12-2**  *The Communication Model*

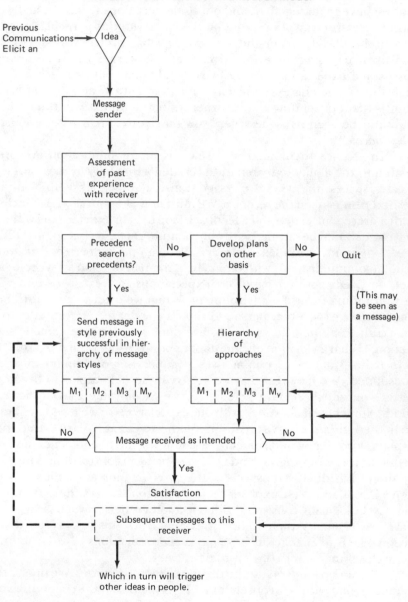

process from the receiver's point of view. Suppose your psychological set has always been that bosses are bad. Suppose you had built up a series of experiences over the years which indicate to you that they are not to be trusted. As you related to "bosses," all the messages would be filtered through the screen of distrust—and you could find enough personal experiences from your friends' and your parents' lives to support your "set." Bosses have, for you, lost their credibility.

Over a period of time, certain groups (such as politicians) have lost credibility. As message senders they are not to be trusted. The famous national "credibility gap" is a case in point. Of all the conclusions derived from experiments in attitude change, one which is considered to be fairly basic and reliable is the conclusion that communication is more effective if attributed to a credible source than to a noncredible one. Therapists, teachers, ministers, statesmen—in essence, most figures who we feel have authority—are generally seen as credible figures. The importance of this "role" concept in the communication and change process has also received considerable research.[29]

The credibility theory also raises the important emerging concept of nonverbal behavior. One of the problems in human communication is that the verbal message may say one thing, but the nonverbal communication offered by body posture or movement may indicate something different. The ability to communicate with authenticity on a total level is the object of a number of sensitivity and encounter movements which stress the "authentic human person." We might add that in "human systems" the "force" that links and alters the system is communication and the nature of the communication. The direction of the change will be related to one's interpretation of the message sent by another part of the system. In a group one acts in response to others' communication. The others then respond to that person's responses in an ongoing interaction chain.

Communication in large organizations is a major source of study.

> Management has long been concerned with getting its message across to the workers, that is, communicating downward throughout the organization. Management often is concerned with its own lack of effectiveness in the communication process. . . .
> Organization structure is definitely tied to communications systems. The relationship is apparent when formal structures, channels, and media are involved. . . .[30]

29.   T. Sorbin and V. Allen, "Role Enactment, Audience Feedback, and Attitude Change," *Sociometry*, vol. 27 (1964), pp. 183–89.

30.   Fremont E. Kast and James Rosenzweig, *Organization and Management: A Systems Approach* (New York: McGraw Hill, 1974), p. 87.

Organizational communication has also been studied from the viewpoint of formal and informal structures within the organization,[31] as well as from the viewpoint of control systems and organizational learning.[32]

New ways to visualize communications have grown out of systems theory and cybernetics. The central themes in cybernetics are communication and control.[33] In order to reap the rewards of the communicative act, the message sender must have some indication of the effectiveness of the message. In large organizational systems communication specific inputs and outputs are seldom clear.

In addition, the number of levels between the person attempting to initiate the communication and the ultimate target, particularly if the target is the director, can be decisive. Patti notes that a greater number of levels increases the degree of resistance that the idea will encounter.[34]

In most small groups communication is more informal. The members also send messages back to the leaders that can be picked up quickly because of the face-to-face situation. This is known as feedback. Even large organizations have built in feedback mechanisms because of the recognition that negative feedback needs to be reckoned with in order for the organization to function optimally and, at times, to survive.

### group cohesion

Group cohesion deals with the degree of attractiveness that a group has for its members. It reflects the nature of the bonds among members. In a cohesive group the members feel they want to belong and they have a part to play. Cohesive groups satisfy some of the security needs of their members. This satisfaction might be due to the high status of the group, its accomplishments, opportunities to participate and be accepted, having a leadership role in the group, or safety from outside attack. On the other hand, too domineering leadership, disrespect for a member's ideas, or constant fighting weakens the group bonds. There is generally a "zone of indifference" within which unhappy members will still maintain a working interest in the group. When things get beyond this zone, however, the members will drop out psychologically and/or physically.

Cohesive groups, because of their appeal, tend to be able to make stronger demands on their members to conform to the group's norms.

31.   Peter Blau and W. Scott, *Formal Organizations* (San Francisco: Chandler Publishing Company, 1962).

32.   R. M. Cyeri and J. G. March, *A Behavioral Theory of the Firm* (Englewood Cliffs, N.J.: Prentice-Hall, Inc., 1963).

33.   Norbert Wiener, *The Human Use of Human Beings* (Boston: Houghton Mifflin Company, 1954).

34.   Rino J. Patti, "Organizational Resistance and Change: The View from Below," *Social Service Review*, 48, no. 3 (Sept. 1974), 378.

Therefore, in a work-oriented situation, cohesive groups will be highly productive. In order to make themselves more attractive to prospective members, groups will offer a wide variety of programs, hoping to meet needs. For example, church groups not only attempt to meet religious needs, but educational and social needs as well. Some groups make themselves appealing by strong restrictions on membership. In an organization aimed at service and advocating democratic principles, such an elite group might alienate a number of staff members and could be counterproductive.

In a work group, such as a group supervision situation, cohesiveness often develops around the agreement on social goals, synergistic techniques for decision making, and minimization of status differentials. The recognition that all members have important contributions to make motivates members to work.

### group norms

Just as role defines the expected behavior for individuals filling certain positions, norms set the expected behavior for *all* the members of the group. Norms are the "rules of the game" that the members of the group evolve for themselves. All groups have some norms to which members must adhere. Clear group norms often help new members learn what is acceptable behavior in the group. The group often helps you determine which line conforms to their norms. In the conformity studies carried out by Ash, participants often "saw" shorter lines drawn on paper as being longer if previous reporters in the group reported them longer. The respondents were not aware that the reporters were paid to report shorter lines as longer.[35]

Groups tend to want and therefore create "conformity" to the norms of the group, not only in actions, but in dress, speech, eating habits, and so on. Conformity, however, should not necessarily be viewed negatively. For example, if the norms of a hospital ward group are such that patients are expected to participate in activities rather than hang around in bed, this can be used for therapeutic purposes. In large institutions, the norms of various sub-groups often differ. Goffman has pointed out that the differences of doctor norms and side norms can immobilize the treatment process.[36]

It is important for the administrator not only to recognize the value of a strong normative system for the agency, but the dangers as well.

35.  Solomon Ash, "Studies of Independence and Conformity—Part I," *Psychological Monographs*, vol. 70. (1956).
36.  Erving Goffman, *Asylums: Essays on the Social Situation of Mental Patients and Other Inmates* (Chicago: Aldine, 1961).

Norms can also create a "yes" orientation at a time that a "no" may be needed. The norm must be for honest responses.

Deviance from the norms of the group presents special problems. The deviant can often force the group to examine its own behavior. The group response can be to (1) mobilize against the deviant, or (2) to change the limits of its own behavior in relation to the deviant. It can of course accept the deviant's ideas.

People belong to numerous groups, and the influences of these groups affect the member's actions in other situations. They often become the person's reference groups. Reference groups are those groups to which a person aspires, and from which he or she tends to take clues for behaving. Members and prospective members try to conform to the expected behavior of their reference groups, which tend to be socializing influences on the individual. Where the expected behavior is fairly clear, as in a professional group, it is easier to learn correct actions.

The expectations that the members have of each other mold many of the norms of the group. As it meets over a period of time, there are recurrent interactions among members. These tend to build up a pool of common symbols—ways of perceiving and thinking—which lead to:

> Common ways of looking at things.
> Consistent modes of communication.
> Shared attitudes.
> Mutually accepted obligations.
> Mutual expectations regarding the behavior of others.
> Common friends and enemies.

### team building

By now it is obvious that a great deal of the work of the organization is achieved through small groups, committees, task forces, departments, and so on. Where the norms of a team are to work toward the clearly stated objectives, that team will be productive.

How can the groups within the agency be helped to work together as a team, rather than to oppose each other. Certain general principles might be suggested:

a.   Each member should know the others—their roles, hopes, and places in the group.

b.   Competitive actions should be avoided.

c.   The goals of the team and the means by which they will be reached should be jointly arrived at—a mutually negotiated contract.

d.   Members should support each other, and provide a community where one member is not permitted to act badly.

e.   The group should be synergistic—no loose decision-making processes should be initiated.
f.   Good relationships among work groups should be fostered by cooperative rather than competitive modes.
g.   Shared leadership, rather than hierarchical structure, should be maintained.
h.   Staff development and consultation should be available.
i.   Realistic work loads mutually determined as far as possible.
j.   "Fair" treatment and rewards for all staff should be the norm.
k.   All members, new or old, wise or befuddled, creative or dull, should be treated with respect and dignity.

Individuals in groups will tend to repeat some of the actions which they developed in their first group—the family. It is therefore important to establish a "community" model in which paternalism and sibling rivalry are avoided. This becomes a vital concern for the administrator who also may start to repeat some of his or her own earlier group experiences, and in fact, enjoy the parental role. The climate establishes the expectations, and it is important to note that in a system—one part—one action will modify the whole system, at least temporarily. The expectations are therefore that all people in the system must reflect on the impact of their actions on the others.

The agency administrator is in a strong position to exert leadership in any task-oriented group or committee. If the group members feel that the administrator is trying to sell his or her ideas, rather than use the committee creatively, they will either go along with those ideas or resist work. Clearly, the work group needs and can use a chairperson who knows group dynamics and understands the task at hand, but the group itself must feel its work is purposeful and not a rubber stamp.

### approaches to staff development

Responsibility for the proper education of staff in order to accomplish the goals of the agency is in the hands of the administrator. Larger social welfare and human service agencies often establish a specific job assignment called Staff Development Specialist. At times the executive or his delegate may assume the responsibilities of this position, which include:[37]

1.   Recruiting and selecting of staff;
2.   Orienting new employees to their positions;

37.   Further material on staff development can be found in Paul Abels, *The Practice of Supervision and Staff Development* (New York: Association Press, 1976).

3. Developing in employees the knowledge, attitudes and skills necessary to do the job;
4. Maximizing the job performance of all employees in the agency; and
5. Consultating with other agencies, departments and organizations about the training needs of staff.

In addition to identifying training needs, administrators must develop, monitor and often conduct the training of staff. Besides understanding how people learn, they have to be teachers, workshop leaders and training program organizers. It is vital for the administrator to examine a number of people during the training and choose some who will be able, with proper instruction, to translate the group learning orientations into work with individuals or smaller learning groups.

Tyler suggests that the major purposes of staff development are:[38]

1. To help staff members develop the understanding, skills, and attitudes required to perform their work effectively.
2. To help them keep up to date where new research and new practices are developing rapidly.
3. To provide opportunities for each individual to develop increased competence and to assume increasing responsibility for improving services.
4. To provide a warm, dynamic environment for growth and improvement by both client and staff.

## THE CREATIVE CLIENT

The power to change lies with the client, but unless this power is engaged, goal-oriented change will not occur. It may be presumptuous, but necessary, to remind the readers of two points previously discussed: 1. the client is part of the system, as well as the reason for the system's existence; and 2. there is a reciprocal-transactional relationship between the staff and the client.

If the worker is truthful, excited, innovative, and creative in his or her work with the client, then the client will pick up this creative metacommunication in his or her own approach to problem solving. Modeling—demonstrating the desired behavior—provides a means for the clients to see first hand the ways of acting that the helper hopes will be beneficial. Modeling has been shown to be one of the most valuable and influential techniques for learning and changing. The creative powers of the clients will also be unleashed in their own behalf. Clients, too, can learn creative

---

38.   Ralph W. Tyler, "In-Service Training Problems and Needs," *Planning In-Service Training Programs for Mental Health*, Region VI Conference, Omaha, Nebraska (Dec. 1963), p. 2.

responses to life's situations. For them, as well as staff, Wheelis' basic law that when things are not going well one must try harder and try something different, holds true.

Client creativity can be developed in a number of ways, such as:

1. By the clients' involvement in agency planning, policy making, soliciting financial support, lobbying, and so on.
2. By mutual exploration of their problems and the treatment plan.
3. By creative helping techniques, such as role plays and role reversals, meditation, and so forth.
4. By growth assignments, logs, homework, diaries, agenda readings.
5. By helping them enroll in courses, find new jobs, join groups, volunteer in agencies.
6. By helping them develop self-help groups, so that at a certain point they have the option of alternative service mechanisms.

Some of these approaches, and we are sure that the reader can think of many more, require a willingness on the part of the agency to risk new, often "alien," treatment approaches. They also recognize the client as a partner of the agency in the self-recreating process.

Increasingly we are becoming aware that some agencies retard the client's ability to use the agency for growth. Some agencies, particularly those serving chronic clients, such as the aged, often become warehouses. Institutional neurosis can occur in hospitals, nursing homes, prisons, or anywhere persons are removed from society and live in rigid, isolated communities. It can also develop in the person's own home if he or she is isolated. The symptoms are: erosion of personality, overdependence, expressionless faces, automatic behavior, and loss of interest in the outside world.[39]

Generally speaking, in the institution, opportunity for interaction, freedom, privacy, and leisure activities is diminished unless creative programs are developed. Some older persons, for example, maintain:

1. We want to make our own decisions regarding our own lives—we don't want other people to make these decisions for us.
2. We want to continue to be involved in life—we don't want to be put on the shelf.
3. We want to be treated with dignity.[40]

With some care and thought,

Facilities for the aged could become places where one goes to be rehabilitated to the greatest extent possible, nurturing the sense of hope and self-esteem

39.   Robert N. Butler and Myrna Lewis, *Aging and Mental Health: Positive Psychosocial Approaches* (St. Louis: Mosby Press, 1977), p. 259.
40.   Butler and Lewis, *Aging and Mental Health*, p. XII.

which can make the last and often most difficult years of life worthwhile, up to the moment of death. Whether in the outside world or within an institution, the older person needs someone to talk to about his/her life, to revise it, to make sense of it, and to come to terms with his/her dying.[41]

Many other minority client groups would also utilize agency services if administrators and staff were more sensitive to the cultural factors, fears, and rebuffs that these groups are subject to. Miranda and Kitano discuss some of the barriers minority groups have encountered in contacts with mental health service. Both Japanese-Americans and Mexican-Americans underutilize these services. "Certainly to be considered within this complex is the tremendous obstacle that bureaucratic-like mental health agencies present. . . ."[42] Life styles, language barriers, fragmented services, lack of information, and inaccessibility all work together to create barriers.

Often "health administrators assign complex tasks to people poorly prepared to handle them"[43] and the use of paraprofessionals is frequently seen as giving less than the best service.

Awareness of these concerns permits the administrator to avoid some of the pitfalls. Creative programming and use of community people on boards and advisory committees can make for more creative clients.

## IMPORTANT WORK

The individual must take pleasure in an activity, its conclusions, and its consequences. Not only must the workplace offer the satisfiers that Herzberg talks about, but there must be both internal and external rewards for creative adaptations. One must gain satisfaction not only from acknowledgment that one's work is valued, but, indeed, from seeing one's ideas put to use. Creative responses that are thwarted through budgetary restraints or "lazy" management act as a retardant to future creativity.

When local and regional funding sources start to cut back on welfare and the community responses seem antiwelfare, the work of the human service staff is undermined and their morale lessened. Even agencies with long-standing, excellent reputations suffer from this community neglect. It is a pervasive destroyer of morale, particularly when funds are tight,

41.    Robert N. Butler, *Why Survive? Being Old in America* (New York: Harper & Row, 1975), p. 299.

42.    Manuel Miranda and Harry H. L. Kitano, "Barriers to Mental Health Service: A Japanese-American and Mexican-American Dilemma," in *Chicanos Social and Psychological Perspective*, ed. Carrol Hernandez, Marsha Haug, Nathaniel Wagner (St. Louis: Mosby Press, 1976), p. 245.

43.    Miranda and Kitano, "Barriers to Mental Health Service," p. 249.

and creates stress for staff and clients, as is suggested by this recent news report.

### Funds removed for a Bellefaire therapy setup
*By John Nussbaum*

> Bellefaire's outpatient child therapy program abruptly lost its funding yesterday because it serves 12 children rather than 16.
>
> The Cuyahoga County Community Mental Health and Retardation Board yesterday allocated more than $8 million in federal state and county mental health and drug abuse funds, and left the Bellefaire program without money as of Saturday.
>
> The action, which does not affect Bellefaire's school and residential treatment, came just two days before the beginning of the new fiscal year.
>
> "You are putting us in a position where we have to tell our clients on June 28 that we cannot serve them after June 30," said Edwin M. Roth, president of Bellefaire. "We do not have the funds even to wind the program down properly."[44]

In such situations, the staff may indeed feel that their work is not valued, and the general social work community, as well as concerned citizens, must fill the gap. They can do this by mobilizing other community resources and proclaiming the public testimony which reaffirms their work. The administrator can often be helpful as a catalytic agent if he or she has maintained community contacts and earlier has done the type of interpretation which attests to the agency's validity.

The creative organization must be able to demonstrate its creativity in the face of threats, as well as when things are moving smoothly. At time of stress, it is often important that the administrator's own support system be available to help him or her over the rough times, to be thoughtful and reflective, and to maintain creative and synergistic response postures, rather than to lash out in anger in a fight-flight response.

Building a creative organization is a complex process[45]. It depends on staff, clients, and a nonmalevolent environment in order to function optimally. The administrator is one important part of that complexity. The administrator's control of the other forces is limited, but, at the very least, he or she can insure that his or her own actions are positive and that the work undertaken by the agency is worthy of being performed.

44.   *Cleveland Plain Dealer*, June 27, 1978, p. 3.

45.   Barry A. Stein and Rosabeth Moss Kanter, "Building the Parallel Organization: Creating Mechanisms for Permanent Quality of Work Life," *Journal of Applied Behavioral Science*, 16, no. 3 (1980), 371.

# CHAPTER 13

---

# the exceptional
# administrator

There are expanding pressures in the human services to pursue the "successful" models of administrative practice prevalent in business and industry. While we have periodic and telling examples that some of these "management" approaches are not that successful, the myth of the efficient manager as coming out of the business management field continues. It will take the truly exceptional administrator to resist a total submission to these pressures and integrate the best of what management theory has to offer with the best of the human services—particularly the democratic heritage and humanistic values which still pervade this area. Only the truly artful administrator can avoid the lure of the hierarchical, pyramiding, colonizing structures that have become the template for many of our social agencies.

In his discussion of the art of management, Siu notes that the philosopher-executive may cover the "whole" of integrated experience with but one triple insight: the dreaming, the understanding, and the acting. Thus the vision must be partialized, analyzed and acted upon. But

he adds that it is important to share in the dreams of the staff. The visions of the organization are the integrated visions of many. From the dreaming emerges understanding and "proper" action. Siu is trying to express the flow that can come with a truly integrated staff involved in creative work. "The direction of human beings is a matter of artistry, rather then procedures and formulae."[1] He sketches out an approach to administration that supports his view that to deal with human beings in a manner which enhances their humanness is indeed an art.

In the human services it has long been recognized that professionalism is both an art and a science; that technology alone cannot provide for the holistic needs of the people we work with and for. Ordway Tead asked, "In what sense is administration an art?" The answer, "because it summons an imposing body of special talents on behalf of a collaborative creation which is integral to the conduct of civilized living today."[2] Tead tried to establish the need for an administrative body of knowledge based on the democratic principles of our country. He was concerned that in a country dedicated to democratic life, organizations did not seem to believe that democratic processes could support productive concerns. His thoughts are echoed today by the charge that our institutions have become too mechanical and have tended to disregard the inputs of the people they were established to serve. The caretakers have stopped caring.

## THE HUMAN ADMINISTRATOR

We have learned from our own quests for help, and from the experiences of our clients, that helpers' suggestions are often resisted, no matter how well-intentioned they are. This seems paradoxical, particularly when the help is aggressively sought and the desire for change proclaimed. We know just how difficult the change processes can be—the ambivalence, the fear, the lack of energy, and the costs. We know, too, the toll it can take on the helper. Yet knowing all of this, we expect that the administrator will come through similar experiences complete, unscarred, and vital. It is important to recognize the vulnerability and humanness of administrators as they carry out their tasks of stabilization and change.

All people are shaped by their environments. Terrell, in an interesting analysis of administrators perceptions of the "New Federalism," points out, "Human service managers, then, reflect many of the basic dilemmas confronting all citizens. . . ."[3] He was referring to how the nature of their

1. R.G.H. Siu, *The Tao of Science* (Cambridge, Mass.: M.I.T. Press, 1957), p. 146.
2. Ordway Tead, *The Art of Administration* (New York: McGraw-Hill Book Company, 1951), p. 6.
3. Paul Terrell "Beyond the Categories: Human Service Managers View the New Federal Aid," *Public Administration Review*, 40, no. 1 (Jan–Feb. 1980), 54.

settings influenced administrators views of the appropriateness of certain conditions that were attached to funding.

The person, who is the social worker who is the administrator, is shaped not only by the facts and myths of the general society, but by the facts and myths of his or her profession as well. Nowhere is he or she made more vulnerable than by society's mystique concerning the "leader." Although reality may indicate the contrary, myths of the "great leader" prevail. Although few people agree with Scott's analysis that "[m]anagers have become largely powerless to affect the organizations they inhabit,"[4] the search for the "great leader" continues. Only the wise administrator can avoid the traps that would force him or her to reenact the myths. It is like a Greek tragedy where, in the first act, we can see the doom awaiting the hero at the play's end.

There are two particular aspects of the "great leader" mystique that may spur the leader to unwarranted and unwise action. The first is the staff's views of the new administrator as having exceptional abilities and, therefore, those necessary to carry out all of their unfulfilled dreams. This myth is maintained and nurtured by our historical recognition of and respect for great leaders. The great leader-heroes of our time are often "hyped" beyond their human origins and capabilities by television, movies, and books. The scenario usually reveals a leader who is loved by the people and who conquers all obstacles in order to help the group or organization to overcome its difficulties. This is the expectation frequently thrust upon administrators and, naturally, since the administrator is usually the product of the same social mythology, she or he will start to believe in the truth of the myth. Reynolds, dealing with some of the dangers inherent in this development, notes,

> When we bury the illusion that an executive must seem to be one of the gods, we may have field work for executives-in-training and take it as much for granted as field work in case work.[5]

A second fantasy that may turn out to be the administrator's undoing is related to the amount of power that seems to go with the office. The leader may believe that holding the office will permit the accomplishment of all his or her dearly held goals. The cold reality that others, too, have their dreams and goals, and that these may often conflict with the goals of the administrator, may be slow to appear, but appear it will.

This desire on the part of the administrator to actualize his or her

        4.   Quoted in Frederick C. Thayer, "Values, Truth, and Administration: God or Mammon?" *Public Administration Review*, 40, no. 1 (Jan.–Feb. 1980), 92.
        5.   Bertha Reynolds, *Learning and Teaching in the Practice of Social Work* (New York: Farrar & Rinehart, Inc., 1945), p. 320.

goals is often at the base of the executives preference for working in a newly established setting. The setting is viewed by the administrator in a very personal way as an opportunity to fulfill his or her personal strivings. "I want to create what I want."[6]

A natural outcome of both of these myths is the tendency for the administrator to attempt to handle more then is humanly possible. This often begins with efforts to carry out as many tasks and goals as possible, quickly, so as to make a mark on the organization. This usually serves to motivate staff, and leads to further increases in ideas and programs. At this point, unless safeguards are built in, the administrator will begin to see him- or herself as indispensible. The executive may, in the course of being overworked, become isolated from the other staff. Freundenberger, who has been a consultant to administrators in the mental health field, describes this process and singles it out as a cause of administrative burnout.

Administrators of alternative organizations, free clinics, and other similar organizations are extremely susceptible to burnout. They must constantly shift between the "deviant" communities in which they may work and the "normal" communities that often supply the funds or threaten the continuation of the programs.[7] Freudenberger defines burnout as a wearing out or exhaustion caused by excessive demands on strength, energy, and resources. Not only does overwork lead to physical fatigue, it leads to boredom as well. The prelude to burnout is often self-doubt and a loss of charisma. The staff start to take the leader for granted and become disappointed in him or her. Then the agency starts to have "normal" problems—perhaps because the administrator has not fulfilled the fantasy of the "great leader."[8]

Administrative burnout, though, is more often due to the tremendous pressures inherited with the position. Role expectations from board, staff, community, and family, in addition to personal developmental stresses, exacerbate the many day-to-day problems. No wonder it is often easier to look for shortcuts or to modify one's own values in order to compromise with the many conflicting demands than to stand firm. For many, it is only the sense of mission, the struggle for a "just society," which keeps them on an even keel.

6. Seymour B. Sarason, *The Creation of Settings and the Future Societies* (San Francisco: Jossey-Bass Publishers, 1976), p. 222.

7. Herbert J. Freudenberger, *The Staff Burn-out Syndrome* (Washington, D. C.: Drug Abuse Council, 1975), pp. 1–10.

8. Burnout is certainly not a syndrome limited to administrators. Freudenberger's major discussion deals with staff. Maslach has also done a great deal of work in this area. Abels attempts to relate burnout to the type of agency service in his paper, "The Psychologically Battered Helper (unpublished paper, School of Applied Social Science, Case Western Reserve University, Cleveland, Ohio).

Florence Kelley, who had worked at Hull House and later became head of the National Consumer's League, once said:

> You know at 20 I signed on to serve my country for the duration of the war on poverty and on injustice and oppression and I take it. . .that it will last out my life and yours and our children's lives.[9]

## THE DEMOCRATIC ADMINISTRATOR

Leadership of organizations requires high moral efforts and acts. Often the administrator becomes the symbol of the "cause" for which the agency exists. Tead suggests that "implicit in democratic leadership has to be the administrator's recognition that he is the custodian of opportunity—opportunity for associated persons to enhance the quality of life by the contribution of their labors."[10]

People want to contribute their labors to worthwhile efforts, and one of the basic questions that an administrator may have to ask him- or herself is, "Is this program—project, effort—worthy of being undertaken?" The goals of the organization need to be of such character that they can win the efforts of the staff. Self-deception, often a result of narcissism or egoism, can occur.

Sarason suggests two basic groupings of leaders in the human services: one group which seeks power, and another which seeks to test ideas. Although both will use the new setting to serve their own purposes, the latter group will provide more substantive issues for the staff to work with, and more opportunities for them to be involved in setting the agency's direction.[11]

We can more easily accept the selfish purposes of the leader who says, "Join with me in testing these ideas," provided that we can also contribute our ideas to the visions to be tested. In essence, we are then talking about a more synergistic democratic administration,

> . . .the direction and oversight of an organization which assures that aims are shared and in the making, that working policies and methods are agreed to by those involved, that all who participate feel both free and eager to contribute their best creative effort, that stimulating personal leadership is assured, and that in consequence the total outcome maximized the aim of the organization while also contributing to the growing selfhood of all involved in terms of clearly realized benefits."[12]

9.   Florence Kelley, quoted in William L. O'Neill, *Everyone was Brave: The Rise and Fall of Feminism in America* (New York: Quadrangle, 1969), p. 239.

10.   Tead, *The Art of Administration*, p. 138.

11.   Sarason, *The Creation of Settings*.

12.   Tead, *The Art of Administration*, p. 134.

Staff participation in setting the policies to which they must adhere is a fundamental issue in the constructive functioning of all organizations in a democratic society. Elliott Jaques points out that in industrial societies ninety percent of the working population gains its livelihood from bureaucratic organizations. He suggests that worker participation is an issue that will remain a major problem.[13]

## THE WISE ADMINISTRATOR

What will the administrator offer the staff—people who are human services workers—when they turn to him or her for guidance? How will this human being respond to another? Can there be a recognition of mutuality between the "governed" and the leader? Otto Kernberg notes some of the difficulties for both leader and led when some of the very human qualities of administrators are warped by the pressures created by unrealistic views of leadership. Sadism, narcissism, and other contemporary mental health problems are often exacerbated when they occur in the person of the administrator. These are often intensified by staff reactions. Although Kernberg's analysis of leader problems tends to be framed in psychoanalytic terms, the approach is informative.[14]

The wise administrator recognizes his or her humanness and that he or she is first and foremost a human being whose hopes, life styles, and, to a great extent, responses are shaped by his or her culture and hopes for the future. For example, many administrators are in their forties and fifties, which may be a crucial, transitional stage of their lives. They may be uncertain about their futures, capabilities, or what direction to take. They question whether they are at a fork in the road, or at a dead end. They themselves may feel alienated from staff because of their over-involvement in the work of the agency. They may see younger, brighter people waiting to replace them, or even attacking their vulnerability. In this sense, we may all be victims of the "press for success," the fear of closeness or rejection from others, or the pressure to be exclusive.

The executive, though not alone in bearing the brunt of external criticisms of the agency, is usually held accountable for its lack of success and errors. Administrators faced with these attacks may react by cloaking themselves in legitimizing myths rather than seeking a common solution in partnership with staff.[15]

13.    Elliott Jaques, "Essential Developments in Bureaucracy in the 1980's," *Journal of Applied Behavioral Sciences*, 16, no. 3 (1980), 443.

14.    See Otto F. Kernberg, "Regression in Organizational Leadership," *Psychiatry*, vol. 42 (Feb. 1979).

15.    Steven J. Taylor and Robert Bogdan, "Defending Illusions: The Institution's Struggle for Survival," *Human Organization*, 39, no. 3 (Fall 1980), 217.

Recognition of the similarity of our own struggles for independence, success, or perserverence, with the struggles of others can bring closer identity with staff and clients, and with our community.

Jules Henry helps us see this important similarity between workers and clients as he concludes his description of patient life:

> As for patients, they live out their last days in long stretches of anxiety and silent reminiscing, punctured by outbursts of petulance at one another, by T.V. viewing, and social life is minimal. . . .There is a yearning after communication, but no real ability to achieve it. In this we are all very much like them.[16]

Many institutions intensify the kind of life which is prevalent in its society, with its residents carrying on best as they can and its staff doing as has been done to them, each alienated from the others. Some staff are isolated and have always been so, others are able or would like to forge close and meaningful ties. But problems face the staff in developing relationships with each other unless the bitter fruits of competition are condemned by the agency administrator.

These "social" relation concerns reflect many of our society's dilemmas. If the new executive is a woman, there are the pitfalls of sexism. If the executive is a younger person, then the bitterness of the passed-over, older staff person may erupt. If the executive is a member of a minority group, then racially oriented resistance may create problems. The outsider creates stress or anger for the inner circle.

We cannot assume however that all responses in the agency to a new executive will be problematic. Within every organization there are powerful forces at work that permit the evolution of healthy solutions to most problems. Mary Follett referred to these types of endeavors as "intergrating" or "unifying," and devoted much of her life to developing concepts of management that would make such solutions possible.[17] When one believes, one can often make things happen; where one is certain of failure, one gives up and failure is then truly certain.

Although he advocates self-actualizing approaches in management, Maslow notes that "Giving people good conditions spoils them for bad conditions.[18] Sensitive use of power by the administrator can shape the behavior of staff in new ways. In order not to repeat the errors of the past, administrators, because of their critical position and the leverage they

---

16.   Jules Henry, *Culture Against Man* (New York: Random House, Vintage Books, 1974), p. 474.

17.   For a review of some of Mary Parker Follett's ideas see, Elliot M. Fox, "Mary Parker Follett: The Enduring Contribution," *Public Administration Review*, 28, no. 6 (Nov.–Dec. 1968).

18.   Abraham H. Maslow, *Eupsychian Management* (Homewood, Ill.: Dorsey Press, 1965), p. 262.

have in controlling the thrust of the relationship among staff and between staff and client, need to use this power for the betterment of the human condition. Thus, to view our society as alienating, or the institution as depersonalizing, is to recognize a truth, but only a partial truth. As much as one is acted upon, one also acts. "With the noose around our neck, there still are options—to curse God or to pray, to weep or to slap the executioner in the face."[19] The risk may be great, and the change slight, but it will make a difference.

## THE REFLECTIVE ADMINISTRATOR

In this book, we have expressed the view that administrative practice needs to reconstruct itself around a new approach to working with people, one that minimizes status differentials and attempts to establish a moral community in which executive and staff, helper and helped, are indeed one. We have suggested that although there are many who share this vision, it is only now beginning to find its way into practice in western organizations. What we have come to realize is that the visions of the agency's administrator are useless unless the visions are shared by all. As Walt Whitman said, "To have great poets there must be great audiences, too."[20]

A normative systems approach to administration can exist without a normative practice, but only as a breakwater maintaining an island of humanism and social justice in a sea of disillusionment. Comments by administrators such as, "[s]ocial workers have the mentality that makes them think they're not accountable to anyone but the client," only lead to an alienated staff, and a separation from the oneness of the agency.[21] Although it is outside the scope of this book to establish a reconstructed practice in the human services, we clearly see this as an important step. Indeed, in their beginnings, the social reform and settlement movements were attempts to establish a normative approach in the human service professions.

### from the east

Possibly because of their centuries of experiences in administration, several prescriptive-normative orientations have grown out of Eastern approaches to administration and governance.

19.   Allen Wheelis, *How People Change* (New York: Harper & Row, Publishers, Inc., 1974), p. 115.
20.   Quoted in R. G. Siu, *The Tao of Science*, p. 137.
21.   *Cleveland Plain Dealer*, Sept. 4, 1977, p. 32.

One such approach was evident in the work of Confucius, who taught a way of life in which morality occupied a supreme position. One of his views on the totality of the human experience, and his extraordinarily contemporary systems view, is reflected by the following:

> The ancients, who wished to preserve the clear and good character of the world, first set about to regulate their national life. In order to regulate their national life, they cultivated their family life. In order to cultivate their family life, they rectified their personal life. In order to rectify their personal life, they elevated their heart. In order to elevate their heart they made their will sincere. In order to make their will sincere, they enlightened their mind. In order to enlighten their mind, they conducted research. Their research being conducted, their mind was enlightened. Their mind being enlightened, their will was made sincere. Their will being sincere, their heart was elevated. Their heart being elevated, their personal life was rectified. Their personal life being rectified, their family life was cultivated. Their family life being cultivated, their national life was regulated. Their national life being regulated, the good and clear character of the world was preserved and peace and tranquility reigned thereafter.

His thoughts on the need for good administrators might be summarized by the following anecdote attributed to Confucius.:

> When asked, "Wouldn't it be good if everyone in the village loved the mayor?" he responded, "It would be better if the good people loved him and the evil ones hated him."[22]

A later development in Chinese thinking was reflected by the work of Lao-tzu in his *Tao-te-ching* or "Tao" (the Way). There was a recognition here too that leadership was important, the state and people fragile, and that the ruler should model himself on the Tao. "One who has the Tao will be inwardly a sage and outwardly a true being."[23]

The basic approach of this Eastern philosophy was that through minimum intervention by the administrator, and through his or her delegation of authority to others, the "best" administration would result:

> Desiring to rule over the people, one must in one's works humble oneself before them; and, desiring to lead the people, one must in one's person follow behind them.[24]

Interesting offshoots of this were writings which could be consulted as guides to proper decision making in regard to one's own life and the process of political life. Although we are not advocating these guides, we do suggest that their demands for reflection on the part of the administrator are important contributions.

22.   R. G. Siu, *The Tao of Science*, p. 139.
23.   Lao-Tzu, *Tao-Te-Ching* (New York: Mentor Books, 1955), p. 33.
24.   Attributed to Confucius.

The *I Ching*, or *Book of Changes*, was one such guide.[25] It was used as a guide to help those in "ruling" positions make "just decisions," thoughtfully and in harmony with what then was the most moral focus of thinking. The "just" decisions were to be in keeping with the natural forces available to the wise administrator. Not only does the *I Ching* link us to the past by illuminating the historical search for help in decision making, but it also shows us that administrator-staff relationships have always called for thoughtful, sensitive handling for the best service to be given. Furthermore it illustrates an important concept for the wise administrator to consider, that is, that approaches to helping that people believe in tend to have potency for them and that the current "fad" may be a valuable tool because it is current and being widely used.

Richard Pascale, who spent a number of years studying Japanese management process, wrote on the significant difference between Japanese and American management styles. In what he refers to as a Zen approach, he notes a great deal more bottom-upward communication in Japanese firms, and a much less confrontative style. In addition, he notes that the Japanese manager falls back on two concepts, "omote" (up front) and "ura" (behind the scenes), and that what takes place up front is extremely important, often ceremonial. Therefore announcements are not made about programs, for example, until a great deal has been done behind the scenes.

He notes as well two other important considerations: 1. a great deal of concern for the individual, conveying not only an acknowledgment by others of a person's unique qualities, but also valuing them in a positive way, and 2. a much greater amount of funds spent on social and recreational facilities than their American counterparts ($48.85 per employee per year versus $14.85).[26]

Peter Drucker has also reported important differences in the two management styles. He notes that in the decision-making process the Japanese spend a great deal of time trying to focus on "what the decision is all about." Secondly, they bring out all dissenting views and focus on alternatives rather than a "right" answer. He seems to feel we are moving more in the Japanese direction.[27]

25. *The I Ching*, trans. Richard Wilhelm (Princeton, N.J.: Princeton University Press, 1973), p. 48. Recently, with our revived interest in other approaches to the good life and in self-actualization, the *I Ching* has once more become a popular source. For example, it has entered the human service literature in relation to supervision through an interesting article by Stambler and Pearlman, who used the *I Ching* as a supervisory-analytic guide for assessment of a case previously reported in a journal. See Morris Stambler and Chester Pearlman, "Supervision as Revelation of the Pattern: I Ching Comments on 'The Open Door,'" *Family Process*, 13, no. 3 (September 1974).

26. Richard Tanner Pascale, "Zen and the Art of Management," *Harvard Business Review* (March–April 1978), p. 161.

27. Peter Drucker, *Management: Tasks, Responsibilities, Practices* (New York: Harper & Row, 1973), p. 470.

We are not suggesting that Eastern approaches to management are "better" than Western ones and should be copied. We are discussing different histories and cultures, but what is "natural" to one (the eastern) group might be incorporated into Western styles because it meets the needs of all people and would have a more universal acceptance. Involvement in decisions and feeling a sense of community within the work place, we feel, would be two such acceptable changes.

Some of the paradoxical therapists use approaches similar to the Taoist doctrines by making positive use of a person's negative forces. These therapists join with the resistance of the client and create a paradox that often leads to client change.[28]

Today, we are faced with administrative concerns that are similar to many of the earlier eastern concerns, mainly the interrelatedness of people in hierarchies and the use or misuse of power. Nor have we found solace in the modern "scientific" guidelines in our own decision-making approaches, for these too often use cost-benefit criteria or efficiency criteria rather than effective, "just" solutions as a base. We are still in need of methods for structuring what one does in a way that achieves agreement with others on both specific supervisory experience and upon its general significance and explanation.

We cannot simply ignore administrative "folklore," but like Stambler and Pearlman, we must reflect on the use of less "scientific" tools. They conclude that "in our opinion, use of I Ching as a consultant/supervisor deserves further exploration."[29] In one sense the I Ching was a tool which was universally used and which Illich would call a convivial tool. We might compare it with a modern compendium or handbook on administrative techniques, the major difference being the element of chance, which meant that the answers were more likely to be seen as "fateful," and therefore carrying an important force to be reckoned with. But perhaps even more important, the apparent success of some of the Japanese approaches to industrial expansions in management is rooted in a belief in these "obsolete-potent" techniques.[30]

Even when faced with industrialization and change, the administration in the East has managed to maintain certain unique, person-oriented approaches. Some Japanese organizations, for example, maintain a "family"-oriented relationship. In some plants, workers are guaranteed their positions and, therefore, security. They, in turn, feel a strong loyalty to the organization. The size of many of these organizations, however, does not permit for the face-to-face communication between

28.   See, for example, Jay Haley, *Problem Solving Therapy* (San Francisco: Jossey Bass, 1976).

29.   Stambler and Pearlman, "I Ching Comments," p. 371.

30.   See, for example, Albert Low, *Zen and Creative Management* (New York: Anchor Books, 1976), pp. 193–219.

staff and administrator that is the norm in most social agencies.

The staff person in the social agency often wants to be part of a community and maintain that face-to-face contact with his or her colleagues. The ability to continue that communication on a positive level may be the crux of the difficulty in building the "just" community the agency might become. Very often, a staff person feels put off by the style of communication of a peer or an administrator. In turn, the perceived slight, can escalate the incident and cut communication among people.

### from the west

A PARADIGM FOR OUR TIMES. Levinson, a psychiatrist concerned with the difficulties people have in communicating, suggests that much of the recent work in psychiatry and sociology on group operations focus on the empathetic manner in which people connect and influence each other. "Yet, however sophisticated our inquiry, the model requires signaling across interpersonal space, and the only instrumentality we know of for that is auditory and visual cues. We wait upon the emergence of a new paradigm which will render 'reasonable' the presently obscure."[31] This new paradigm will require a complete reorganization of our concepts of relationship. A new view is necessary to explain how we are, all—people, birds, trees—connected to each other, thus making up an organic whole.

Levinson's statement, in addition to calling for interpersonal reorganization, illustrates that his structural approach melds into a system's ecological model. But how does one get signals across interpersonal space? Our evolutionary forefathers' signals were initially related to safety. "Simpler" animals, perhaps even the first humans, passed on signals more instinctively.[32]

The communications needed to transform a staff group from a nonwork, self-oriented inception, to a creative, adaptive, and socially oriented practice must mediate the cognitive orientation of the staff involved in that experience. Staff engaged in developing their capabilities for helping are part of a vast network of interrelated acts—past, present, and future—which impact on both their clients and themselves. The more holistic the view staff can take, the more relevant the action can be to the client, that is, the more the client will feel that the staff sees him or her as a human being and not just a problem or a case. The worker can also more easily discern whether a proposed solution will alter other parts of the client system in such a way that the solution creates more problems than it solves.

31. Edgar Levinson, *The Fallacy of Understanding* (New York: Basic Books, 1972), p. 221.

32. Julian Jaynes, *The Origin of Consciousness in the Breakdown of the Bicameral Mind* (Boston: Houghton Mifflin Company, 1977).

What wise administrators need to know is that no matter what stance they take in working with staff, staff will interpret the action in terms of their own needs, not the administrators' visions. Building on Levinson's work, administrators' best actions would be to explain why they do what they do, recognizing that staff may not see it their way. What this tends to do is to allow the recognition with staff, of their motivations, as well as the probability that staff will see it differently, and their right to do so.

Administrators must also work on themselves, just as they work on staff development. They must have empathy, which means not only being able to put themselves in the place of staff, but to know how staff feel about them. This is a skill that administrator's need to develop.

Even when staff disagree, they will have respect for the manner in which the disagreement is handled. They will also have learned that often the disagreement is not on the issues, but on their own ideas, idiosyncratic needs, or misconceptions. This self-knowledge can help the staff in their own growth, as well as help them to appreciate the dilemmas of the administrator and the client.

We are living in a world in which people need each other in order to survive. Large institutions have increasingly taken the place of the family and the small community, which formerly took care of those in need. Yet many of these institutions have developed into warehouses or businesses in which the profit motive outweighs the service orientation. Administrators who were once people of vision and valor have been replaced by managers who are expert at figuring out cost-benefit analyses and who disguise their incompetence and greed in phrases such as "business is business." The manager can excuse his or her actions by this response, and it is often accepted at face value. We have learned these patterned responses. They have become acceptable because we have learned to accept them.

Running an agency in a magnificent manner, with mutual respect and dignity among people, is no easy matter because it is hard work to alter the patterns of resistance, fear, and obsequiousness that workers show to "bosses," no matter what the setting. The wise administrator can find ways to restructure the nature of the relationship among staff. He or she can help them learn new patterns of behavior through a number of processes, and can help staff maintain their own visions of why they entered the helping arena. Staff are most likely to appreciate these efforts when they feel that the administrator also shares these visions and is working to accomplish them.

There is a growing discontent with organizations and their increased amount of institutionalization. In the mental health area, for example, there is a movement to deinstitutionalize, and turn to the community as a support and refuge for mental patients. However, resistance from the community because of fear of the "mentally ill" has tended to slow this process, has brought forth new roles for administrators related to interpretation and cooperation. These developments are harbingers of some of the changes the future will bring.

## THE FUTURE-ORIENTED ADMINISTRATOR

All people are concerned about the future and, to varying degrees, make decisions and take current actions based on their hopes for future rewards. To that extent, we are all futurists. A bright spot in human evolution has been the realization, in this century, that people can indeed control their environment and their future. Our greatest disillusionment is the growing feelings of hopelessness resulting from having done it poorly—having lost control. It is only within the past decade that an identifiable, professional futurist group has emerged, and its members have provided the roots for a transdisciplinary futurist profession. The wise administrator must not only have a sense of what the future needs may be for agency programs, but must understand the nature of changing values and their impact on his or her staff.

There is a growing self-help "movement" of people who conclude that the only way to save the future is, indeed, to start to plan for it—to become shapers of the social structure—rather than become the pigeons of the profit makers and power seekers. They believe that by assessing the changes, directions, and alternatives and selecting a direction or "alternative future" that they hope to realize, they could shape the future. These "futurists" have, through their writings, speeches, forecasting, methodology, political action, and courses at all academic levels, begun to alert people to the political alternatives of the future.[33] They are action oriented, utopian, and creative. They seek a just society in which all people are treated with dignity, and are free to achieve their human potential. Their major message is that by working for preferred alternatives, people can recapture a sense of influencing their own destinies and increase their hopes for the future. Certain changes in society should be highlighted in order to visualize the planning an administrator may have to contemplate.

Briefly, a few of the emerging trends that will seriously impact our future are:

1. Shifts in population size, age groupings, and demographic changes are already altering our lives. It is not necessarily the number of people, but their ages that will make the difference. As fertility declines in the

33. Alvin Toffler, *Future Shock* (New York: Bantam Books, 1970).

United States, the median age of the population will increase. Currently the median age is approaching thirty, and the aged make up 8 percent of our population. By 2020 the median age will reach thirty-five and 15 percent of the population will be over sixty-five. What this means is that we are becoming an older population. Brazil, in contrast, has a population of which over 70 percent is in their teens. Some of the consequences have already been felt in the closing of hospital maternity wards, and teacher over-supply.

The shifts of population to the west and south will have implications for the older cities, and employment and living patterns. St. Petersburg, Florida, for example, tried to limit its population size; Oregon deters tourists.

2. Developments in automation and technology will influence and control some socio-health areas of controversy, such as gender selection, intelligence, artificial organs, and the extension of life. Experiments with recombinant DNA may create new life forms and computers may control human behavior.

3. Changing patterns of family life, acceptance of "deviant" life styles, and the growing movements advocating more freedom for women and other minority groups will create positive growth, but also create challenging alterations in social relations and societal needs. The "group" will emerge as a bastion of strength in a computerized, individualistic society. It is through one's group that identity and support will be found.

An additional factor seems to be a growing trend toward institutionalism and the consequent minimizing of involvement of people with each other in decision making. Rather, there is a tendency to permit the institutions to make the decisions. A response to this trend is a turn to self-help groups and shared communities as attempts to counter the alienation and sense of powerlessness created by large institutions. Proposals for this "transformation" scenario as a major life style of the future are generally held to be unrealistic. Bell's postindustrial paradigm seems the one most likely to be adopted by society.[34]

This is not an extensive nor detailed list, but it is important to note that any modifications in age groupings, technological advancement, or genetic controls may have far-reaching developments. For example, the extension of life has led to people being more productive in their later years, and to laws raising the retirement age, which has led in turn to concerns about job blockages for younger people, possible conservative management in corporations, concerns about unproductive university professors, a growing political base for the aged in this country, many lonely and disheartened older people, and a new nursing home industry even listed on the stock exchange. This *cross-impact analysis* is an important tool in any assessment of future technologies and trends. It is particularly

34.   Daniel Bell, *The Coming of Post Industrial Society* (New York: Basic Books, 1973).

important for the administrator who will be faced with job modifications or maintaining older workers' productivity. New services will need to be developed that support an increasingly aging population and/or jobless youth population. Intergenerational stress may increase with consequent societal problems.

### attempts to influence the future

Professional groups, as well as government, business, cities, and industries, have attempted to assess future trends in order to prepare and modify their organizations appropriately.[35] Mazade reports on a conference of 100 mental health administrators and educators who were brought together to: 1. identify changes—trends which would be influencing mental health administrators in the future; 2. examine what problems would they create for mental health administration; and 3. determine what knowledge and skill will be required of mental health administrators in order to deal with these changes.[36]

The priority issues were broken down into a number of areas:

1. *Funding priorities*: Methods and limited resources will create restrictions on the administration. This may lead to more competition, the squeezing out of smaller agencies, and reduced flexibility for the administrator. The administrator will need the technical competencies of cost analysis, grantsmanship and interorganizational skills.

2. *Accountability*: More detailed information will be required by service recipients, funding sources, and governing bodies. There will be an increased level of community participation in mental health planning. The administrator will need skills to assess these demands for accountability, particularly in its impact on budget, staff, and services.

3. *Services*: The conferees expected the "trend toward community-based care to continue, but that some regional institution would be required in the future to meet the needs of the most severely ill." Administrators will need to know budgetary processes, innovative service delivery models, and how to "integrate mental health services with primary and 'realistic' health systems."[37]

The conferees also noted the difficulty of forecasting future policy in an environment shaped by momentary political realities. Their emphasis

35. Some examples include: Ervin Laslo, *Goals for Mankind: A Report to the Club of Rome on the New Horizons of Global Community* (New York: E. P. Dutton, 1977); *The Next 25 Years* (Washington, D.C.: World Future Society, 1975); Alvin Toffler, *Learning For Tomorrow* (New York: Vintage Books, 1974).

36. Noel A. Mazade, "Future Issues in Mental Health Administration: A Report," *Administration in Mental Health*, 6, no. 2 (Winter 1978), 154–60.

37. Mazade, "Future Issues in Mental Health," p. 160.

seemed to be the recognition of the impact of the external forces on the agency, and the need for administrative personnel to possess behavioral skills in order to deal with these external forces.

The concern in the human services with being able to deal with the future and the need for the profession to respond and, indeed, to be proactive, is illustrated by courses and articles on the future of social work by Paul Abels and others,[38] as well as by the NASW's recently formed "Futures Commission" under the chairleadership of Bertram M. Beck. This commission held its organizational meeting in March 1979 and has been active in formulating the issues and alternatives open to our profession as they view societal-professional trends. The results of their findings will have important implications for administrators in the human services area.

Some indications of what some of these problems might be are reflected in an article in the October 1977, *The Futurist*. The first two societal problems listed are, "Malnutrition—Induced Mental Deficients Leading to Social Instability" and "The Cultural Exclusion of the Aged." Others include: "The Effects of Stress on Individuals and Society," "Changing Family Forms," and "The Limits to the Management of Large Complex Systems."[39]

If, as we have suggested above, various factors external to the agency and its immediate environment will in the future impact the agency's ability to fulfill its service or create new needs, it behooves the administrator, as the key leadership person, to establish some means of becoming aware of these changes and their implications. The hoped for result being, naturally, that the information will permit the agency to develop resources to adapt to these changes.

Administrators need, then, to function with one eye on the future. A number of technological processes have been developed which permit the administrator to do such "future planning." Like the administrator's utilization of the normative stance, most futurists are concerned with what "ought to be," and some authors suggest that all futures research may be normative, too.[40] Through the use of forecasting techniques, they attempt to anticipate the future in order to plan for a more Utopian way of life.[41]

38.  See Paul Abels, "Terra Incognita: The Future of the Profession," *Social Work*, 20, no. 1 (Jan. 1975), 25; "A Social Work Course on the Future" (unpublished paper presented at the Council on Social Work Education annual meeting, March 1975); and "The Future of Helping" (unpublished paper presented at the International Conference on The Future, Toronto, June 1980).

39.  "Forty-one Future Problems," *The Futurist* (October 1977), pp. 275–78.

40.  See Wayne I. Boucher, *The Study of the Future: An Agenda for Research* (Washington, D.C.: National Science Foundation, 1973), p. 75.

41.  Forecasting techniques are discussed in Chapter 7.

# THE RESPECTFUL ADMINISTRATOR

It seems somehow fitting to end our book with a reaffirmation of the basic themes of our presentation. If we are to take holistic thinking seriously, acknowledging that it recognizes the interrelationship of people, actions, and organizations, as well as the actions of professionals charged with some guidance within that change system, then we cannot fail to see that all the efforts, no matter how small or seemingly unimportant, that are directed at developing more respectful administrative practices will have an impact.

The administrator who is concerned that the staff with whom he or she works are autonomous beings, entitled to freedom in keeping with the principles of our democracy, needs to see that these principles are respected within the organization. They cannot be delayed until more "prosperous" times, or when the board is "ready" or the case loads smaller, or the staff more experienced. Public service administrators are subject to debilitating handicaps; "agency managers are almost literally in the position of having to beg for every dollar, every worker and every piece of equipment."[42]

Numerous authors have noted the failure of our organizations and of our leadership. We can begin now to help our staff to operate with more freedom for themselves and for their clients. Follett refused to discuss what to do if her integrative solutions wouldn't work in some organizations, saying that they should at least be tried, and that no second-best approaches would do. We, too, must keep trying until we are able to find a unity with staff so that they can join us in our dreams. As Allen Wheelis has noted, when things do not go well in helping situations, try harder, and do something different.[43]

The inability of an organization to function at an efficient level is an extremely serious problem, particularly when we consider the extent of power some institutions have over people's lives. Romano-V notes that:

"On any given day during 1969 in the state of California, virtually 8 million people from an estimated population of 19,800,000 were under some form of institutional care or in some institutional program or were employed to provide the care and administer the programs."[44]

42. John Darnton, "Middle Management in City Government Held to Be in Crisis," *New York Times*, Sept. 23, 1975. p. 1, col. 2.

43. Allen Wheelis, *How People Change*, pp. 110–116.

44. Octavio I. Romano-V, "Institutions in Modern Society: Caretakers and Subjects," *Science*, vol. 183 (22 Feb. 1974).

Thus, we see that administrators play an important part in the lives of people. Clients are dependent on institutions for their education, their livelihood and their health. Both administrative functioning and the agency's professional service need to be at a level approaching the current state of the art.

While this commitment to provide optimal service is itself a heavy burden to place on the administrator, the importance of the work to staff members adds another dimension to the administrator's responsibilities. Like the clients, the staff depend on the organization's proper functioning and maintenance for their well being. In times of fiscal austerity the social effects of staff reduction become important. While we are familiar with the problems created by retirement, we are less aware of the impact of unemployment on the lives of people.

There is a growing amount of evidence showing that increases in unemployment lead to increases in the incidence of murder, death, and suicide. The work of Prof. M. Harvey Brenner as reported in the New York Times suggests that the correlation between unemployment and death and criminal behavior is strong.[45]

While there has been a great deal of study concerning the impact of unemployment on the economy and on the worker and his or her family, very little research has been done of the stress placed on the administrator who has the task of carrying out dismissals during organizational crises.

The 1980s are a period of intense agency competition for scarce financial resources. In the competition among agencies, we believe the creative organization has a good chance to survive, partly because of its wise leadership and partly because of the staff's ability to work synergistically. While some organizations faced with shrinking resources will tend to see staff or service cuts as one of the first steps in meeting a tightened budget, we believe the creative agency will look for new ways to meet the crises and in fact increase its services in order to meet new needs.[46] A major factor in finding solutions to the problems will be the ability of administration and staff to work together.

Many administrative problems can be overcome if the administrator soundly understands that people want to be:

1. valued;
2. treated with respect and dignity;
3. involved in the kind of work that they feel is valued and worthwhile;
4. helpful to growth of the agency.

45.   Nancy Hicks, "U.S. Study Links Rise in Jobless to Deaths, Murder and Suicide," *The New York Times*, Oct. 31, 1976, p. 1, col. 6.

46.   One proposal for such a project, developed by Richard E. Isralowitz and Paul Abels, was *Minimizing the Stress of Threatened Unemployment and Unemployment in the Cleveland Area* (unpublished paper, Human Services Design Laboratory, School of Applied Social Sciences, Case Western Reserve University, Cleveland, Ohio, March 1980).

So we have come full circle, back to the concepts of freedom, respect and dignity that are the basic tenets of our approach to normative administration.

The continuing struggle of freedom versus control is one with which we in the human services are familiar. The values of the profession have been those which hold with the rights of the clients to live their lives, to receive help and to use it as they will with the least possible amount of outside control or interference in their lives. This has been a continuous battle waged against those who hold that the giving of funds or services carries the right to impose control over the lives of the clients. In a climate of service cutbacks, retrenchment and shrinking funding sources the movement to restrict assistance to those who "deserve" it, according to narrow guidelines, or who will do as we wish, can be expected to gain momentum.

As human service workers we must renew our belief in the dignity and worth of the individual and the right to freedom. We must continue to resist attempts to control others' lives through rules or restrictive programs. The wise and respectful administrator embodies the best in democratic and humanistic principles and is an example for staff, client and community.

The axiom that giving people good conditions spoils them for bad conditions suggests that our organizations can improve. They reflect our evolutionary movement from authoritarian to democratic principles, from rule by status to governance by contract.

In essence, people are asking for a new social contract. Just as clients, students, minorities, and women have started to demand equal participation, members of organizations are likewise seeking new patterns of interaction—a new contract with the agency. The wise administrator can work to meet that magnificent challenge.

# NAME INDEX

# SUBJECT INDEX